This book is dedicated to
my supportive
mother,
Babs.

acknowledgments

I raise a toast in thanks to my agent, June
Clark, and all the people at Adams Media.
I'm very grateful for their hard work.

THE
EVERYTHING®
BARTENDER'S BOOK
4TH EDITION

Dear Reader,

Whether you have a desire to learn how to mix one drink at a home party or many drinks working as a bartender at a local establishment, this book gives you the information you need to get started or brush up on your mad whiskey-slingin' skills.

Being the bartender at a home-party bar or at a local bar can be fun and requires a well-groomed appearance and a sociable personality (or at least one inside itching to come out).

The Everything® Bartender's Book, 4th Edition is filled with everything the beginner, middlin', or expert bartender needs to know about the stylish bar and cocktail world. This book overflows with over 1,000 recipes that range from the classics and historic cocktails (from the 1800s to the early 1900s) to modern and contemporary cocktails found in craft bars of today.

If you have any questions, don't hesitate to e-mail me at *Cheryl@misscharming.com* or visit my website: *www.miss charming.com.*

Cheers!

Cheryl Charming

The EVERYTHING® Series

These handy, accessible books give you all you need to tackle a difficult project, gain a new hobby, comprehend a fascinating topic, prepare for an exam, or even brush up on something you learned back in school but have since forgotten.

We now have more than 400 *Everything*® books in print, spanning such wide-ranging categories as weddings, pregnancy, cooking, music instruction, foreign language, crafts, pets, New Age, and so much more. When you're done reading them all, you can finally say you know *Everything*®!

PUBLISHER Karen Cooper

MANAGING EDITOR, EVERYTHING® SERIES Lisa Laing

COPY CHIEF Casey Ebert

ASSISTANT PRODUCTION EDITOR Alex Guarco

ACQUISITIONS EDITOR Eileen Mullan

SENIOR DEVELOPMENT EDITOR Brett Palana-Shanahan

ASSOCIATE DEVELOPMENT EDITOR Eileen Mullan

EVERYTHING® SERIES COVER DESIGNER Erin Alexander

Visit the entire Everything® series at *www.everything.com*

THE
EVERYTHING
BARTENDER'S
BOOK
4TH EDITION

Your complete guide
to cocktails, martinis,
mixed drinks, and more!

Cheryl Charming

Adams Media
New York   London   Toronto   Sydney   New Delhi

Adams Media
An Imprint of Simon & Schuster, Inc.
100 Technology Center Drive
Stoughton, MA 02072

An Everything® Series Book.
Everything® and everything.com® are registered trademarks of Simon & Schuster, Inc.

ADAMS MEDIA and colophon are trademarks of Simon & Schuster, Inc.

For information about special discounts for bulk purchases, please contact Simon & Schuster Special Sales at 1-866-506-1949 or business@simonandschuster.com.

The Simon & Schuster Speakers Bureau can bring authors to your live event. For more information or to book an event contact the Simon & Schuster Speakers Bureau at 1-866-248-3049 or visit our website at www.simonspeakers.com.

Manufactured in the United States of America

10 2021

Library of Congress Cataloging-in-Publication Data
Charming, Cheryl.
  The everything bartender's book / Cheryl Charming. – 4th edition.
    pages cm
  Includes index.
  ISBN 978-1-4405-8633-0 (pb) – ISBN 1-4405-8633-0 (pb) – ISBN 978-1-4405-8634-7 (ebook) – ISBN 1-4405-8634-9 (ebook)
  1. Bartending–Handbooks, manuals, etc. 2. Alcoholic beverages–Handbooks, manuals, etc.
  3. Cocktails–Handbooks, manuals, etc. I. Title.
  TX951.R47 2015
  641.87'4–dc23
                        2014042337

ISBN 978-1-4405-8633-0
ISBN 978-1-4405-8634-7 (ebook)

contents

top 10 things
bartenders should know

1. No one knows where the cocktail was invented.

2. The first known written reference to the cocktail was in 1803.

3. The first known written definition of the cocktail was in 1806.

4. Jerry Thomas (1800s) was the first known celebrity bartender. He traveled the world and wrote the first known bartender book, *How to Mix Drinks*, in 1862.

5. Most professions are either physical or mental. Bartending is both.

6. Bartending is not typically an entry-level position. Most positions are filled from within.

7. You don't have to memorize hundreds of recipes to be a bartender. There are only about fifty recipes to know—all the rest are spinoffs from those.

8. There are about 1.5 million bartenders in America alone and most work at local bars.

9. A real martini is made with gin and dry vermouth. And since James Bond ordered a vodka martini in the film *Dr. No* in 1962, vodka and dry vermouth has become acceptable as well.

10. Absinthe is pronounced *AB-sinth*, cognac *CONE-yak*, Cointreau *KWAN-troh*, Courvoisier *core-VAH-see-A*, crème de cacao *krem de kuh-KOW* or *kuh-KAY-oh*, and Pernod *pur-NO*.

introduction

Standing behind the bar is one fine place to be. As the bartender and host at a home party or in the workplace, it's your job to keep the good times rollin'—and with this book you'll be prepared. Above all, you'll be able to dip into the book for information, tips, ingredients, and recipes. You'll find everything—glassware, tools, spirits, beer, wine, mixers, garnishes, party ideas, and techniques.

The Everything® Bartender's Book, 4th Edition begins with a brief history of alcohol, spirits, cocktails, and the bartending profession. It goes on to give you all the basics you need in order to concoct a cocktail. You'll find that there's no great mystery to making one. You only need to grasp the differences between drink families and the basics of shaking, blending, and mixing drinks.

For the sake of understanding—and sampling—the basic contents of drinks, a chapter is devoted to each spirit that makes cocktails possible: vodka, gin, rum, tequila, and whiskey. Some of the greatest drinks ever invented are made with one liquor and one mixer, and you'll find them in their respective chapters.

If you are going to be an Everything® bartender, you have to be hip to what's current and wise enough to know what's classic, so this book gives you the best of what's timeless—the Whiskey Sour, Tom Collins, Old-Fashioned, and other favorites with their variations and mutations. There is a special classic symbol Y by each classic cocktail so that you know the difference between a mutation and the original classic. All bartenders should know these classic drinks in their basic forms.

Other chapters include shots and shooters, specialty and multispirit drinks, beer, wine, aperitifs and cordials, holiday drinks and punches, and homemade recipes. The shots and shooters chapter includes the hottest and hippest shooters found in nightclubs—classics, layered, flaming, and even more shots. Drinks like the Long Island Iced Tea, which contains vodka, gin, rum, and tequila, will be found in the multi-spirit chapter. The wine chapter covers recipes made from many wine-based alcohols, such as champagne, port, sherry, cider, cognac, and brandy. Aperitifs with a wine base such as vermouth bleed over into the aperitif and cordial chapter. There's even a chapter of recipes where you can learn to make, for example, your own coffee liqueur, Irish cream, syrups, and more!

Finally, you'll find many tidbits peppered throughout the book—bar- and cocktail-related jokes, trivia, hints, bar tricks, and more. As a whole, *The Everything® Bartender's Book, 4th Edition* provides you with a well-rounded perspective on what it takes to be a bartender. Now go out and shake things up!

history of alcohol and bartending

Alcohol consumption dates back almost to the dawn of human civilization. Over time, alcohol developed into a major trade item. Some regions developed specialty drinks that we still drink today, such as tequila and champagne. Through it all, there always had to be someone on hand to host and serve the alcohol. The duty of tending bar truly reaches back to ancient times.

An Alcohol Timeline

No one knows the exact moment, year, century, or even period when alcohol was first discovered. It's believed that alcohol has been around since at least 10,000 B.C.E. because archaeologists unearthed Stone Age beer mugs from the Neolithic period.

Ancient Alcohol

Long before the dawn of the Common Era, ancient civilizations around the world brewed and distilled alcohol using whatever ingredients were available to them. The Chinese made wine as early as 7000 B.C.E., and rice-based sake spread through Japan around 200 B.C.E. The Babylonians recorded their recipes for beer on ninety-two stone tablets in 4300 B.C.E., and rice and barley beer were brewed in India by 800 B.C.E. Archaeological evidence suggests that alcohol was an important part of ancient life. People depended on it for commerce and celebrated deities such as Bacchus, the Roman god of wine.

Water Into Wine

Alcohol became a common drink, but apparently it wasn't as plentiful as one happy wedding couple in Cana would have hoped. They ran out of wine for their guests, and Jesus of Nazareth performed a miraculous transformation of water into wine.

Ancient people also recognized problems associated with alcohol consumption. Alcohol had its first brush with the law in 50 B.C.E. when King Burebista of Thrace became the first to ban alcohol. Religions from Christianity to Hinduism to Buddhism encouraged drinking in moderation, and Islam forbade it altogether.

Medieval Alcohol

The fall of the Roman Empire brought changes to all of Europe. Infrastructure crumbled, but trade still allowed new techniques and products to circulate. Around C.E. 900, Viking ships disguised as *barcos rabelos*—wine merchants' vessels—entered the Douro River in Portugal. Monasteries became the keepers of alcohol; they had the resources to uphold the labor-intensive process of making it. French monks, forced inland by Viking raids, cultivated Chardonnay grapes and made Chablis wine circa C.E. 800.

Medieval Innovations
Persian and Arab alchemists pioneered the conventional process of distillation in the Middle Ages, and the new types of alcohol it produced were used for medicinal purposes at first.

During the Black Death plague epidemic in the fourteenth century, some people believed that drinks made from juniper berries (gin) could save them. Others believed that consuming alcohol in moderation was the key to warding off the plague.

In the 1400s, so many alchemists were distilling alcohol that England's King Henry IV ruled that only the monasteries could continue the practice. Meanwhile, German brewers perfected the lager method, and the first export of Russian vodka was recorded in the sixteenth century.

Alcohol in the New World

Alcohol played a large role in travel and exploration. In the New World, Columbus found Native Americans making beer from corn and black birch sap. Ferdinand Magellan, captain of the first ship to sail around the world, spent more money on sherry than weapons when stocking his ship for a voyage to the New World. Sir Walter Raleigh brewed the first beer in Virginia and then sent a request for better beer back to England. Colonists made wine from strawberries, blackberries, gooseberries, and elderberries. They also planted non-native apple trees, which yielded cider.

> **Tequila**
> The Aztecs used the blue agave plant to make alcoholic beverages long before the Spanish discovered the plant and created tequila. The first tequila distilleries opened in Mexico in the seventeenth century.

Modern Beginnings

The popular brands we know today began to appear on the scene in the eighteenth century. In 1759, Arthur Guinness signed a 9,000-year lease for a brewery in Dublin. The Guinness Storehouse welcomes tourists, and a tour of the Storehouse culminates with a complimentary pint of Guinness in the Gravity Bar, which provides a 360-degree view of Dublin. Richard Hennessy founded Hennessy Cognac in 1765, and across the Atlantic, some historians claim that the Reverend Elijah Craig created a new whiskey formula of corn, rye, and barley malt, and established the Jim Beam distillery in 1789.

History of the Cocktail

The origin of the word *cocktail* will probably never be known because there are many stories of where it came from. These origination accounts include a woman named Betsy Flanagan putting a rooster tail in drinks (cock-tail); an American tavern keeper pouring alcohol into a ceramic rooster, then guests would tap the tail when they wanted a drink; and a possible derivation from the French word *coquetel*. The very first known mention of the word *cocktail* was found in an early American newspaper, the *Farmer's Cabinet*, on April 28, 1803. It read, "Drank a glass of cocktail—excellent for the head. . . . Call'd at the Doct's. found Burnham—he looked very wise—drank another glass of cocktail."

In 1806, the definition of the word first appeared in print in the Hudson, New York, publication *The Balance, and Columbian Repository* as a political stab against Democrats. It ran, "Cocktail is stimulating liquor composed of spirits of any kind, sugar, water, and bitters. It is vulgarly called a bittered sling and is supposed to be an excellent electioneering potion, inasmuch as it renders the heart stout and bold, at the same time that it fuddles the head. It is said, also to be of great use to a Democratic candidate: because, a person having swallowed a glass of it, is ready to swallow anything else."

Keeping Cocktail History Alive
The historical cocktail has recently come back into vogue. Much of this is due to great cocktail historians and authors who are passionate about preserving the history of the cocktail. The main contributions come from the Museum of the American Cocktail (*www.cocktailmuseum.org*) and Tales of the Cocktail (*www.talesofthecocktail.com*).

Jerry Thomas, the first celebrity bartender, published the first drink recipe book to contain cocktails, *How to Mix Drinks*, in 1862. He marveled at the inventiveness of the nineteenth-century world, of which mixology was a part. "A new beverage is the pride of the Bartender, and its appreciation and adoption his crowning glory," Thomas wrote in the 1876 edition. The book contained several drinks that are still familiar to many people today. *How to Mix Drinks* included three different Tom Collins recipes, although the rest of the Collins family is not mentioned. Recipes for the Manhattan and Whiskey Sour were printed, and Thomas included what he termed "temperance drinks"—drinks without alcohol.

Alcohol in the Twentieth Century

Resistance to alcohol grew during the nineteenth century. Religious and conservative groups worried about the effects of alcohol abuse on individuals and communities. In 1874, the first national convention of the Women's Christian Temperance Union was held. The union promoted the movement for prohibition in the United States and tried to shut down saloons. They blamed male drinking for prostitution, child abuse, and poverty.

Prohibition

The temperance movement steadily gained a huge following worldwide, resulting in bans on alcohol. Canada, Finland, Iceland, Norway, Russia/Soviet Union, and the United States all enacted bans on alcohol in the first decades of the twentieth century. In the United States, the Eighteenth Amendment prohibited the sale and production of alcoholic beverages beginning in 1920. Nearly fourteen years and three constitutional amendments later, Congress repealed the Eighteenth Amendment, but not before Prohibition wreaked havoc on the American alcohol industry. Breweries, distilleries, and wineries were forced to shutter themselves, damaging an emerging market. But Prohibition proved impossible to enforce. Americans continued to consume alcohol, smuggled in illegally from neighboring countries or produced illegally within U.S. borders. Speakeasies flourished; there were more speakeasies during Prohibition than there were legitimate bars before the Eighteenth Amendment went into effect.

Pop Alcohol

The American alcohol market rebounded after 1933, and the twentieth century saw floods of new products and cocktails. A fictional British agent named James Bond put a handsome face to the Martini. In Ian Fleming's original 1952 novel, Bond orders a dry martini served in a deep champagne goblet with three measures of Gordon's gin, one of Gordon's vodka, and half a measure of Lillet dry vermouth shaken very well until ice-cold, with a garnish of lemon peel. This is the first reference to combining both vodka and gin in a martini.

Public awareness of the dangers of overindulgence remains an issue. In 1980, Candy Lightner founded Mothers Against Drunk Drivers (MADD) after a drunk driver killed her thirteen-year-old daughter, Cari. The United States set the legal drinking age at twenty-one years in 1984.

The last two decades have seen an onslaught of new drinks. Malt beverages hit store shelves in the 1990s. Smirnoff Ice debuted in 2001 in the United States and quickly captured the market. In the world of cocktails, bartenders strove to invent quirky new drinks to keep patrons interested, aided by exotic products like Blavod black vodka.

Bartending Beginnings

There has always been a person in charge of making beverages and serving them. In ancient times, it was a postproduction job for women. The men grew and harvested the raw materials and women took the responsibility of cooking and preparing it into food and drink.

Media Bartenders
Today in movies, television, music, and novels, bartenders are typically portrayed providing solace to the downtrodden, offering psychological advice to the confused, supplying private detectives with information, or being the life of the party.

As serving meals became an occupation and watering holes opened for people to gather, familiar features began to appear. Someone standing behind a structure—a barrier (bar for short)—

serving food and drink has been recorded throughout history. Romans called their structures *thermopoliums*. Their bar tops had holes, and jars of alcohol were set down into the bar and served with ladles.

The Art of Modern Bartending

By the 1950s, thanks to new household-appliance technology and war-free times, women began entertaining in their homes. Lo and behold, the cocktail party came into its own. In the 1960s and 1970s, casual dining restaurant/bar chains permeated the nation, introducing sweetened froufrou drinks that resulted in the decline of bartending as an art and the incline of sales. The 1988 film *Cocktail* created a new category of bartender—one who puts on a show and entertains customers by flipping glasses and bottles.

Before They Were Famous
Many famous people tended bar—Bill Cosby, Bruce Willis, Sandra Bullock, Dave Matthews, and Ellen DeGeneres, to name a few.

The 1990s produced high-end beer, wine, and spirits that set the foundation for higher-quality cocktails created by bar chefs and mixologists at the turn of the century. Today you'll find bartenders specializing in blowing fire, flipping bottles, dancing half-naked on a bar top, and using only fresh ingredients. There's also your reliable average Joe down the street at your local bar. Just know that the majority of bartenders are the latter.

Behind-the-Bar Etiquette

Being behind the bar is like living in a fishbowl. Some refer to it as being on stage. Basic bar etiquette applies to both the real-world bartender and the home-party bartender.

The Real-World Bartender

The best real-world bartenders make an art form out of their profession. Successful professional bartenders possess many skills and personality traits.

- A good personality and an ability to interact well with people are two of a bartender's best assets. A sense of humor is invaluable.
- A well-groomed appearance helps bartenders seem more approachable and professional.
- Physical strength is required for long hours standing behind the bar and lifting heavy boxes.
- Basic math skills allow bartenders to make change and measure drinks accurately and quickly.
- Bartenders need to be able to remember everything from drink recipes to customers' names.
- Multitasking is a must! Bars are busy, and the bartender must make sure everything runs smoothly.
- A great smile is key since bartenders smile a lot.

Bartenders must be aware of everything around them at all times. They know the drink levels of everyone's beverage, and they see new customers as they approach the bar. A second set of eyes in the back of their heads would be a remarkable evolutionary improvement; failing that, bartenders need to be constantly alert.

The Home-Party Bartender

The bartender can literally make or break a party. Though private-party bartenders must be very organized with plenty of backup, once everything is in place they can relax and just be the life of the party, since the hassle of running tabs and dealing with credit cards is nonexistent. The home-party bartender's main job is to smile, be happy, and set the tone for the party.

Service Tips

There are thousands of tips a bartender can learn through the years to help make her job easier and more efficient. There are far too many to list, but a few will illuminate the way.

- When a guest sits at the bar, always greet him with eye contact and a smile as you lay down a cocktail napkin. If you cannot get to him right away, let him know that you'll be right with him. Guests don't mind waiting if they are recognized.
- Keep the bar top clean for customers.
- Always think of sanitation. Don't let your fingers touch drinking surfaces—the top of the straw, the rim of a glass, the ice, and the tops of bottles.
- When you are given a tip, always make eye contact and say "Thank you."
- Always serve the woman first, then the man. If a group of women are at the bar, it's customary to serve the oldest first and so forth.
- People love to hear their names. Try to remember names.

bartending 101

Bartender (bär´ ten dur) n. One who mixes and serves alcoholic drinks at a bar, lounge, or tavern. Also called barkeeper, barkeep, barmaid, barman, tavern keeper, whiskey slinger, mixologist, and tapster. Bartending basics start with the lingo. It's also essential to recognize the glassware. The next things a bartender needs are the proper tools to make the cocktail: ice, alcohol, mixers, and the crowning touch, the garnish.

The Five Drink Families

It can be mind-boggling for the bartending newbie to glance through cocktail recipes, but they really only break down into five categories—juicy, creamy, sour, hot, and carbonated. There are a few extensions from the categories, notably the tropical, highball, stick, and classic variations.

Juicy: Juicy drinks are made with any type of cold juice. Popular examples are Screwdriver, Cape Cod, and Bloody Mary.

Creamy: Creamy drinks use cream, half-and-half, Irish cream, and similar liquids to give them a heavier texture. Popular examples are White Russian, Mudslide, Creamsicle, Grasshopper, and Bushwhacker.

Sour: Sour drinks are made with the tang of citrus juice. Popular examples are Whiskey Sour, Amaretto Sour, Tom Collins, Margarita, Sour Appletini, and Long Island Iced Tea.

Highballs
Originally, when a guest walked up to the bar and asked for a highball, the bartender grabbed a bottle of rye whiskey and mixed it with ginger ale. Today a highball just means a drink containing a spirit mixed with a carbonated mixer.

Hot: These are made with coffee, hot apple cider, tea, hot chocolate, and other similar hot beverages. Popular examples are Irish Coffee, Hot Toddy, Keoke Coffee, and Coffee Liqueur and Coffee.

Carbonated: Carbonated drinks take advantage of soda's fizzy bubbles. These are basic highballs like Vodka and Soda, Vodka and Tonic, Gin and Tonic, Rum and Coke, Bourbon and Coke, and Seven and Seven.

Bartending Terms

If you grasp these techniques, you'll be able to stand proud behind the bar with confidence.

Blended Cocktail: This is the type that you mix in a blender. Some people call it a frozen drink. The trick is to not put too much ice into the blender in the beginning; you can always add more to reach the desired consistency.

Built Cocktail: This one is the easiest to make. Start with a glass of ice. Pour in your spirits and follow with the mixer. You're done. You've made a drink "on the rocks."

Chilled Cocktail: Pouring a cold drink into a warm glass is not a crime, but it should be. If refrigerator or freezer space allows, squeeze the glasses in along with the ice cream. If not, fill a glass with ice and water to chill it before you mix the drink.

Flamed Cocktail: The most popular flamed drinks are topped with 151 proof rum, taking advantage of its flammability. Always use extreme caution when handling fire, and make sure the flame is blown out before consuming the drink.

Float: To float means to pour some alcohol on top of a drink. The float adds flavor and character to a drink. Don't confuse it with the layered drink. The quantity of alcohol used in a float is less than that required for a layered drink. About half an ounce will suffice.

Layered Drink: Different types of alcohol have different weights (densities). This allows them to be layered on top of one another.

For shots, you simply pour the spirit onto something like a bar spoon to break its fall so that it goes into the glass slowly. This way it layers on top of the spirit layer below it.

Muddled Cocktail: To muddle, you crush your ingredients to release their flavors.

Neat Drink: *Neat* is pouring straight from the bottle into a glass. Ice or mixers are not added.

Rolled Cocktail: You roll a cocktail by building a drink and then shifting it back and forth once with another glass or shaker tin.

Shaken Cocktail: You shake a cocktail by putting ice and your ingredients in a shaker tin and shaking the drink to make it cold.

Strained Cocktail: You are chilling the drink and straining it over ice or straight up. The most popular use of this method is with straight-up shots and shooters. The term *straight up* refers to something that is chilled and served without ice.

Stirred Cocktail: One stirring technique is to build a cocktail and then stir it with a straw. The other way is used when you're making a classic Manhattan or Martini: You fill a bar glass (pint glass) with ice, pour in your ingredients, stir with a bar spoon, and strain.

Glassware

In some cases there are essential reasons for the choice of glass. A cocktail glass is held by its stem so the hand does not warm the drink. A brandy snifter is rested in the palm, so the hand warms the liquid and releases its aroma.

The pint glass can also be used as a mixing glass or all-purpose glass. Beer, specialty drinks, sweet teas, or tropical drinks may all be served in a pint glass. Beer can be served in a mug, pint glass, stein, pilsner-style glass, yard (very tall beer glass), goblet, pitcher, or tankard. All are best chilled.

Brandy snifters range considerably in size, from 5 to 25 ounces, so use your personal preference as a guide. The brief stem allows your hand to warm the brandy. The mouth of the snifter, narrower than the base, holds the aroma. Cordials and liqueurs can be served in them, as well as high-end single malt Scotch, whiskey, rum, and tequila.

Champagne is served in either a 4- to 6-ounce stemmed, wide-mouthed glass (coupe) or a 7- to 8-ounce flute, and the style does make a difference. The open surface of the wide-mouthed glass allows the carbonation to escape, while the narrow flute preserves the bubbles. There are also two styles of flutes, called tulip and trumpet (named for their shape).

The cocktail glass is the symbol of drinking establishments throughout the world. Its size ranges between 4 to 12 ounces and comes in many vintage and modern shapes. The larger-sized glasses are meant for cocktails made with added mixers like a Lemondrop Martini. Smaller cocktail glasses are meant for spirit-only cocktails like a Classic Martini.

A highball glass, the most universally used glass, holds 8 to 12 ounces of on-the-rocks drinks (highballs) like Scotch and Soda or Gin and Tonic and other two-ingredient, on-the-rocks drinks like Vodka and Orange Juice or Moscow Mule.

The Irish coffee mug is a soul-warming glass container for all hot drinks. At 6 to 8 ounces, it offers enough volume for the right proportions of spirits and nonalcoholic ingredients, and its handle allows you to hold the glass while the drink is still properly hot.

Irish Coffee History
Joe Sheridan, an Irish airport bartender, invented the Irish Coffee at what is now Shannon Airport in Ireland. In 1952, a San Francisco reporter named Stanton Delaplane took the recipe back to Jack Koeppler, who owned the Buena Vista Cafe. Today, the bar claims to serve 2,000 Irish Coffees a day.

A 1-ounce **liqueur glass** is also known as a *cordial* glass or a *pony*. You'll find them in different shapes, but they all hold 1 ounce of liquid.

The **old-fashioned glass** is for the venerable Old-Fashioned, but it's also used for most cocktails when they are requested on the rocks. That's the story behind its alias, the rocks glass. Ranging from 4 to 8 ounces, the old-fashioned is the short, squat member of the glass team. A lot of bars will use this glass for their highballs.

A 3- to 4-ounce **sherry glass** holds many of the before- and after-dinner drinks, such as sherry, port, and various aperitifs. These are, by definition, small drinks, and the size of the sherry glass is right for the portion.

The 1- or 2-ounce **shot glass** does double duty as a measurer and a serving glass. Many bars don't use shot glasses as much anymore because they tend to get stolen.

The 8- to 20-ounce **red wine glass** is balloon-shaped; the 8- to 20-ounce **white wine glass** is quite a bit slimmer, but there's no need to be a stickler about these dimensions. Unless perfection is a prerequisite, all-purpose wine glasses are acceptable. Most bars use one all-purpose wine glass.

The Stemmed Boob?

It's an urban legend that the coupe-style champagne glass was modeled after Marie Antoinette's breasts so everyone could drink from them. However, this cannot be true because this style glass was invented in the 1600s and Marie wasn't born until the 1700s.

Cool Tools

Bottom line, equipment matters and bartending is no exception. If you are equipping a home bar, think about the drinks you and your guests like the most and prioritize which tools to purchase.

Bar spoon. A bar spoon is used to stir classic Manhattans and Martinis and other cocktails in a mixing glass and to layer drinks. To layer, simply break the fall with the spoon or pour the alcohol down the spiral.

Blender. A bar without a blender is a bar without frozen Daiquiris. The heavier the motor, the better for crushing ice.

Waiter's version

Wingtype

Corkscrew. The most professional corkscrew (wine tool) is the "waiter's" version, a two-in-one gadget that opens wine bottles and beer bottles. This is the only corkscrew a real bartender uses. Here's how to use it to open a wine bottle: Remove the foil around the top of the cork with the knife on the corkscrew. Insert the screw (worm) into the center of the cork and twist until it's nearly all the way into the cork. Set the pry bar on the lip of the bottle and pry the cork straight up out of the bottle. The knife will also come in handy for many things when working as a bartender.

Ice scoop. An ice scoop is very important. A 24-ounce scoop is your best bet because it keeps nasty bacteria-infested hands out of the ice. Always stab the scoop into the ice handle-up so that you're only touching the handle. Never underestimate the power of ice. It's the second thing you need when making a cocktail. It's needed to melt the necessary water into the drink as well as keep it cold. The ice needs to be extremely clean at all times (and preferably made from filtered water).

Jigger. This measuring device is double-sided with different measures on each end. The most popular has 1½ ounces on one side and ½ ounce on the other, but you can buy many other sizes to meet your needs.

 Juice extractor and citrus reamer. Fresh juice is a small effort that goes a long way. An extractor or a reamer is the most common way to get fresh juice behind the bar when making a cocktail to order.

 Mixing glass. This clear pint glass is used to make classic Martinis and Manhattans (or any stirred cocktail) and used to muddle. It can also be used as one of the pieces of a Boston shaker.

 Muddler. This stick can be made of wood, plastic, or a combination of materials. It's used to crush mint, sugar, fruit, and herbs.

 Pour spouts. Pour spouts are pushed into bottle openings, allowing you to speed-pour your liquor and liqueurs. They are essential when tending bar or else you would be screwing caps off and on all night. After a party at home, simply take them out and put the caps back on the bottles.

Shaker tins. There are two types of shaker tins: cobbler and Boston. The cobbler shakers consist of three pieces—a tumbler, a lid with a built-in strainer, and a cap to cover the strainer. These are popular among amateur bartenders because they are easy to use, but busy bartenders favor Boston shakers. The Boston shaker consists of two pieces that fit inside each other. One piece is stainless steel, and the other piece is either a smaller stainless steel tin or a mixing glass. You shake your drink, then tap where they meet to break the seal and pour the drink. The two-part design allows for quicker pouring.

Strainer. There are three types of strainers: the Hawthorne, the julep, and a conical mesh strainer. The handheld conical mesh strainer is used in conjunction with the Hawthorne strainer as a double strainer (strain with the Hawthorne strainer into the mesh strainer). The Hawthorne has a coil around it and is used with a shaker tin. The julep strainer is placed in a convex position inside a mixing glass.

Zester. A zester (also called a channel knife) makes long curly twists out of citrus fruit peel. Simply set the zester on the fruit, apply pressure, and slice off a long piece.

Alcohol

Marines, Boy Scouts, and bartenders should always be prepared. Stocking a bar should be a matter of personal taste, lifestyle, and finances. But unless having a drink is always going to be a solitary pleasure, the person behind the bar should be prepared for guests.

How prepared you are is up to you. If Uncle Michael, who always visits at Christmas, only smiles with a glass of Irish whiskey in his hand, buy one bottle. If cognac inspires camaraderie among your friends, make the investment. If beer does the trick, stick to what works. Here are two suggested lists, one for a basic home bar and another that goes beyond basic to complete.

Basic Bar	Add for Complete Bar
Bourbon	Port
Brandy and Cognac	Canadian Whiskey
Gin	Dark and/or Spiced Rum
Rum	Coffee Liqueur
Scotch	Aged Tequila
Tequila	Grand Marnier
Vodka	Flavored Vodka
Whiskey (Irish)	Single Malt Scotch
Blended Whiskey or Rye	

Mixers

Mixers provide the flavor and balance that combine with liquor to give a drink its distinctive taste. Mixers range from plain water to club soda, from flavored sodas (like cola and lemon and lime) to fruit juices (orange, pineapple, cranberry, grapefruit, and tomato, and others). When it comes to mixers, fresher is always better.

Sugar

Sugar is a powerful partner in many drinks, but its presence is behind the scenes, never tasted distinctly, and never, never felt as granules. Unless granulated sugar is specified, confectioners' sugar, referred to in this book as fine sugar, should always be used. Some bartenders go a step further and prepare a "simple syrup" of sugar and water to use instead of dry sugar. To make a simple syrup, heat 2 cups of water in a saucepan and slowly add 2 cups of granulated sugar until it is completely dissolved. Boil for 5 minutes and then cool. The syrup can be stored in a bottle in a cool place for about a year. See Chapter 14 for more syrup recipes.

Popular Mixers
Popular mixers include orange juice, cranberry juice, pineapple juice, grapefruit juice, lemon and lime juices, Bloody Mary mix, strawberry mix, olive juice, V8 juice, tomato juice, simple syrup, grenadine, coconut cream, honey, gomme, orgeat, lime juice cordial, hot sauce, Worcestershire, beef bouillon, Clamato juice, clam juice, milk, cream, half-and-half, ice cream, hot chocolate, unsalted butter, eggnog, egg white, all sodas, coffee, espresso, tea, and hot water.

Get Fresh!

With this book's bias for "fresher is better," it is difficult to be objective. Fresh ingredients make a difference you can taste, but it may not be possible for you to make all of your own mixes. You can buy prepared mixes for Daiquiris, Margaritas, and, of course, Bloody Marys, among others. They come in bottled and powdered form. Some are excellent and some are not. Let the bartender beware and be the judge. "Sour" mixes, which contain lemon juice, sugar, and some egg white, are a special case. Whenever a recipe in this book calls for sugar and fresh lemon or lime juice, sour mix can be substituted in the amount indicated on the product's label.

Be Bitter!

While the sound of *bitters* is not appealing, the little bottles are a wonderful witch's brew of roots and barks, berries, and herbs. Bitters add a kick of flavor to the mixed drinks they accompany, always in small amounts—dashes, to be approximately exact. The most common type of bitters is Angostura, made in Trinidad. Two that are sometimes used are Peychaud's, from New Orleans, and Regans' orange bitters. Bitters do have an alcohol content and should not be served to anyone who abstains totally. Tasting them plain is not recommended either.

Condiments: The Little Things in Life

Sugar and spice and everything nice are all needed at the bar. Drinks are a delicate balance of ingredients, a microcosm of flavors. When the drink that is being created only totals three to eight ounces, every dash, splash, and fraction of a teaspoon counts. Condiments are like the little things in life—they make all the difference. Stocking the bar with them is not an exaggerated effort, but as basic as buying the liquor. For some people, a Martini does not exist without an olive, and a Margarita is naked without its salt. A Gibson is, in fact, defined by its cocktail onion. A collection of condiments is dependent on personal needs. The accompanying list includes items such as celery stalks and horseradish for Bloody Marys that you cannot keep at the bar waiting but must be available when the drinks are made. However, kosher salt for Margaritas can be ready at any time. Here are some condiments you can try:

Brown sugar	Cinnamon	Raw sugar
Cayenne pepper	Chili pepper	Salt
Celery salt	Kosher salt	Spicy seasonings
Cloves	Nutmeg	Sugar
Cocoa powder	Pepper	Sugar cubes
Coconut flakes	Powdered sugar	White pepper

Garnishes

The most popular garnishes are the lime, lemon, cherry, and olive. Runners-up are the orange, pineapple, cocktail onion, celery, mint, strawberry, and banana. You'll see other garnishes mentioned in this book, but you'll have to go out and explore to find some of the most outlandish. Pickled okra, edible pearl dust, and oysters on the half shell have all been used as unlikely garnishes.

Cutting garnishes can be intimidating for some people, but it's really easy. Just make sure you always wash your hands well first or wear rubber gloves when handling garnishes. After making a cut, always lay the flat side of the fruit down to create a stable base for cutting.

The Wedge: To cut the essential wedge, slice a lime (or lemon) in half lengthwise and cut each half into four wedges. When serving, squeeze the juice into the drink, rub the fruit side around the rim of the glass, and drop the slice in.

The Slice: If you prefer to set the fruit on the edge of the glass, cut it into eighths and make a slit in the meat of each slice.

The Twist: There are a few ways to make twists (usually lemon). One is to cut off both ends of the fruit so the inside meat shows. Make a slit in the fruit from end to end. Squeeze a bar spoon beneath the skin and scoop out the fruit. Cut the peel widthwise into ¼" strips. Another technique is to cut slits all around a whole citrus fruit and cut off one end. You can then peel off a twist to order. The proper way to garnish with a twist is to twist the peel, colored side down, over the drink, so the oils will release. Then, rub the colored side around the rim and drop the twist into the drink. Using a zester can make a long curly twist. Simply set the zester on the fruit's peel, apply pressure, and slice off a long piece.

Sometimes guests will ask for a soda water with a twist. This means that they want a lime wedge and not a lemon twist.

The Quarter: Quarter cuts work best when muddling. Cut the fruit in half through the middle. Lay both pieces flat and then cut twice, making a cross. This will yield four quarters per piece.

The Wheel: Cut off the ends of the fruit, then cut a ¼"-deep slit lengthwise (this slit makes it easy for you to set it on the rim of the glass). Hold the fruit firmly and cut 4 or 5 wheels.

Cutting Tools

A serrated knife is the best knife to use when cutting garnishes, and a cutting board that is not used for cutting meat is preferred. As a safety precaution, place a wet bar towel under the cutting board to avoid slippage.

The Zest: The zest is the cut that really helps you show off. It's an oval-shaped rind slice from a piece of citrus that can be squeezed over a drink and combined with a flame to make an attention-getting burst. This happens because the oil of the rind meets the flame. Most often the zest is made from an orange. Don't confuse this with the kind of zesting done to citrus fruits in cooking and baking. That type of zesting results in bitty shreds of peel that nobody would want floating in a drink.

Rimming

Glass rims can be dipped in something wet or sticky and then dipped into something edible. Rimming always makes a great presentation. Margaritas look better with kosher salt around their rims, and Chocolate Martinis are appetizing in chocolate-rimmed glasses.

Drinking glasses can be rimmed with sugar of all types and colors, salt of all types and colors, cocoa powder, hot chocolate powder, shaved chocolate, coconut flakes, Pop Rocks, sprinkles, edible gold flakes, Cajun spices, crushed Oreo cookies, crushed graham crackers, and anything else your imagination can conjure up.

Measurements Matter

Since the metric system measures the world, except in the United States, here are some equivalents and charts to help avoid confusion. When measuring ingredients for a drink, remember that the balance is important, so for weaker or stronger drinks, adjust all of the components accordingly.

BARTENDER MEASURES		
Bar Measurements	Standard	Metric
1 dash	.03 ounce	0.9 milliliter
1 splash	.25 ounce	7.5 milliliters
1 teaspoon	.125 ounce	3.7 milliliters
1 tablespoon	.375 ounce	11.1 milliliters
1 float	.5 ounce	14.8 milliliters
1 pony	1 ounce	29.5 milliliters
1 jigger	1.5 ounces	44.5 milliliters
1 cup	8 ounces	237.0 milliliters
1 pint	16 ounces	472.0 milliliters
1 quart	32 ounces	946.0 milliliters
1 gallon	128 ounces	3.78 liters

METRIC SIZES FOR SPIRITS AND BEER AND WINES		
Name of Container	Standard	Metric
split	6.3 ounces	187.0 milliliters
half	12.6 ounces	375.0 milliliters
fifth	25.3 ounces	750.0 milliliters
quart	33.8 ounces	1 liter
magnum	50.7 ounces	1.5 liters
jeroboam	101.4 ounces	3 liters
nebuchadnezzar	3.96 gallons	15 liters
keg	7.75 gallons	29.3 liters

These measures are great to look up when having a cocktail party. Experienced bartenders—through repetition—learn to eyeball everything, but if you are in doubt, then there's nothing wrong with measuring. The main things to keep in mind are that you can get 3 or 4 servings from a bottle of wine, 20 to 25 shots of alcohol from a fifth, and 30 to 35 shots of alcohol from a liter.

CHAPTER 3

beer: the oldest alcohol known to man

Man has been brewing beer since the moment he remained in one place long enough to grow grain. Scientists and archaeologists have noted that beer dates back to 7000 B.C.E. Ninety-two Babylonian tablets have been found with beer recipes carved into them, and over twenty types of beer recipes have been found on Sumerian tablets. Beer was used for food, medicine, and bartering, and was key in ceremonies and celebrations.

Beer History

The Egyptians were the first to refine the texture and taste of beer. After that, the Greeks and Romans carried on the beer-making tradition when there weren't grapes to make wine. Ancient Germans (Teutons) took their beer very seriously, even using it as a sacrifice to their beer gods.

During medieval times, monastery monks focused intently on making the best beer possible. Hops were first used in the 1000s, and it must have improved beer tremendously because priests baptized children with the beer made with it. By the 1200s beer was classified as ale (top-fermenting) or lager (bottom-fermenting). Germany brewed cold-temperature lagers, storing them in caves, while England brewed room-temperature ales and stored them in cellars. In 1519, the Reinheitsgebot was enacted in Bavaria, Germany, requiring that all beer be made only from barley, hops, and water. By the early 1600s a way to bottle beer with a cork was perfected, the most popular drinking song in England was "John Barleycorn," and there were over 17,000 taverns in England alone.

The Two Types of Beer
Beer is classified as ale or lager. Ale is made by adding yeast on top of the brewing mixture. Types of ales include stout, porter, bitter, wheat, lambic, brown, pale, Belgian, barley wine, amber, and cream. Lager is made by adding yeast on the bottom of the brewing mixture. Types of lagers include bock, dry, light, ice, pilsner, and malt.

In 1978, U.S. President Jimmy Carter signed a bill legalizing home brewing of beer for the first time since Prohibition. People began experimenting, making their own home brews. Handcrafted beer combined with a high-tech era resulted in microbrews. Microbreweries sprouted up all over the country. The Institute for Brewing Studies reported explosive growth in this industry in the 1980s—and that growth was based on smallness. Comparing these beers to the corporate kind is to liken a hunk of rich-textured, whole-grain, home-baked bread to a slice of supermarket white. Words like *tangy*, *full-bodied*, *robust*, and *flowery* have real meaning in this context. Today, there are microbreweries producing craft beer in every state.

Beer Recipes

Beer cocktails are libations that contain beer. Beer can be used as a base ingredient or as a substitution for a carbonated mixer. Today, craft beer is made from a variety of ingredients such as pecans, chocolate, coconut, chilies, sweet potatoes, fruits, coffee, herbs, pumpkin, and more. Using these craft beers in cocktails enhances the flavor and also allows people to get creative in combining flavors when mixing with other mixers, spirits, and liqueurs.

Afternoon Melon Delight

Watermelon ice cubes

12 ounces light- to medium-bodied beer

Make watermelon ice cubes by blending fresh ripe watermelon in a blender, then straining to make watermelon juice. Add simple syrup to the juice to taste, then freeze in ice cubes trays. Fill a tall glass with watermelon ice cubes and slowly add the beer.

Ale Punch

14 ounces ale

1/2 ounce brandy

1/2 ounce sherry

1/4 ounce simple syrup

Dash ground cloves

1 lemon slice

Pour the brandy and sherry into the ale, then add the simple syrup, ground cloves, and lemon slice. Gently stir.

Baltimore Zoo

1/2 ounce vodka

1/2 ounce rum

1/2 ounce grenadine

Stout to fill

Pour all the ingredients into a pint glass or beer mug.

Bee Sting

12 ounces dark beer

3 ounces orange juice

Pour the orange juice into the beer. Stir gently to mix.

Beer Buster

2 ounces chilled vodka

14 ounces chilled light beer

Pour the vodka into a chilled mug and add the beer.

Beermato

2 ounces Clamato juice

1/2 ounce lemon juice

2 dashes Worcestershire sauce

12 ounces light beer

Pour all the ingredients into a pint glass or beer mug.

Bittersweet

1 ounce Campari

4 ounces orange soda

4 ounces light beer

Fill a tall glass with ice and add all the ingredients. Stir gently.

Black and Tan

8 ounces pale ale (such as Bass)

8 ounces stout (such as Guinness)

Pour the pale ale into the glass, then slowly pour the stout on top of the ale to create a layer. Use a spoon bowl to break the fall (bars with stout on tap come with black and tan spoons).

Black Shandy

8 ounces stout

8 ounces cola

Pour ingredients into a pint glass or beer mug.

Black Velvet

6 ounces chilled champagne or sparkling wine

6 ounces chilled stout or dark porter

This was invented in honor of Prince Albert after he died at age forty-two in 1861. You simply float the stout on top of the champagne. Do not stir.

Popular Ales

The most popular ale brands are Bass, Red Hook, Guinness, Full Sail, Sierra Nevada, Pete's Wicked Ale, Pyramid Hefeweizen, Sam Adams Cream Stout, Sam Adams Cherry Wheat, and Sam Adams Boston Ale.

Bloody Beer

14 ounces lager

2 ounces Bloody Mary mix

Dash Tabasco (optional)

Dash Worcestershire (optional)

Pour the Bloody Mary mix into the beer. Embellish with a dash of Tabasco and a dash of Worcestershire if you like.

Blow My Skull Off

15 ounces stout

1 ounce rum

Dash cayenne pepper

Lime slice

Pour the rum into the stout. Sprinkle the cayenne pepper in and mix gently. Squeeze the juice from the lime and drop it into the beer.

Boilermaker

15 ounces light beer

1 ounce whiskey

Combine the beer and whiskey in a beer mug using your preferred method. Emily Post would sip this drink after pouring the shot into the beer (pinky finger raised). Other people might drop the shot, glass and all, into the filled beer mug and chug-a-lug before the foam hits the floor.

Bourbon Bacon Ale

14 ounces dark ale

1 ounce Grade B maple syrup

1 ounce bourbon

1 crispy slice of maple bacon

Pour the maple syrup and bourbon into the beer and gently stir. Garnish with crispy slice of maple bacon.

Broadway

11 ounces light beer

5 ounces cola

Combine the beer and the cola gently because both are carbonated. This is a popular mixture in Japan.

Butterscotch Float

12 ounces chocolate stout

2 ounces butterscotch schnapps

1 scoop butter pecan ice cream

Pour the schnapps into the beer and then add the ice cream on top.

Caribbean Night

15 ounces light beer

1 ounce coffee liqueur

Pour the coffee liqueur into the beer. Stir gently to mix thoroughly.

Cheeky Tractor

1 ounce Irish cream

1/2 ounce sambuca

8 ounces dark beer

Pour the Irish cream and sambuca into a glass. Fill with the dark beer.

Cherry Ale Blossom

1 ounce elderflower liqueur

12 ounces cherry ale

Pour ingredients into a chilled beer mug.

Where to Find Craft Beer

Every medium to large American city has a small selection of craft beer in grocery stores. You'll find a larger selection in large liquor stores, but if you are looking for a boutique selection of craft beer worldwide, then just search on the Internet for craft beer stores in your area.

Cherry Russian Ale

15 ounces stout

1 ounce cherry vodka

Pour ingredients into a pint glass or beer mug.

Chew Brew

12 ounces light beer

7 orange gummy bears

Pour the beer into a chilled glass and drop in the gummy bears.

Chocolate-Covered Cherry

12 ounces cherry beer

1 ounce white crème de cacao

Pour the crème de cacao into the beer and gently mix.

Chocolate Raspberry Beer

12 ounces raspberry beer

1 ounce white or dark crème de cacao

Pour the crème de cacao into the beer and gently mix.

Chocolate Russian Ale

15 ounces stout

1 ounce chocolate vodka

Pour ingredients into a pint glass or beer mug.

Chocolate Truffle

14 ounces stout

1 ounce raspberry liqueur

1 ounce chocolate liqueur

Pour ingredients into a pint glass or beer mug.

Corona Limon

12-ounce bottle Corona

1½ ounces Bacardi Limon

Drink a little of the beer from the bottle, then add the Bacardi Limon.

Corona with Training Wheels

Lime slice

12-ounce bottle Corona

Kosher Margarita salt

Rub the lime on the neck of the Corona bottle to moisten. Sprinkle kosher salt on the neck. Push the lime into the bottle. Lick salt before or after you take a sip. In some parts of America this is referred to as a dressed Corona.

Cream of Wheat

8 ounces stout

8 ounces hefeweizen

Pour ingredients into a pint glass or beer mug.

Danish Pastry

1 ounce Cherry Heering

12 ounces Danish pale lager (such as Carlsberg)

Lime wedge

Pour liquid ingredients into a pint glass or beer mug. Squeeze the lime into the mixture before dropping it into the glass.

The Five Steps in Making Beer

(1) Harvest barley and soak it, allowing it to germinate to create malt. (2) Clean and grind malt, then optionally mix it with corn grits; cook to create wort. (3) Boil wort with the herb hops. (4) Cool wort and add either top- or bottom-fermenting yeast. (5) Add flavors, filter, and pasteurize. Store in cans, bottles, or kegs.

Dark Port

14 ounces stout

2 ounces port

Pour ingredients into a pint glass or beer mug.

Depth Charge

2 ounces chilled peppermint schnapps

14 ounces light beer

Pour the chilled peppermint schnapps into a frosted mug. Top off with beer.

Dog's Bollocks

8 ounces lager

1 ounce melon-flavored vodka

1/2 ounce lime juice cordial

Pour the vodka and lime juice cordial into a glass of lager.

Dr. Pepper

14 ounces light beer

1 ounce amaretto

1/2 ounce 151 rum

1/4 ounce grenadine

Pour the amaretto, rum, and grenadine into the beer.

Figgy Apricot

2 ounces fig purée

1 ounce amaretto

8 ounces apricot ale

Add the purée to a 16-ounce glass, and then pour in the amaretto and mix together. Add ice then the apricot beer and gently stir.

Florida Sunshine Beer

12 ounces light beer

3 ounces orange juice

1/2 ounce simple syrup

Pour all ingredients into a glass and mix gently.

Lager Characteristics

Bock: can be light or dark in color but always has a hoppy taste and has a high alcohol content. Pilsner: light-colored (yellow) and light-bodied. Dry: light in color and body with a clean, crisp taste. Ice: light in color and body with a high alcohol content.

Ginger Blueberry

Handful of blueberries

5 ounces ginger beer

5 ounces blueberry beer

Drop the blueberries in the bottom of a 16-ounce glass and gently muddle. Add ice. Pour in the ginger beer and blueberry beer and gently stir.

Ginger Shandy

8 ounces chilled ginger beer

8 ounces chilled light beer

In a beer glass, mix ginger beer with the light beer.

Hazelnut Coffee

1 ounce hazelnut liqueur
12 ounces coffee stout

Pour ingredients into a pint glass or beer mug.

Hot Beer

14 ounces light beer
1 ounce cinnamon schnapps
1/2 ounce grenadine

Pour the beer, cinnamon schnapps, and grenadine into a glass. Slightly stir.

Isar Water

1 ounce blue curaçao
2 ounces apple juice
13 ounces wheat beer

Chill all of the ingredients. Pour the curaçao and apple juice into a glass. Fill with the wheat beer.

Jamaican Me Thirsty

12 ounces Jamaican beer
1 ounce dark Jamaican rum
1 ounce banana liqueur

Pour the rum and liqueur into the beer and gently stir.

Lager and Lime

16 ounces light lager (pilsner)
1/2 ounce lime juice cordial

Add the lime juice cordial to the lager. Examples of a pilsner are Budweiser, Coors, and Miller.

Lagerita

1 1/2 ounces tequila
1 ounce triple sec
1 ounce lime juice
16 ounces light Mexican beer

Shake the tequila, triple sec, and lime juice with ice, then strain into a tall, chilled, half-salted rimmed glass. Add the beer on top.

Ale Characteristics

Stout: very dark (almost black) with a very full body. Brown ales: medium-bodied, buttery, and smooth. Porter: dark and hoppy. Wheat: light, creamy, and fruity. Pale ale: medium-bodied with a slight bitterness. Cream ale: light-bodied with a malty flavor. Amber: medium-bodied and hoppy.

Light Lunch Box

11 ounces light beer
1 ounce amaretto
4 ounces orange juice

Pour the amaretto and orange juice into the beer. Stir gently to mix.

Liverpool Kiss

15 ounces dark beer
1 ounce crème de cassis

Pour the crème de cassis into the dark beer. Stir gently to mix.

Mexican Cherry

16-ounce bottle Corona
½ ounce grenadine
1 maraschino cherry

Pour out a little of the beer from the bottle. Add the grenadine and garnish with a cherry on top.

Michelada

7 ounces light beer
1 ounce tequila
1 ounce lemon juice
Dash Tabasco
Dash Worcestershire
Pinch salt and pepper

Pour the beer into a glass of ice. Add the tequila, lemon juice, Tabasco, Worcestershire, and salt and pepper.

Orange-Spiked Lager

1 ounce orange liqueur (such as triple sec)
15 ounces light beer

Pour the orange liqueur into a glass. Fill with beer. To make the beer appear green, replace the orange liqueur with blue curaçao, which still has an orange flavor.

Passion Beer

14 ounces light beer
½ ounce passion fruit juice
1 ounce passion liqueur

Pour all ingredients into a glass. Gently mix.

Peach-Spiked Brew

1 ounce chilled peach schnapps
15 ounces chilled light beer

Pour the peach schnapps into a glass. Fill with beer.

United States Beer Firsts

In 1587, Sir Walter Raleigh brewed the first beer in Virginia. In 1757, the future first president, George Washington, wrote about his personal beer recipe and titled it To Make Small Beer. In 1876, Anheuser-Busch sent out the first fleet of double-walled refrigerated railroad cars across the United States. In 1935, Krueger Cream Ale was the first canned beer. In 1959, Coors was the first beer to be packaged in lightweight aluminum cans. In 1963, the Schlitz Brewing Company introduced the pop-top beer. In 1974, Miller Lite Beer became the first light beer. In 1984, Labatt Brewing Company introduced the twist-off cap.

Pecan Float

12 ounces pecan beer

1 ounce vanilla syrup

1 scoop pralines and cream ice cream

Pour the vanilla syrup into the beer, then top with the ice cream.

Pizza Beer

14 ounces lager or 14 ounces wheat beer

2 ounces Bloody Mary mix

Pepperoni slice

Mozzarella cube

Olive

Pour the Bloody Mary mix into the beer and gently stir. Garnish with pepperoni slice, mozzarella cube, and olive on a skewer.

Pumpkin Black and Tan

8 ounces pumpkin ale

8 ounces stout

Pour the ale into the glass and slowly pour the stout on top of the ale to create a layer.

Raging Bull

12 ounces Mexican beer

3 ounces Red Bull

1 ounce tequila

Pour ingredients into a pint glass or beer mug.

Raspberry Russian Ale

15 ounces stout

1 ounce raspberry vodka

Pour ingredients into a pint glass or beer mug.

Red Eye

14 ounces lager

2 ounces tomato juice

Lemon slice (optional)

Pour the tomato juice into the beer. You can embellish it with a lemon slice if you desire.

Red-Headed Stepchild

14 ounces light beer

1 ounce whiskey

1/2 ounce grenadine

Pour all ingredients into a glass. Gently mix.

Rise and Shine

1 ounce whiskey

1 ounce lemon juice

1 ounce Grade B maple syrup

1 organic egg white

5 ounces beer of choice

Beef jerky

Shake the first four ingredients with ice and strain into a tall chilled glass. Fill with beer and garnish with beef jerky.

Beer Trivia

In the 1490s, Columbus found Native Americans making beer from corn and black birch sap. In 1876, Louis Pasteur learned the secrets of yeast in the fermentation process and also learned to pasteurize beer twenty-two years before the same was done to milk. In 1909, Teddy Roosevelt took 500 gallons of beer on safari in Africa. In 1963, the stainless steel beer keg was introduced.

Rotten Apple

8 ounces stout
8 ounces apple cider

Pour ingredients into a pint glass or beer mug.

Rotten Pear

8 ounces stout
8 ounces pear cider

Pour ingredients into a pint glass or beer mug.

Ruby

15 ounces stout
1 ounce ruby port
Dash nutmeg

Pour the ruby port into the stout. Sprinkle with nutmeg.

Rushing Russian Ale

15 ounces stout
1 ounce espresso vodka

Pour ingredients into a pint glass or beer mug.

Russian Ale

15 ounces stout
1 ounce vodka

Pour ingredients into a pint glass or beer mug.

Sake Bomb

1 ounce sake
15 ounces Japanese beer

Pour the sake into a shot glass and the beer into a pint glass. Drop the shot glass into the beer. For a fun variation, balance the shot of sake over the beer with a pair of chopsticks. Slam the table to make the shot fall into the beer and drink.

Scotland Yard

12 ounces light beer
1 ounce Drambuie

Pour the Drambuie into the beer and gently stir.

Shandy

8 ounces chilled Sprite or 7UP
8 ounces chilled light beer

In a beer glass, mix Sprite or 7UP with the beer.

Beer and Health Benefits
There are some health benefits based on many scientific studies on beer. Beer makes bones stronger because of its high silicon levels. Beer prevents kidney stones in men. Moderate beer consumption lowers risk of heart disease, and those who do consume it moderately are less likely to develop high blood pressure.

Skip and Go Naked

½ ounce gin
½ ounce sweet-and-sour mix
Beer to fill

Shake the gin and sweet-and-sour mix with ice. Pour into a highball glass of ice. Fill with beer.

Skippy

2 ounces vodka
6 ounces lemonade
8 ounces lager

Pour the vodka and lemonade into a glass. Fill with the lager.

Snake in the Apple Tree

8 ounces chilled stout
8 ounces chilled apple cider

Mix the stout and apple cider in a beer glass.

Sneaky Pete

15 ounces light beer
1 ounce applejack

Pour beer into a chilled mug and add applejack. Stir slightly.

South Wind

15 ounces light beer
1 ounce melon liqueur

Pour the melon liqueur into the beer. Stir gently to mix thoroughly until a pretty green.

Spiced Beer

12 ounces light beer
2 ounces ginger ale
¼ ounce simple syrup
¼ teaspoon ground ginger
Pinch nutmeg
Dash bitters

Pour the beer and ginger ale into a glass. Add the simple syrup, ginger, nutmeg, and bitters.

Strawberry Pimm's Cup

1½ ounces Pimm's No. 1
1 ounce simple syrup
1 ounce fresh lemon juice
5 ounces strawberry beer
Cucumber slice
Seasonal fruit

Pour the Pimm's No. 1, simple syrup, and lemon juice into a 16-ounce glass, then add ice. Top with strawberry beer and gently stir. Add a cucumber slice and seasonal fruit for a garnish.

Sugar and Spice and Everything Nice

Bottle or can chilled Guinness stout

1/4 cup chilled sweetened condensed milk

Pinch cinnamon

Pinch nutmeg

1 packet cocoa mix

Pour the chilled Guinness stout beer into a bowl. Add chilled condensed milk, cinnamon, nutmeg, and cocoa mix and stir until blended. Pour into a tall beer glass and enjoy.

Sweet Potato Pie

12 ounces sweet potato ale

1 ounce toasted marshmallow syrup

1/2 ounce cinnamon schnapps

1 large marshmallow

Pour the syrup and schnapps into the beer and stir gently, then top with a marshmallow. Use a chef's torch to toast the marshmallow.

Tomahawk

8 ounces stout

1 ounce vodka

7 ounces Smirnoff Ice

Pour the vodka into the stout. Fill with Smirnoff Ice.

Tropical Beer

11 ounces light beer

3 ounces ginger ale

1 ounce lemon-flavored rum

1/2 ounce lime juice cordial

1/4 ounce peach schnapps

1/2 ounce grenadine

Pour all ingredients into a tall glass in the order given. Stir once, gently.

Vanilla Russian Ale

15 ounces stout

1 ounce vanilla vodka

Pour ingredients into a pint glass or beer mug.

Whistle Belly

14 ounces ale

1 ounce dark rum

1 ounce molasses

Pour the rum and molasses into the beer and gently mix.

CHAPTER

4

wine, champagne, cider, cognac, and brandy

Wine is a fermented beverage made from fruits—and not necessarily grapes. Wine is most definitely a blast from the past. The first written account of it is in the Bible, which notes that Noah planted a vineyard and made wine. Before that, wine was probably discovered by accident due to grape spoilage. Researchers say that social wine drinking probably began around 6000 B.C.E. In some cultures, beer was for the villagers and workers and wine was reserved for royalty. The Romans are truly responsible for expanding the wine culture in the Old World, mainly due to the sheer size of the Roman Empire.

Through the Grapevine

There are four types of wine: still, aromatized, sparkling, and fortified. Aromatized and fortified wines are described in the chapter on aperitifs, and sparkling refers to the champagne in this chapter. Still wines are the familiar red and white varieties that range in taste from dry and semidry to sweet.

Choosing Wine

Facing the forest of wine bottles at the liquor or grocery store can be daunting. The following list describes wines in the most general way with the barest descriptions. The best way to learn about wine is to investigate and experiment yourself. Individual taste is the best standard for personal pleasure. White wines are served chilled and red wines are served at room temperature. Also, the name of a wine clues you in to the type of grapes used. For example, a Cabernet Sauvignon is made from Cabernet Sauvignon grapes.

Popular Wines

Popular red wines include Cabernet Sauvignon (full-bodied and dark), Merlot (medium-bodied and lighter than Cabernet), Burgundy (heavy and dark), Beaujolais (light-bodied, with a better taste when chilled), Pinot Noir (light-bodied and mild), Zinfandel (medium-bodied and spicy), Petite Sirah (rich berry flavor), and Chianti (soft and smooth).

Popular white wines include Chardonnay (dry and crisp), Sauvignon Blanc (dry and citrusy), Chenin Blanc (fruity), Chablis (light and woody), Riesling (fruity and sweet), and Gewürztraminer (spicy sweet).

American Beauty

1 ounce rose vodka

5 ounces rosé wine

Rose petals, for garnish

Fill a large wine glass half full with ice. Add the liquid ingredients. Stir. Garnish with rose petals.

Bishop

2 ounces orange juice

1 ounce lemon juice

1 teaspoon sugar

4 ounces red wine

Pour juices and sugar into a mixing glass nearly filled with ice. Strain into a highball glass over ice. Fill with red wine.

Blue Sangria

4 ounces white wine

1 ounce blue curaçao

2 ounces white grape juice

2 ounces soda water

Seasonal fruits, for garnish

Fill a tall glass or large wine glass with ice and add the liquid ingredients. Garnish with slices of seasonal fruits.

Cactus Berry

3 ounces merlot

1 ounce blanco tequila

1 ounce Cointreau

1 ounce fresh lime juice

1 lime wedge

Combine liquid ingredients in a shaker half filled with ice. Shake well. Strain into a cocktail glass. Garnish with lime wedge.

Cardinal

1 ounce crème de cassis

Red wine to fill

Fill half of a wine glass with ice. Add the crème de cassis. Fill with red wine.

Elderflower Wine

5 ounces dry white wine

1 ounce elderflower liqueur

1 ounce soda water

Fill a highball or small wine glass with ice and add all the ingredients. Stir.

Glogg

7 ounces red wine

½ ounce fresh lemon juice

1 teaspoon sugar

1 cinnamon stick

Warm up the first three ingredients on the stove or in a microwave. Pour into a mug or Irish coffee glass. Garnish with cinnamon stick.

Kir

½ ounce crème de cassis (or to taste)

4 ounces dry white wine

1 lemon twist

Pour the crème de cassis into a large wine glass. Add the wine. Serve with a lemon twist.

Mulled Wine

Zest from a quarter of an orange

Zest from a quarter of a lemon

1 tablespoon sugar

1 cinnamon stick

2 whole cloves

4 ounces water

5 ounces red wine

Slices from a quarter of an orange

Slices from a quarter of a lemon

Put the fruit zest, sugar, cinnamon stick, cloves, and water into a small pot and bring to a slow boil. Remove from heat and add the wine. Add the orange and lemon slices and warm on low heat for 40 minutes (do NOT boil). Strain and serve.

Red Velvet Grapes

1 ounce white crème de cacao

5 ounces red wine

Red grapes, for garnish

Fill a large wine glass with ice and add the liquid ingredients. Stir. Garnish with red grapes still on the stem and draped over the rim.

Wine Words to Know

Aging = Effects of maturation. Alcoholic fermentation = The process by which yeast and sugar in grapes react to produce alcohol. AC = Appellation d'Origine Contrôlée, the quality control designation on French wine. Claret = English term for red wine. Demi-Sec = Medium sweet. Doux = Sweet. Fortified wine = Wine with a high-strength spirit added.

Rose Petal Sangria

4 ounces rosé wine

1 ounce rose syrup

2 ounces white grape juice

2 ounces soda water

Rose petals, for garnish

Fill a tall glass or large wine glass with ice and add the liquid ingredients. Garnish with rose petals.

Rosy Navel

1 ounce peach schnapps

1 ounce fresh orange juice

5 ounces rosé wine

2 ounces soda water

Fill a large wine glass with ice and add all the ingredients. Stir.

Sangria #1 ♉

4 ounces red wine

1 ounce blackberry brandy

1/2 ounce orange juice

1/2 ounce pineapple juice

Soda water or Perrier to fill

Sliced seasonal fruits, for garnish

Fill a tall glass or large wine glass with ice and add the first four ingredients. Fill with soda to 1" from the rim. Garnish with slices of seasonal fruits.

Sangria #2

Makes 8 glasses

2 bottles red wine

2 ounces brandy

1 cup orange juice

1/2 cup pineapple juice

1/2 cup cherry juice

2 tablespoons sugar

3 cups maraschino cherries

1 orange, thinly sliced into wheels

1 lemon, thinly sliced into wheels

1 lime, thinly sliced into wheels

Fruits of your choice, for garnish

Combine the liquids, sugar, cherries, and half of the sliced citrus fruit. Chill. When ready to serve, add the rest of the citrus fruit. Garnish each glass with a piece of fruit. To make a nonalcoholic version, use grape juice. You are not limited to these fruits. All fruits are acceptable in sangria, so experiment.

Tangerine Bubbles

1 ounce tangerine vodka

1 ounce fresh tangerine juice

Dry champagne to fill

Pour the vodka and juice into a champagne glass, then fill with the dry champagne. Stir slightly.

Valentine

4 ounces Beaujolais

2 ounces cranberry juice

Combine ingredients in a shaker half filled with ice. Shake, then strain into a wine glass.

Vanilla Pear Mimosa

1 ounce vanilla vodka

1 ounce pear nectar

Dry champagne to fill

Pour the vodka and nectar into a champagne glass, then fill with the dry champagne. Stir slightly.

Vino Crush

4 ounces white wine

1 ounce Grand Marnier

Orange soda to fill

Fill a tall glass with ice and pour in the wine and Grand Marnier. Fill with the orange soda.

Whiny Beach

1 ounce coconut rum

2 ounces white wine

2 ounces cranberry juice

Fill a large wine glass with ice and add all the ingredients. Stir.

White or Red Wine Cooler

5 ounces wine
Sprite or 7UP to fill
Lemon or lime wedge, for garnish

Pour wine and soda over ice into a large wine glass. Stir gently. Garnish with fruit wedge.

White or Red Wine Spritzer

5 ounces red or white wine
Club soda or sparkling water to fill
Lemon or lime wedge, for garnish

Pour wine and soda over ice into a large wine glass. Stir gently. Garnish with fruit wedge.

No Rules for Sangria

There are no real rules for sangria except that it needs to have wine and fruit in it. For the White Sangria, you can easily add or substitute clear liquids such as white (clear) cranberry juice, white grape juice, champagne (for carbonation), and any seasonal fruits you desire. It's all up to you.

White Sangria #1

4 ounces white wine
$\frac{1}{2}$ ounce apple brandy
1 ounce apple juice
$\frac{1}{4}$ teaspoon ground cinnamon
Soda water or Perrier to fill
Sliced seasonal fruits, for garnish

Fill a tall glass or large wine glass with ice and add the first four ingredients. Fill with soda to 1" from the rim. Garnish with slices of seasonal fruits.

White Sangria #2

Serves 6

1 cup water
$\frac{1}{2}$ cup sugar
6 cinnamon sticks
1 bottle nondry white wine
1 cup sparkling water
1 cup apple juice
$\frac{1}{2}$ cup orange juice
3 oranges cut in wheels
Cherries, to taste
3 apples cut in chunks

Heat the water, sugar, and cinnamon sticks to a simmer. Continue to simmer for 5 minutes. Remove from heat. Let cool to room temperature. Remove the sticks; mix in white wine, sparkling water, apple juice, and orange juice. Chill overnight in the refrigerator. Add the fruit on top for presentation.

A Touch of Bubbly: Champagne

Champagne is sexy, no doubt about it. Its bubbles are flirtatious, and its fizz is a sultry invitation to hold hands, sigh, and exchange glances. *Champagne* is a term often used to describe any sparkling wine, but that is technically incorrect. Genuine champagne is only produced in France, in the chalky hills and valleys near the River Marne that make up the Champagne region. But the champagne method (*méthode champenoise*) of fermenting wine in the bottle it is sold in can be used anywhere to make still wine sparkle.

The method for making champagne begins with a *cuvée*, a vineyard's blend of dry white wines. The blend is bottled with yeast and sugar for a second fermentation to create the bubbles. In the process a sediment is formed. *Mon Dieu!* No matter how fine the wine, gunk in the bottle will not do. So the second step ingeniously collects the sediment. The bottles are tilted and turned so that the sediment clings to the cork. In the third step, the cork (along with the unsightly muck) is removed, a bit of sugar is added, and the bottle is recorked. The typical mushroom-shaped cork is a result of ramming two-thirds of a cork wider than the neck into the bottle. Under pressure, the cork forms a perfect seal. The wire on top is to prevent any overexuberant bubbles from popping their cork.

A champagne bottle should be opened with the same caution used in handling a dangerous weapon. Imagine the bottle as a gun and your finger as the safety catch. Always keep a thumb or finger over the cork. First remove the foil and wire, with your thumb hovering over the cork. Then point the bottle at a 45-degree angle away from everybody. Grip the cork firmly in one hand and pull the bottle with the other. As the internal pressure loosens the cork, continue to hold it firmly.

Champagne offers choices and clear descriptions. Created in a range from dry to sweet, the contents of the bottles are conveniently labeled. *Brut* is very dry; extra dry or *sec* is not as dry; *demi-sec* is the half-and-half of champagne, slightly sweet and dry; and *doux* is the sweetest of all.

Bellini

1 ounce chilled white peach purée
Prosecco sparkling wine to fill

Pour the purée into a champagne flute and fill with Prosecco. You can buy the purée or hand-make some. A lot of people use champagne and a peach nectar or liqueur, but this recipe stays true to the original 1948 concoction.

Black Velvet

6 ounces chilled stout or dark porter
6 ounces chilled champagne or sparkling wine

Float the chilled stout on top of the chilled champagne. Do not stir. This drink was created in honor of Queen Victoria's husband, Prince Albert, after his death in 1861.

Champagne and Chambord

1 ounce Chambord raspberry liqueur
Chilled champagne to fill

Pour the Chambord into a champagne flute and fill with champagne.

Champagne Antoine

1 ounce gin
1 ounce dry vermouth
1/8 ounce Pernod
Chilled dry champagne to fill
1 lemon twist

Shake the gin, vermouth, and Pernod with ice. Strain into a champagne flute. Fill with champagne and add a lemon twist.

Wine Words to Know

Jug wine = American term for table wine. Sec = Dry. Tannin = Natural component in skins, seeds, and stems of grapes that creates a dry, puckering sensation in the mouth. Varietal = Grape variety; wines made from a single grape are varietals, and labeled with that grape. Vintage = Defines the grape harvest of a single year.

Champagne Cocktail

6 ounces chilled champagne
1 sugar cube
3 dashes Angostura bitters
1 lemon twist

Pour a glass of champagne. Soak a sugar cube with the bitters. Drop the cube into the champagne and add the twist.

Champagne Fizz or Diamond Fizz

2 ounces gin
1 ounce lemon juice
1 teaspoon sugar
Chilled champagne to fill

Combine gin, lemon juice, and sugar in a shaker half filled with ice and shake. Strain into a highball glass over ice. Fill with champagne.

Champagne Flamingo

¾ ounce vodka
¾ ounce Campari
Chilled champagne to fill
Zest of orange, for garnish

Shake vodka and Campari with
ice and strain into a champagne
flute. Fill with champagne.
Garnish with zest of orange.

Champagne Mint

½ ounce green crème de menthe
Chilled champagne to fill

Pour crème de menthe into a
flute and fill with champagne.

Death in the Afternoon

1 ounce absinthe
Chilled champagne to fill

Pour absinthe into a champagne
flute. Fill with champagne.

Bubbly Bath
Rumor has it that Marilyn
Monroe once filled up her
tub with 350 bottles of champagne and took a bath.

Flirtini

½ ounce pineapple vodka
1 ounce pineapple juice
Champagne to fill

Shake the vodka and pineapple
juice. Strain into a champagne
flute. Fill with champagne.

French 75

1 ounce gin
1 ounce lemon juice
½ ounce simple syrup
Chilled champagne to fill
1 lemon twist

Build gin, lemon juice, and simple syrup into a champagne flute
and top with chilled champagne.
Garnish with lemon twist.

Kir Royale

1 ounce crème de cassis
Chilled champagne to fill
1 lemon twist

Pour the crème de cassis into a
champagne flute and fill with
champagne. Garnish with lemon
twist.

Make Believe

½ ounce dark rum
½ ounce ginger syrup
½ ounce fresh lime juice
5 ounces dry champagne

Pour the ingredients into a champagne glass and gently stir.

Melon Mimosa

1 ounce melon liqueur

1 teaspoon lime cordial

5 ounces chilled champagne

Combine ingredients in a champagne flute or white wine glass. Stir gently.

Mimosa

¼ of a champagne flute of freshly squeezed orange juice

Champagne to fill

1 strawberry

Fill a champagne flute a quarter of the way with orange juice. Fill with champagne and garnish the rim with a strawberry.

Miss Beehavin'

1 ounce pear brandy

½ ounce honey

5 ounces dry champagne

Pour the first two ingredients into a champagne glass and stir until honey dissolves. Fill with dry champagne.

Moulin Rouge

1 ounce Chambord raspberry liqueur

½ ounce Grand Marnier

5 ounces French champagne

Red pinwheel, for garnish (optional)

Pour all liquid ingredients into a wine glass. Garnish with the red pinwheel if desired.

Pimm's Royale

¼ ounce Pimm's Cup

Chilled champagne to fill

1 cucumber spear

Pour the Pimm's Cup in a champagne flute. Fill with chilled champagne and garnish with cucumber spear.

Poinsettia

½ ounce cranberry juice

¼ ounce triple sec

Chilled champagne to fill

1 lime twist

Pour the juice and the triple sec in a champagne flute. Fill with chilled champagne and garnish with lime twist.

Serving Champagne

Keep the cork pointed away from anything it could hurt or break if it accidentally comes out (at 100 miles per hour!). Release the cork by gripping the cork tightly with one hand and twisting the bottom of the bottle with the other hand. You should hear a soft hiss and pop. To pour, hold the bottom of the bottle with your thumb into the punt (the dent in the bottom of the bottle) and your fingers spread underneath.

Hard Cider and Fruit Wine

Cider is unfiltered fruit juice that is sold still or sparkling. Hard cider is plain cider that has been fermented to create an alcoholic beverage; technically, you can say it's a fruit wine. It can also be found still or sparkling and can be classified by dry to sweet. Hard cider can include added flavors from flowers and herbs. Today, the most common hard cider is made from apples or pears, but in ancient times hard cider was also made from such fruits as quince, hawthorn, and loquats.

Angry Strawberry

2 ripe strawberries

2 basil leaves

2 lime wedges

½ ounce simple syrup

1 ounce strawberry vodka

4 ounces Angry Orchard Crisp Apple Hard Cider or Woodchuck Pear Hard Cider

Drop the first three ingredients into a large glass and muddle for five seconds. Add the simple syrup and vodka, then fill the glass with ice. Pour in the cider and gently stir.

Apple Pie Float

1 ounce Tuaca

5 ounces hard apple cider

1 scoop vanilla bean ice cream

Pour the Tuaca and cider into a glass, then top with the ice cream.

Bourbon Ginger Cider

1 ounce bourbon

1 ounce ginger liqueur (such as Domaine de Canton)

5 ounces Angry Orchard Apple Ginger Hard Cider

Fill a 16-ounce glass with ice, add all the ingredients, and gently stir.

Burning Apples

2 dashes hot sauce

12 ounces hard apple cider

Dash the hot sauce into the bottom of a 12-ounce glass, then add the cider.

Caribbean Cider

1 ounce dark rum

1 ounce banana liqueur

5 ounces hard pear cider

Fill a 12-ounce glass with ice and add all the ingredients, then gently stir.

Cinnamon Cider

1 ounce cinnamon whiskey (such as Fireball)

5 ounces hard apple cider

Cinnamon stick

Fill a 12-ounce glass with ice and add all the liquid ingredients, then gently stir. Garnish with cinnamon stick.

Crock-Pot Cider

4 bottles hard apple (or pear) cider

8 ounces pear vodka

4 ounces brown sugar

2 cups cranberry juice

2 cinnamon sticks

Rind of 1 orange studded with whole cloves

Put all in a large Crock-Pot set on low for 4 hours. Serve warm.

Ancient Cider

Hard cider rose to fame in c.e. 1066 thanks to the Norman Conquest of England. The invasion of French soldiers brought a variety of apples to England, and cider quickly became the most popular drink of the time.

Green Fairy Cider

1/2 ounce absinthe (preferably Lucid)

1/2 ounce lime juice

4 ounces Angry Orchard Green Apple Hard Cider

Mint sprig

Fill a 12-ounce glass with ice and add all the liquid ingredients, then gently stir. Garnish with mint sprig.

Green Melon Cider

1 ounce melon liqueur

1/2 ounce lime juice

4 ounces Angry Orchard Green Apple Hard Cider

Green apple slice

Fill a 12-ounce glass with ice and add all the liquid ingredients, then gently stir. Garnish with green apple slice.

Hard Rickey

2 ounces gin

1/2 ounce lime juice

3 ounces hard apple cider

Lime slice

Fill a highball glass with ice and add all the liquid ingredients, then gently stir. Garnish with lime slice.

Jäger Bomb Cider

5 ounces hard apple cider
1/2 ounce Jägermeister
1/2 ounce Grand Marnier

Pour the apple cider into a 16-ounce glass, and then pour the Jägermeister and Grand Marnier into a shot glass. Drop the shot into the glass of cider and drink quickly.

Peaches and Pears

12 ounces hard pear cider
1 ounce peach schnapps

Pour the hard cider into a glass and add the schnapps.

Presidential Cider

Both George Washington and Thomas Jefferson owned apple orchards and were known to make hard apple cider in 1789. Abraham Lincoln didn't own an orchard, but sold hard apple cider in his tavern called Berry & Lincoln in 1833. Other Presidents that loved hard cider were William Harrison and John Adams.

Pear Collins

1 ounce gin
1 ounce lemon juice
1 ounce simple syrup
5 ounces hard pear cider

Fill a 12-ounce glass with ice. Shake the gin, lemon juice, and simple syrup, then strain into the glass of ice. Top with the hard pear cider and gently stir.

Smokey Cider

1 ounce Scotch
1 ounce amaretto
1/2 ounce lemon juice
12 ounces hard apple cider

Fill a 16-ounce glass with ice. Shake the Scotch, amaretto, and lemon juice with ice, then strain into the glass of ice. Add the hard cider and gently stir.

Sour Apple

12 ounces hard apple cider
1 ounce sour apple schnapps

Pour the hard cider into a glass and add the schnapps.

Sparkling Appletini

1 ounce lemon vodka
1 ounce sour apple schnapps
1/2 ounce lemon juice
3 ounces hard apple cider

Shake the vodka, schnapps, and lemon juice with ice. Strain into a martini glass. Top with the hard apple cider.

Cognac and Brandy

Cognac and brandy are distilled wines. All cognacs are brandy, but not all brandies are cognacs. Brandy can be made from any fruit (including grapes). Cognac must be made in the Cognac region of France from grapes grown in the same place. Cognacs are distilled twice and stored in oak casks made from the wood of the trees grown in the Cognac region. The length of the aging process varies and distillers offer a guide for the buyer. There are three general classifications to separate cognacs from each other—VS (*very special*, aged at least two years), VSOP (*very special old pale* or *very superior old pale*, aged at least four years), and XO (*extra old*, aged at least six years).

Aside from cognac, there are many types of brandies. The vintners of California distill brandies from their own grapes, which tend to be lighter and smoother. There is a dry Italian brandy called *grappa*; apple brandies such as *calvados*; kirschwasser, or *kirsch*, made from cherries; *Poire Williams*, made from pears; *framboise*, made from raspberries; *fraise*, made from strawberries; and *slivovitz*, made from plums. These are true brandies, distilled directly from fruits. Other fruit-flavored brandies may actually be liqueurs created from a variety of liquors. They are not necessarily inferior, just not made directly from fruit or grape wine.

Ambrosia

1 ounce applejack

1 ounce brandy

Dash triple sec

Juice from ½ lemon

Chilled champagne to fill

Pour the first four ingredients into an ice-filled shaker. Shake well and strain into a highball glass over ice. Fill with champagne and stir gently.

Apricot Sour

2 ounces apricot brandy

3 ounces sour mix

1 cherry

Pour the brandy and sour mix into a shaker tin of ice. Shake and strain over a highball glass of ice. Garnish with cherry.

B&B

1 ounce Bénédictine

1 ounce brandy

Pour the Bénédictine and the brandy into a brandy snifter.

Baby Doll

2 ounces cognac

1½ ounces Grand Marnier

Juice from ½ lemon

Sugar, for rimming

Pour the cognac, Grand Marnier, and lemon juice into a shaker tin of ice. Shake and strain into a sugar-rimmed cocktail glass.

Beautiful

1 ounce cognac

1 ounce Grand Marnier

Pour ingredients into a brandy snifter and serve.

Angel's Share

"Angel's share" is a wine-making term for the portion of cognac that is lost to evaporation. Legend says that when you visit the Cognac region of France you can actually smell the cognac in the air.

Between the Sheets

¾ ounce light rum

¾ ounce brandy

¾ ounce triple sec

½ ounce lemon juice

1 lemon twist

Pour all liquid ingredients into shaker. Shake with ice. Strain into a martini glass and garnish with lemon twist.

Bombay Cocktail

1 ounce brandy

½ ounce dry vermouth

½ ounce triple sec

½ ounce sweet vermouth

1 lemon twist

Pour liquid ingredients into a cocktail shaker nearly filled with ice. Shake, then strain into a cocktail glass. Garnish with lemon twist.

Brandy Alexander

1½ ounces brandy

1 ounce dark crème de cacao

1 ounce cream or half-and-half

Sprinkle of nutmeg, for garnish

Combine liquid ingredients in a shaker nearly filled with ice. Shake, then strain into a cocktail glass. Sprinkle with nutmeg. This cocktail can also be prepared in the blender.

Brandy Cassis

1½ ounces brandy

¼ ounce crème de cassis

1 ounce lemon juice

1 lemon twist

Combine liquid ingredients in a shaker nearly filled with ice. Shake, then strain into a cocktail glass. Serve with a lemon twist.

Brandy Manhattan

1½ ounces brandy

1 ounce sweet vermouth

1 teaspoon sugar

Dash bitters

Pour all ingredients into a shaker of ice and shake. Strain into a cocktail glass.

Brandy Milk Punch

1 ounce brandy

4 ounces whole milk

1 teaspoon powdered sugar

1 teaspoon vanilla extract

Combine the ingredients in a cocktail shaker with ice. Shake and strain into a highball glass filled with crushed ice.

Brandy Vermouth Classic

2 ounces brandy

½ ounce sweet vermouth

Dash bitters

Combine ingredients in a mixing glass half filled with ice and stir. Strain into a cocktail glass.

Calvados Cocktail

1½ ounces calvados apple brandy

2 ounces orange juice

1 orange twist

Combine liquid ingredients in a shaker filled with ice. Shake, then strain into a cocktail glass. Serve with an orange twist.

Combustible Edison

1 ounce Campari

1 ounce fresh lemon juice

2 ounces brandy

Shake the Campari and lemon juice with ice and strain into a cocktail glass, filling to 1" from the rim. Pour the brandy in a snifter and heat it for 10 seconds in the microwave. Light the brandy with a match, then pour the flaming stream into the cocktail glass.

Creamy Mocha Alexander

1 ounce brandy

1 ounce coffee liqueur

1 ounce dark crème de cacao

2 scoops vanilla ice cream

Put all ingredients into a blender and blend without ice. Pour into a tall glass.

Napoleon

Napoleon loved cognac. As a matter of fact, he made the Courvoisier distillery his headquarters during the French Revolution. Today, Courvoisier makes a Napoleon cognac as a tribute.

Delovely

1 ounce brandy
1 ounce calvados
¼ ounce lemon juice
¼ ounce grenadine

Shake the ingredients with ice in a cocktail shaker. Strain into a cocktail glass.

Dirty Mother

1 ounce brandy
1 ounce coffee liqueur

Build the ingredients in a rocks glass of ice.

Dirty White Mother

1 ounce brandy
2 ounces cream or half-and-half
1 ounce coffee liqueur

Shake the ingredients with ice in a cocktail shaker. Strain into a highball glass of ice.

Dream Cocktail

2 ounces brandy
1 teaspoon anisette
½ ounce triple sec

Combine ingredients in a shaker nearly filled with ice. Shake and strain into a cocktail glass.

Fancy Brandy

2 ounces brandy
¼ ounce Cointreau
¼ teaspoon sugar
Dash bitters
1 lemon twist

Pour liquid ingredients into a mixing glass nearly filled with ice and stir. Strain into a cocktail glass. Serve with a lemon twist.

French Passion

1 ounce cognac
1 ounce Alizé Red Passion liqueur

Build in a rocks glass of ice.

Sniffing Cognac

The experts say that sniffing cognac is done in three stages: held at your chest, then at your neck, and finally at your nose. When sniffing, a wine glass works better than a snifter.

Jack Rose

1½ ounces apple brandy

1 ounce fresh lime juice

½ ounce grenadine

Combine ingredients in a shaker nearly filled with ice. Shake and strain into a cocktail glass.

Kama Sutra Martini

1 ounce Alizé cognac

1 ounce Alizé Red Passion liqueur

1 ounce orange juice

Shake well with ice and strain into a martini glass.

Alizé

Alizé (al-la-ZAY) is a blend of cognac and passion fruit. Even though it first hit the American market in 1986, it wasn't until Tupac Shakur mentioned a drink named "Thug Passion" in a 1990s rap song that it skyrocketed to fame among the hip-hop generation. Today there are many flavor varieties of Alizé.

Keoke Coffee (also called Coffee Nudge)

½ ounce brandy

½ ounce coffee liqueur

Hot black coffee to fill

Pour the ingredients into a mug or Irish coffee mug.

Poire Man's Cobbler

1½ ounces Poire Williams pear brandy

½ ounce fresh lime juice

½ ounce simple syrup

Soda water to fill

1 pear slice

Pour liquid ingredients into a highball glass of ice. Stir and garnish with pear slice.

Rimmed Brothers Grimm Cocoa

1 teaspoon sugar

½ teaspoon cinnamon powder

1 ounce Irish cream

1 packet hot cocoa

Hot water to fill

Whipped cream, for garnish (optional)

Miniature marshmallows, for garnish (optional)

Mix the sugar and cinnamon together on a saucer. Wet the rim of a mug and dip it in the cinnamon-sugar mix. Pour the Irish cream and the cocoa into the mug. Fill with hot water and stir. Garnish with whipped cream or mini marshmallows if desired.

Separator

1 ounce brandy

1 ounce coffee liqueur

2 ounces cream or half-and-half

Build in a rocks glass of ice.

Sidecar 🍸

2 ounces brandy
½ ounce Cointreau
1 ounce fresh lemon juice

Combine ingredients in a shaker nearly filled with ice. Shake and strain into a cocktail glass.

Sidewinder

Sugar for rimming
2 ounces pear brandy
1 ounce Cointreau
1 ounce fresh lemon juice

Rim a cocktail glass with sugar. Pour liquid ingredients into a shaker of ice and shake. Strain into the sugar-rimmed cocktail glass.

Sonata

1 ounce cognac
1 ounce amaretto

Pour both ingredients into a brandy snifter, then swirl to mix.

Stinger 🍸

1 ounce brandy
¼ ounce white crème de menthe

Build in a rocks glass of ice.

Witch Doctor

1½ ounces brandy
2 ounces cream
¼ ounce dark crème de cacao
¼ ounce simple syrup
¼ ounce vanilla extract

Shake all the ingredients in a shaker tin with ice, then strain into a chilled cocktail glass.

Stock Up on Ice

In order to have ice available at all times, keep a large container in the freezer to hold your special ice. Or if you plan to host a party, start saving ice a couple of weeks before the big event.

aperitifs, cordials, and liqueurs

An *aperitif* (uh-pair-a-TEEF) is an alcoholic drink taken before dinner. Aperitifs are meant to stimulate your appetite. Cordials and liqueurs are often used as after-dinner drinks to aid digestion.

Aperitifs and Nightcaps

Leisurely get-togethers allow guests to savor their conversation and their drinks while they wait for their meal. Aperitifs include sherry, port, vermouths, Lillet, Dubonnet, Becherovka, and cocktails made with Campari, pastis, ouzo, and Cynar. The first five mentioned are wine based but were not talked about in the preceding wine chapter because they are more pertinent to this chapter.

After-dinner drinks often help with digestion. Europeans drink shots of limoncello, minted schnapps, grappa, and anise liqueurs. Today, after-dinner drinks tend to be either creamy, hot, or a neat measure of spirit. Nightcaps can be a hot drink or a single spirit that is sipped to make you feel warm and cozy inside. If you like the taste of anise/licorice (pastis), there are many other choices for you—Galliano, anisette, ouzo, sambuca, pastis, Ricard, Pernod, or absinthe.

Absinthe (AB-sinth) has an intriguing history. Absinthe originated in Switzerland and legend says that the inventor was Dr. Pierre Ordinaire. *Absinthe* means *wormwood* in French. It was one of the original ingredients in the first believed cocktail, the Sazerac. But absinthe also had a darker, more dangerous side. This pastis had a high alcohol content and was made with wormwood, which caused slight hallucinations, earning it the nickname the Green Fairy (*La Fée Verte*).

By 1906, absinthe was banned in Brazil and Belgium. Other countries followed—Switzerland in 1908 and the United States and France in 1912. It was eventually outlawed worldwide except in England, Sweden, and Norway. After relegalization of absinthe in most of the world in the late 1990s and early 2000s, producers use clever marketing, extravagant claims, and flashy and hip labels to sell less-than-worthy imitations. In July 2007, a New Orleans absinthe historian, chemist, and environmental microbiologist named T.A. Breaux proved to be instrumental in lobbying the American Congress into allowing the first legal absinthe (after being banned for ninety-five years) into America. The name of this absinthe is Lucid.

Adirondack Mint

1 ounce Godiva Milk Chocolate Liqueur

1 ounce peppermint schnapps

5 ounces hot chocolate

Whipped cream, for garnish

Pour liquid ingredients into an Irish coffee glass or mug and stir. Top with whipped cream.

Affair

1 ounce strawberry schnapps

1 ounce cranberry juice

1 ounce orange juice

Pour all ingredients into an ice-filled mixing glass. Stir well, then strain into a cocktail glass.

After Five

1 ounce Irish cream liqueur

1 ounce Kahlúa

1 ounce peppermint schnapps

Pour all ingredients into an ice-filled rocks glass. Stir gently.

Afternoon Delight

1 ounce banana liqueur

1 ounce white crème de cacao

1 scoop banana ice cream

1 scoop chocolate ice cream

Add all ingredients into a blender and blend. For a creamier drink, add cream or milk little by little while the blender is on. Pour into a tall glass.

Almond Joy

1 ounce Coco Lopez coconut cream

1 ounce amaretto

1 ounce crème de cacao

2 ounces half-and-half

Pour ingredients into a shaker with ice. Shake, then strain into a highball glass of ice.

Americano

1 ounce Campari

1 ounce sweet vermouth

Pour Campari and sweet vermouth into a rocks glass filled with ice and stir.

The Americano

It's said that the Americano was created by Italian Gaspare Campari at his bar, Café Campari, in the 1860s. It originally had another name, but Gaspare noticed that the American tourists loved the drink so he renamed it.

Armagnac Lillet

2 ounces Lillet Blanc

2 ounces Armagnac

1 orange wedge

Pour Lillet Blanc and Armagnac over crushed ice in a champagne glass. Garnish with orange wedge.

Banshee 🍸

1 ounce banana liqueur

1 ounce white crème de cacao

2 ounces cream

Combine ingredients in a shaker tin of ice. Shake, then pour into a cocktail glass.

Baronial

2 ounces Lillet Blanc

1 ounce gin

¼ ounce Cointreau

Dash bitters

Pour all ingredients into an ice-filled mixing glass. Stir well, then strain into a cocktail glass.

Liqueur Brands

There are many liqueur brands on the market, but the top four that make crèmes, schnapps, cordials, and liqueurs are DeKuyper, Bols, Marie Brizard, and Hiram Walker.

Big Bamboo

2 ounces Canton ginger liqueur

5 ounces ginger ale

Fill a tall glass of your choice with ice. Pour in the ingredients and stir.

Bittersweet Cocktail

1 ounce sweet vermouth

1 ounce dry vermouth

1 lemon twist

Pour liquid ingredients into a mixing glass nearly filled with ice and stir. Strain into a cocktail glass. Add a lemon twist.

Black Honey

1½ ounces Drambuie

Hot coffee to fill

1 tablespoon honey

Whipped cream (optional)

Pour the Drambuie into a coffee mug and fill with coffee. Add the honey and stir to dissolve. Top with whipped cream if you desire.

History of Drambuie

On every Drambuie bottle you'll find its story. In 1746, Prince Charles Edward Stuart gave Captain John MacKinnon the recipe in appreciation for taking care of him during the prince's (unsuccessful) bid for the British throne. The word is Gaelic for "the drink that satisfies."

Black Russian 🍸

1 ounce Kahlúa

1 ounce vodka

Build in a short glass of ice.

Blue Velvet

2 ounces blue curaçao

2 ounces white crème de cacao

Pour both ingredients into a shaker of ice and shake. Strain into a chilled cocktail glass.

Butterscotch Coffee

1 ounce butterscotch schnapps

½ ounce Frangelico

Hot coffee to fill

½ ounce hazelnut creamer

Pour the schnapps and the Frangelico into a coffee mug. Fill with coffee. Add the hazelnut creamer and stir.

Caramel Appletini

1 ounce sour apple schnapps

1 ounce butterscotch schnapps

1 ounce apple-flavored vodka

Pour all ingredients into a shaker tin of ice. Shake, then strain into a cocktail glass.

Charming Proposal

1 ounce sour apple schnapps

¼ ounce grenadine

1 ounce passion liqueur

Ginger ale to fill

Pour the first three ingredients into a tall glass of ice. Stir, then fill with the ginger ale.

> **Flavors of Liqueurs**
>
> Absinthe = anise/licorice; advocaat = eggnog; amaretto = almond; anisette = anise/licorice; aquavit = caraway; Baileys Irish Cream = vanilla, chocolate, and Irish whiskey; Bärenjäger = honey; Bénédictine = herbs and spices; blue curaçao = orange; Chambord = black raspberry; Chartreuse = herbs and spices; Cherry Heering = cherry; coffee liqueur = coffee.

Chocolate Monkey

1 ounce coffee liqueur

1 ounce crème de banana

1 ounce chocolate syrup

5 ounces cream

1 banana

Blend all ingredients in a blender with a cup of ice.

Colorado Bulldog

1 ounce coffee liqueur

1 ounce vodka

2 ounces cream

Cola to fill

Pour coffee liqueur, vodka, and cream into a shaker. Shake, then pour into a highball glass of ice and fill with cola.

Come Hither

1 ounce vodka
1 ounce white crème de cacao
½ ounce Galliano
2 ounces cream

Pour all ingredients into a shaker tin of ice. Shake and strain into a cocktail glass.

Coronation

3 ounces dry sherry
½ ounce dry vermouth
Dash bitters
1 lemon twist

Combine liquid ingredients in a shaker half filled with ice. Shake well. Strain into a cocktail glass and garnish with lemon twist.

Cortés

1 ounce Kahlúa
1 ounce light rum
Dash lemon juice

Combine all ingredients and serve over cracked ice in a brandy snifter.

Crimson and Clover

2 ounces Southern Comfort
5 ounces cranberry juice
Sprinkle of ground cloves

Shake all ingredients and strain into a short glass of ice.

Diablo Cocktail

1 ounce brandy
1 ounce dry vermouth
1 ounce Cointreau
Dash Angostura bitters
Dash Regans' orange bitters

Combine ingredients in a shaker half filled with ice. Shake well. Strain into a cocktail glass.

Dry Negroni

1 ounce Campari
1 ounce gin
1 ounce dry vermouth

Pour ingredients into an old-fashioned glass over ice. Stir gently.

Flavors of Liqueurs

Kahlúa = coffee; Lichido = litchi; Licor 43 = citrus vanilla; limoncello = sweet lemon; Malibu = coconut; manzana = apple; Midori = honeydew melon; Parfait d'Amour = violets, rose, vanilla, and spice; Passoã = passion fruit; patxaran = sloe berry, coffee bean, and vanilla; Pernod = anise/licorice; Pisang Ambon = banana; prunelle = plum.

Dubonnet Cocktail

1 ounce Dubonnet
1 ounce gin
1 lemon twist

Combine liquids in a shaker half filled with ice. Shake well. Strain into a cocktail glass and garnish with lemon twist.

Dubonnet Rouge

2 ounces Dubonnet Rouge
1 ounce applejack
1 lemon twist

Combine Dubonnet and applejack in a shaker half filled with ice. Shake well. Strain into a cocktail glass and garnish with lemon twist.

Foreign Affair

2 ounces sambuca
1 ounce brandy

Pour both ingredients into a shaker tin of ice. Shake and strain into a cocktail glass.

Frog in a Blender

1 ounce coffee liqueur
1 ounce green crème de menthe
2 ounces cream
1/2 ounce red cinnamon schnapps

Put a cup of ice into a blender. Pour in the first three ingredients and blend. Pour into a tall glass and add the red cinnamon schnapps on top. This drink can also be shaken and strained into a cocktail glass.

Frozen Girl Scout Cookie

1 ounce dark crème de cacao
1/2 ounce Frangelico
1/2 ounce Irish cream
1/2 ounce butterscotch schnapps
1/4 ounce cinnamon schnapps
2 scoops vanilla ice cream
Whipped cream, for garnish

Combine all ingredients except the whipped cream in a blender and blend. Pour into a tall glass and top with whipped cream.

Flavors of Liqueurs

Razzmatazz = raspberry; Rumple Minze = peppermint; sambuca = anise/licorice; sloe gin = sloe berry; Southern Comfort = peach, apricot, and honey; Strega = herbs, mint, fennel, and saffron; Tequila Rose = strawberry cream; Tia Maria = coffee; triple sec = orange; tsipouro = anise/licorice; Tuaca = caramel, vanilla, orange; Whidbeys = loganberry; xtabentun = anise/licorice/honey; Yukon Jack = honey.

Fuzzy Navel

2 ounces peach schnapps
Orange juice to fill

Pour the peach schnapps into a highball glass of ice and fill to the top with orange juice.

Godfather

1 ounce amaretto
1 ounce Scotch whisky

Pour amaretto and Scotch into a rocks glass with ice. Stir gently.

Godmother

1 ounce amaretto
1 ounce vodka

Pour amaretto and vodka into a rocks glass with ice. Stir gently.

Golden Cadillac

1 ounce Galliano
1 ounce white crème de cacao
2 ounces cream

Pour all ingredients into a shaker. Shake, then pour into a cocktail glass.

Good Karma

1 ounce raspberry liqueur
1 ounce melon liqueur
1 ounce pineapple juice
1 ounce sweet-and-sour mix

Pour all ingredients into a shaker tin of ice and shake. Strain into a cocktail glass.

Grasshopper

1 ounce green crème de menthe
1 ounce white crème de cacao
2 ounces cream

Pour all ingredients into a shaker tin of ice. Shake and strain into a cocktail glass. This drink can also be served frozen and made with vanilla ice cream instead of cream.

Green-Eyed Blonde

1 ounce melon liqueur
1 ounce banana liqueur
1 ounce Irish cream
2 ounces cream or milk

Pour all ingredients into a shaker tin of ice. Shake and strain into a cocktail glass.

Sweetly Seductive

Served straight in its own glass, a liqueur is sweetly seductive. Indeed, with a 2.5 percent minimum sugar content, liqueurs are the dessert of drinks. Many are even sweeter, and the crèmes, whose creamy consistency stems from high sugar content, are the richest of all. But their sweetness never overwhelms their fruit or herb character, so all liqueurs will add intense, distinctive flavors to mixed drinks.

Honeymoon Suite

1 ounce Irish cream

1 ounce hazelnut liqueur

½ ounce coffee liqueur

½ ounce honey

2 ounces cream or milk

2 chocolate kisses

Pour all liquid ingredients into a shaker tin of ice. Shake and strain into a cocktail glass. Unwrap the two chocolate kisses and drop them into the cocktail.

Love Potion

1 ounce Parfait d'Amour

1 ounce raspberry vodka

White (clear) cranberry juice and club soda to fill

1 sprig of purple seedless grapes

Pour Parfait d'Amour and vodka into a tall glass of ice. Fill with equal parts of white (clear) cranberry juice and club soda. Garnish with the grapes.

Lucky Charm

1 ounce Tequila Rose

1 ounce white crème de menthe

3 ounces milk

Lucky Charms cereal marshmallows

Pour the liquid ingredients into a shaker tin of ice and shake. Strain into a cocktail glass and add the Lucky Charms marshmallows on top.

Nuts and Berries

1 ounce Frangelico

1 ounce Chambord raspberry liqueur

Cream or milk to fill

Pour the Frangelico and Chambord into a short glass of ice. Fill with cream or milk.

Nutty Irishman

1 ounce Frangelico

1 ounce Irish cream

Cream or milk to fill

Pour the Frangelico and Irish cream into a short glass of ice. Fill with cream or milk.

Orgasm

1 ounce coffee liqueur

1 ounce amaretto

2 ounces Irish cream (optional)

2 ounces cream (optional)

Pour ingredients into a shaker. Shake and pour into a short glass of ice. Cream can be added if desired.

Peppermint Pattie

1 ounce dark crème de cacao

1 ounce white crème de menthe

2 ounces cream (optional)

Pour the ingredients in a short glass of ice. Cream can be added if desired.

Picon Fizz

1/2 ounce Amer Picon

1/2 ounce cognac or brandy

1/4 ounce grenadine

Club soda to fill

Pour the first three ingredients into a highball glass of ice. Fill with club soda.

What Is Schnapps?

Schnapps is made from grains, fruit, or herbs fermented and distilled together. Liqueurs are made by steeping herbs and fruits in an alcohol that had already been fermented and distilled. This is the reason schnapps can have a high alcohol content.

Pimm's Cup

1 1/2 ounces Pimm's No. 1

Club soda to fill

1 lemon wedge

1 cucumber slice

Pour the Pimm's into a highball glass of ice. Fill with club soda. Garnish with lemon wedge and cucumber slice.

Pink Squirrel

1 ounce crème de noyaux

1 ounce white crème de cacao

2 ounces cream

Shake all ingredients in a shaker tin half filled with ice. Pour into a cocktail glass.

Platinum Blonde Coffee

1 1/2 ounces Godiva White Chocolate Liqueur

Hot black coffee to fill

Whipped cream, for garnish

Pour the Godiva liqueur into a coffee mug and fill with coffee. Garnish with whipped cream if desired.

Queen Elizabeth

1 ounce Bénédictine

2 ounces sweet vermouth

Pour both ingredients into a shaker tin of ice and shake. Strain into a cocktail glass.

Root Beer Float

1 ounce Galliano

1 ounce vanilla schnapps

1 ounce cream

Root beer to fill

Whipped cream, for garnish

Fill a tall glass with ice and pour in Galliano, schnapps, and cream. Fill with root beer and garnish with whipped cream.

Ruby Sipper

1½ ounces DeKuyper Hot Damn! cinnamon schnapps

Hot apple cider to fill

Pour the cinnamon schnapps into a coffee mug. Fill with hot apple cider.

Sambuca

2 ounces sambuca

3 coffee beans

Pour sambuca into a brandy snifter or cordial glass. Add coffee beans.

Scarlett O'Hara

2 ounces Southern Comfort

3 ounces cranberry juice

Build in a short glass of ice and stir.

Smith and Kearns

2 ounces coffee liqueur

2 ounces cream

Club soda to fill

Pour coffee liqueur and cream into a shaker. Shake and pour into a highball glass of ice. Top with club soda.

Coffee Beans

Sambuca gets three coffee beans when served to savor. You can leave them out if you are serving it for shots. The beans are good luck and mean many things to many people. The most popular meanings are health, happiness, and prosperity.

Smith and Wesson

1 ounce coffee liqueur

1 ounce vodka

2 ounces half-and-half

Club soda to fill

Pour the first three ingredients into a highball glass of ice. Top with club soda.

Sombrero

2 ounces Kahlúa

2 ounces cream

Build in a short glass of ice. Serve layered.

Southern Hospitality

2 ounces Southern Comfort

2 ounces peach schnapps

Fill a shaker tin with ice and add the Southern Comfort and peach schnapps. Shake for about 20 seconds. Strain into a cocktail glass.

Sugared Ginger

Sugar for rimming

2 ounces Canton ginger liqueur

1 ounce fresh lemon juice

Rim a cocktail glass with sugar. Pour liquid ingredients into a shaker of ice and shake. Strain into the sugar-rimmed cocktail glass.

Sweet Vermouth on the Rocks

2 ounces sweet vermouth

Lemon twist

Pour over ice in a short glass. Add a lemon twist.

Vermouth

Vermouth is a fortified wine flavored with herbs, spices, barks, and flowers. The flavors can be added through infusion, maceration, or distillation. There are many brands of vermouth produced in both Italy and France.

Toasted Almond

1 ounce coffee liqueur

1 ounce amaretto

2 ounces cream

Shake ingredients together. Pour into a short glass of ice.

Tootsie Roll

1 ounce coffee liqueur

1 ounce dark crème de cacao

3 ounces orange juice

Pour all ingredients into a shaker tin of ice. Shake and strain into a cocktail glass or pour over a short glass of ice.

Vermouth Cassis

2 ounces dry vermouth

1 ounce crème de cassis

Club soda to fill

Combine vermouth and crème de cassis in a highball glass filled with ice. Fill with club soda.

White Caramel Apple Cider

1 ounce Dooley's toffee liqueur

½ ounce Tuaca

Hot apple cider to fill

Whipped cream, for garnish (optional)

Pour the Dooley's toffee liqueur and Tuaca into a coffee mug. Fill with hot apple cider. Top with whipped cream if you desire.

White Russian

1 ounce Kahlúa

1 ounce vodka

2 ounces cream

Shake all ingredients and pour into a short glass of ice.

Crème versus Cream

A cream liqueur is not to be confused with a crème liqueur. If it says cream, it includes dairy cream. The best example is Baileys Irish Cream. Crèmes have a lot of sugar added, giving them a syrup-like consistency. Crème refers to the consistency. Examples are crème de cacao, crème de menthe, and crème de banana.

XTC

2 ounces X-Rated Fusion liqueur

½ ounce triple sec

4 ounces cranberry juice

Fill a tall glass of your choice with ice. Pour in all the ingredients and stir.

vodka: the spirited neutral

Milk comes from cows, wool comes from sheep, and vodka comes from potatoes. Not so fast. Yes, some vodka is made from potatoes. But unlike many spirits, vodka can be made anywhere in the world with practically anything that contains sugar or starch. Common ingredients (aside from potatoes, of course) include beets and grains such as corn and rye.

Vodka History

Legend says that in the 1300s, Genoese merchants en route to Lithuania brought this *water of life* (*aqua vitae*) to Moscow. Other sources contend that vodka originated in Poland and Russia without any assistance from the Genoese. By the 1700s, people were infusing vodka with herb and fruit flavors like sage, cherry, dill, blackberry, and caraway. (And we thought our modern society created flavored vodka!) Vodka didn't make it into American liquor cabinets until the 1930s—and the brand was Smirnoff. The classic cocktail Moscow Mule became popular in the 1950s despite its association with the menacing Communists on the other side of the Iron Curtain. In 1962, the first James Bond film showed 007 ordering a Martini made with Smirnoff, and vodka skyrocketed straight to the top. It has remained the number-one spirit in America since.

Vodka is a profound silent partner. Because it is chameleon-like, taking on the tastes of anything around it, flavored versions have flourished since the turn of the twenty-first century. New high-end vodkas are constantly produced with their own little gimmicks—vodka made with ice harvested from icebergs, black-colored vodka, vodka filtered multiple times, vodka infused with rose petals, vodka distilled from organic grains . . . the list goes on. Unfortunately, vodka's smooth taste makes it the number-one training-wheel spirit. Inexperienced drinkers tend to learn the hard way that tasteless does not equal painless. As always, moderation is the key to enjoying your white whiskey.

Banana Baybreeze

1½ ounces banana vodka

Equal parts of cranberry and pineapple juice to fill

Pour all the ingredients into a highball glass of ice and stir.

Banana Seabreeze

1½ ounces banana vodka

Equal parts of cranberry and grapefruit juice to fill

Pour all the ingredients into a highball glass of ice and stir.

Barmarche Honey Sour

1½ ounces Belvedere vodka

1½ ounces honey

¼ ounce B&B

1 ounce lemon juice

Half an egg white

Dash bitters

Orange and cherry flag, for garnish

Stir together the vodka and honey to start this award-winning cocktail. Stir in the rest of the ingredients except the flag. Shake and strain into a rocks glass of fresh ice or into a cocktail glass. Garnish with orange and cherry flag. Invented by Clark Clark of Barmarché in New York City.

Baybreeze

1½ ounces vodka

Equal parts of cranberry and pineapple juice to fill

Pour all ingredients into a highball glass of ice.

Berry Bordello

1 ounce strawberry vodka

½ ounce raspberry vodka

½ ounce raspberry liqueur

Cranberry juice to fill

Berries of choice, for garnish

Pour the first three ingredients into a tall glass of ice. Fill with cranberry juice and stir. Garnish with berries.

Black Goose

1 ounce Grey Goose vodka

1 ounce coffee liqueur

Pour both ingredients into a short glass of ice and stir.

Black Magic

2 ounces Blavod black vodka

½ ounce grenadine

7UP to fill

1 maraschino cherry

Pour vodka and grenadine into a tall glass of ice. Fill with 7UP and stir. Garnish with maraschino cherry.

Black Martini

1 ounce Blavod black vodka

1 ounce raspberry liqueur

1 ounce triple sec

2 ounces sweet-and-sour mix

Pour ingredients into a shaker tin of ice. Shake and strain into a martini glass. This black drink looks nice with a white-sugared rim.

Bloody Caesar

1½ shots vodka

¼ shot fresh lime juice

Celery salt, pepper, Tabasco sauce, Worcestershire sauce, to taste

Clamato juice (half tomato juice/half clam juice) to fill

Celery stalk

Combine all liquid ingredients and spices with ice and stir. Strain into a tall glass filled with ice. Garnish with celery stalk.

Bloody Mary

2 ounces vodka

Bloody Mary mix to fill

Celery stalk and lime wedge, for garnish

Combine vodka and Bloody Mary mix; stir with ice. Strain into a tall glass filled with ice. Garnish with celery stalk and lime wedge.

Bloody Mary History

Tomato juice followed quickly on the heels of the juicer, which was introduced in 1921. The Bloody Mary, a simple concoction of vodka and tomato juice, has disputed origins. Bartender Fernand Petiot claimed to have invented the drink in the late 1920s in Paris. Another contender, George Jessel, said he mixed the drink for himself to cure a hangover. It is unknown who the Bloody Mary's namesake was, but the drink was not named for the Catholic Tudor queen who earned the grisly nickname after ordering Protestant purges.

Blueberry Baybreeze

1½ ounces blueberry vodka

Equal parts of cranberry and pineapple juice to fill

Pour all the ingredients into a highball glass of ice and stir.

Blueberry Cosmopolitan

1½ ounces blueberry vodka

½ ounce Cointreau

¼ ounce lime juice or freshly squeezed lime

1 ounce cranberry juice

Lemon twist, orange twist, or lime wedge, for garnish

Pour all liquid ingredients into a shaker tin of ice. Shake and strain into a cocktail glass. Garnish with lemon twist, orange twist, or lime wedge.

Blueberry Seabreeze

1½ ounces blueberry vodka

Equal parts of cranberry and grapefruit juice to fill

Pour all the ingredients into a highball glass of ice and stir.

Blue Lagoon

1 ounce raspberry vodka

1 ounce blue curaçao

Sprite to fill

Pour vodka and curaçao into a highball glass over ice. Fill with Sprite and stir.

Bull Shot Y

1½ ounces vodka

4 ounces chilled beef bouillon

Dash Worcestershire sauce, salt, and pepper

Combine ingredients in a shaker half filled with ice. Shake well. Strain into a highball glass over ice.

Caipiroska

½ lime

2 teaspoons sugar

2 ounces vodka

Muddle the lime and sugar in a mixing glass. Add the vodka and ice. Shake, then strain into a rocks glass of cracked ice.

Cape Codder/Cape Cod

1 ounce vodka

Cranberry juice to fill

1 lime wedge (optional)

Fill a highball glass with ice. Add the vodka. Fill with cranberry juice. Garnish with lime wedge if desired.

The Cape Codder

The Cape Codder gets its name from the mixer used—cranberry juice. It refers to the cranberries that grow in and around Cape Cod in Massachusetts. In the fall, the berries turn a bright red color.

Cherry Baybreeze

1½ ounces cherry vodka

Equal parts of cranberry and pineapple juice to fill

Pour all the ingredients into a highball glass of ice and stir.

Cherry Cosmopolitan

1½ ounces cherry vodka

½ ounce Cointreau

¼ ounce lime juice or freshly squeezed lime

1 ounce cranberry juice

Lemon twist, orange twist, or lime wedge, for garnish

Pour all liquid ingredients into a shaker tin of ice. Shake and strain into a cocktail glass. Garnish with lemon twist, orange twist, or lime wedge.

Cherry Seabreeze

1½ ounces cherry vodka

Equal parts of cranberry and grapefruit juice to fill

Pour all the ingredients into a highball glass of ice and stir.

Cherry White Russian

1 ounce cherry vodka

1 ounce coffee liqueur

2 ounces cream

Shake all ingredients and pour into a short glass of ice.

Chi-Chi

1½ ounces vodka

4 ounces Piña Colada mix

1 pineapple slice and 1 cherry

Pour liquid ingredients into a blender with a cup of ice. Blend. Pour into a tall glass of your choice. Garnish with pineapple slice and cherry.

Chiquita

1½ ounces vodka

½ ounce banana liqueur

¼ ounce amaretto

½ ounce lime juice

¼ cup sliced bananas

Combine ingredients in a blender with a cup of ice. Pour into a tall glass of your choice.

Chocolate Pudding Pop

1 ounce chocolate vodka

1 ounce coffee liqueur

1 ounce Irish cream

2 scoops chocolate ice cream

Cream, to blend

1 Fudgsicle fudge pop

Put the chocolate vodka, coffee liqueur, Irish cream, and ice cream in a blender. Blend, adding the cream little by little until a smooth consistency is achieved. Pour into a tall glass and garnish by sticking in a Fudgsicle fudge pop.

Coconut Baybreeze

1½ ounces coconut vodka

Equal parts of cranberry and pineapple juice to fill

Pour all the ingredients into a highball glass of ice and stir.

Coconut Brownie with Nuts

1 ounce coconut rum

1 ounce vanilla vodka

1 ounce hazelnut liqueur

1 scoop chocolate ice cream

1 scoop vanilla ice cream

1 packet powdered hot chocolate

1 ounce Coco Lopez

1 ounce shredded coconut

Pour the coconut rum, vanilla vodka, hazelnut liqueur, chocolate and vanilla ice cream, powdered hot chocolate, and Coco Lopez into a blender. Blend until drink reaches a smooth consistency. Pour into a tall glass and sprinkle shredded coconut on top.

Coconut Concubine

1 ounce coconut rum

1 ounce vanilla vodka

1 ounce Coco Lopez

Pineapple and orange juice to fill

Splash grenadine

1 pineapple slice and 1 cherry

Pour the first three ingredients into a tall glass of ice. Fill with the pineapple and orange juice. Splash in the grenadine. Stir. Garnish with pineapple slice and cherry.

Coconut Cosmopolitan

1½ ounces coconut vodka

½ ounce Cointreau

¼ ounce lime juice or freshly squeezed lime

1 ounce cranberry juice

Lemon twist, orange twist, or lime wedge, for garnish

Pour all liquid ingredients into a shaker tin of ice. Shake and strain into a cocktail glass. Garnish with lemon twist, orange twist, or lime wedge.

Coconut Seabreeze

1½ ounces coconut vodka

Equal parts of cranberry and grapefruit juice to fill

Pour all the ingredients into a highball glass of ice and stir.

Disaronno Amaretto

They say that in 1525, a church in Saronno, Italy, commissioned artist and da Vinci student Bernardino Luini to paint its sanctuary with frescoes. Luini needed a model for the Madonna and chose the young widowed innkeeper. To show her gratitude, she steeped apricot kernels in brandy, which resulted in the liqueur Disaronno amaretto. Oh, they may have also been lovers.

Coconut White Russian

1 ounce coconut vodka

1 ounce coffee liqueur

2 ounces cream

Shake all ingredients and pour into a short glass of ice.

Copabanana Split

1 ounce vanilla vodka

1 ounce strawberry vodka

1 banana, cut in half lengthwise

2 scoops vanilla ice cream

Cream, to blend

1 ounce dark crème de cacao

1 ounce strawberry syrup

Whipped cream, for garnish

Nuts, for garnish

Maraschino cherry, for garnish

Put the vodkas, half of the banana, and ice cream into a blender and blend. Slowly pour in cream until you reach a smooth consistency. Pour the dark crème de cacao in the bottom of a tall glass and insert the other banana half standing in the glass. Fill halfway with the blended mixture. Add the strawberry syrup. Continue to fill the glass with blended mixture. Add whipped cream, nuts, and a cherry on top of the drink.

Cosmopolitan

1½ ounces lemon vodka

½ ounce Cointreau

¼ ounce lime juice or freshly squeezed lime

¼ ounce cranberry juice

Lemon twist, orange twist, or lime wedge, for garnish

Pour all liquid ingredients into a shaker tin of ice. Shake and strain into a cocktail glass. Garnish with lemon twist, orange twist, or lime wedge.

Creamsicle

1 ounce vanilla vodka

½ ounce triple sec

Equal parts of orange juice and half-and-half to fill

Pour the alcohol into a tall glass. Fill with orange juice and half-and-half. Pour into a shaker. Shake, then strain into another tall glass of ice.

Death by Chocolatini

½ ounce chocolate

1 strawberry

1 swirl chocolate syrup

1½ ounces vanilla vodka

1½ ounces chocolate liqueur

2 ounces cream

Melt the chocolate in a microwave; then dip the strawberry in the chocolate. Cool in the freezer. Swirl chocolate syrup inside a martini glass. Set the martini glass in the freezer. Pour the vodka, liqueur, and cream into a shaker tin. Shake, then strain into the chilled glass. Garnish the rim with the chocolate-covered strawberry.

Desert Rose

2 ounces rose vodka

1 ounce agave nectar

1 ounce fresh lemon juice

1 rose petal

Shake the liquid ingredients in a shaker tin with ice, then strain into a chilled cocktail glass. Garnish with rose petal.

Dirty Girl Scout Cookie

1 ounce vodka

1 ounce coffee liqueur

1 ounce Irish cream liqueur

¼ ounce green crème de menthe

Combine ingredients in a shaker half filled with ice. Shake well. Strain into an old-fashioned glass with ice.

Distill My Heart

1 ounce strawberry vodka
1 ounce raspberry liqueur
1 ounce pineapple juice
1/2 ounce fresh lemon juice

Shake all the ingredients in a shaker tin with ice, then strain into a chilled cocktail glass.

Salty Snacks

Back in saloon times, proprietors offered free lunches, most of which were overly salted, forcing the thirsty diner to buy an alcoholic drink. Many bars now offer peanuts and salty snacks for the same reason.

Espressotini

2 ounces Van Gogh Double Espresso vodka
1 ounce crème de cacao
2 ounces half-and-half (optional)

Pour all ingredients into a shaker of ice and shake. Strain into a chilled cocktail glass.

Espresso White Russian

1 ounce espresso vodka
1 ounce coffee liqueur
2 ounces cream

Shake all ingredients and pour into a short glass of ice.

Florida Sunset

1 1/2 ounces orange-flavored vodka
1/2 ounce grenadine
Orange juice to fill
1 orange slice

Fill a tall glass with ice. Pour in the orange-flavored vodka and the grenadine. Slowly fill the glass with orange juice. The result will be a red layer on the bottom mixing with the orange layer. Garnish with orange slice.

Georgia Peach

1 1/2 ounces peach vodka
1 ounce peach-flavored brandy
1/4 ounce lemon juice
1 teaspoon peach preserves
1/2 fresh peach, cut up

Combine ingredients in a blender with ice. Blend thoroughly. Pour into a tall glass.

Georgia Rose

Sprig of mint
1 1/2 ounces rose vodka
1/2 ounce peach brandy
2 ounces peach nectar

In a short glass, drop in the mint and pour in the rose vodka. Muddle. Pour the minted rose vodka, peach brandy, and peach nectar into a shaker of ice. Shake and strain over a short glass of crushed ice.

Grape Baybreeze

1½ ounces grape vodka

Equal parts of cranberry and pineapple juice to fill

Pour all the ingredients into a highball glass of ice and stir.

Wet Your Whistle

One explanation for the origin of this phrase is that English pubs used to have cups with whistles built into them. A patron in need of a refill would use the whistle to get the barmaid's attention. However, you'd be hard-pressed to find any of these whistling vessels in London today—probably because they never existed in the first place. There is no archaeological evidence of these cups.

Grape Cosmopolitan

1½ ounces grape vodka

½ ounce Cointreau

¼ ounce lime juice or freshly squeezed lime

1 ounce cranberry juice

Lemon twist, orange twist, or lime wedge, for garnish

Pour all liquid ingredients into a shaker tin of ice. Shake and strain into a cocktail glass. Garnish with lemon twist, orange twist, or lime wedge.

Grape Seabreeze

1½ ounces grape vodka

Equal parts of cranberry and grapefruit juice to fill

Pour all the ingredients into a highball glass of ice and stir.

Grapefruit Cosmopolitan

1½ ounces grapefruit vodka

½ ounce Cointreau

¼ ounce lime juice or freshly squeezed lime

1 ounce cranberry juice

Lemon twist, orange twist, or lime wedge, for garnish

Pour all liquid ingredients into a shaker tin of ice. Shake and strain into a cocktail glass. Garnish with lemon twist, orange twist, or lime wedge.

Green Apple Baybreeze

1½ ounces green apple vodka

Equal parts of cranberry and pineapple juice to fill

Pour all the ingredients into a highball glass of ice and stir.

Green Apple Cosmopolitan

1½ ounces green apple vodka
½ ounce Cointreau
¼ ounce lime juice or freshly
squeezed lime
1 ounce cranberry juice
Lemon twist, orange twist, or lime
wedge, for garnish

Pour all liquid ingredients into a
shaker tin of ice. Shake and strain
into a cocktail glass. Garnish with
lemon twist, orange twist, or
lime wedge.

Green Apple Seabreeze

1½ ounces green apple vodka
Equal parts of cranberry and grapefruit
juice to fill

Pour all the ingredients into a
highball glass of ice and stir.

Greyhound

1½ ounces vodka
Grapefruit juice to fill

Fill a glass of your choice with
ice and pour in the vodka, then
fill with grapefruit juice.

Hairy Navel

1 ounce vodka
1 ounce peach schnapps
Fresh orange juice to fill

Pour the vodka and peach
schnapps into a highball glass of
ice. Fill with orange juice.

Harvey Wallbanger

1½ ounces vodka
Orange juice to fill
1 ounce Galliano

Pour vodka into a tall glass of
ice. Fill with orange juice to ½"
from the rim. Top with the
Galliano.

Hollywood

1 ounce vodka
1 ounce raspberry liqueur
Pineapple juice to fill

Pour the vodka and raspberry
liqueur into a highball glass of
ice. Fill with pineapple juice.

Hunka Burning Love

1 ounce raspberry rum or vodka
1 ounce hazelnut liqueur
½ ounce raspberry liqueur
2 scoops banana ice cream
Milk, to blend
½ banana, cut lengthwise
1 ounce 151 rum

Put the raspberry rum or vodka,
hazelnut liqueur, raspberry
liqueur, and banana ice cream
into a blender. Add the milk little
by little to reach a smooth consistency. Pour into a tall glass
and stick the banana into the
glass standing up. Pour the 151
rum all over the banana and
light.

I Dream of Genie Martini

2 ounces cherry-flavored vodka

3 ounces pink lemonade

Splash grenadine for color

Large cube of food-grade dry ice

Shake the liquid ingredients in a shaker tin of ice. Strain into a martini glass. Using tongs, drop in a large cube of food-grade dry ice to activate your Genie Martini. Be extremely cautious—do not touch or drink the ice. Use a cocktail straw in your martini glass as a safety precaution.

Dry Ice

Dry ice is frozen carbon dioxide (the stuff you breathe out). Buy it from your local ice company. The most common use is to put a chunk of it in a punch to get an eerie foggy effect. Keep dry ice chunks as large as possible because you never want to swallow it. Also, you never want to store it in an airtight container or touch it with your bare hands, lips, or any skin, especially if they're wet. Follow these simple precautions and you'll be fine.

Itsy Bitsy Teenie Weenie Yellow Polka Dot Martini

½ ounce dark chocolate

1 ounce raspberry or strawberry vodka

1 ounce limoncello

1 ounce lemon juice

½ ounce simple syrup

Melt the dark chocolate in the microwave. Carefully dip your finger in the chocolate and make polka dots on the inside of a martini glass. Set the glass in the freezer for a minute to harden the chocolate. In a shaker tin of ice add the other ingredients. Shake, then strain into the glass.

Lavender Fields

2 ounces pear vodka

1 ounce lavender syrup

1 ounce fresh lemon juice

Shake all ingredients in a shaker tin with ice, then strain into a chilled cocktail glass.

Lemondrop Martini

Sugar for rimming

1½ ounces citrus-flavored vodka

½ ounce triple sec or Cointreau

1 ounce lemon juice

½ ounce simple syrup

1 sugar-coated lemon wedge

Rim a martini glass with sugar. Pour liquid ingredients into a shaker. Shake, then strain into the glass. Garnish with sugar-coated lemon wedge set on the rim.

Lemon Love Shack Shake

1 ounce lemon vodka
1 ounce Cointreau
2 ounces cream
1 big scoop Italian lemon ice

Put all ingredients into a blender and blend. Add more lemon ice for more of a lemony taste. To make it creamier, add more cream.

Liquid Viagra

1 ounce vodka
1/2 ounce blue curaçao
1/2 ounce apricot brandy
1/2 ounce lime juice

This drink can be made on the rocks or straight up. Pour all ingredients into a shaker tin of ice. Shake, then strain into a glass of your choice with or without ice.

Love Potion #9

1 ounce mandarin vodka
1 ounce Parfait d'Amor
White (clear) cranberry juice to fill
Sprig of purple seedless grapes, for garnish

Pour vodka and Parfait d'Amour into a tall glass of ice. Fill with white (clear) cranberry juice. Garnish with the grapes.

Madras 🍸

1 1/2 ounces vodka
Equal parts of orange and cranberry juice to fill

Pour the vodka into a highball glass of ice. Fill with the juices. Stir.

Mandarin Baybreeze

1 1/2 ounces mandarin vodka
Equal parts of cranberry and pineapple juice to fill

Pour all the ingredients into a highball glass of ice and stir.

Mandarin Bloom

1 ounce mandarin vodka
1 ounce elderflower liqueur
1/2 ounce fresh lemon juice
Sprite or 7UP to fill
Nontoxic flower petals

Pour liquid ingredients into a large glass of ice and garnish with nontoxic flower petals.

Mandarin Cosmopolitan

1 1/2 ounces mandarin vodka
1/2 ounce Cointreau
1/4 ounce lime juice or freshly squeezed lime
1 ounce cranberry juice
Lemon twist, orange twist, or lime wedge, for garnish

Pour all liquid ingredients into a shaker tin of ice. Shake and strain into a cocktail glass. Garnish with lemon twist, orange twist, or lime wedge.

Mandarin Seabreeze

1½ ounces mandarin vodka

Equal parts of cranberry and grapefruit juice to fill

Pour all the ingredients into a highball glass of ice and stir.

Mango Baybreeze

1½ ounces mango vodka

Equal parts of cranberry and pineapple juice to fill

Pour all the ingredients into a highball glass of ice and stir.

Mango Cosmopolitan

1½ ounces mango vodka

½ ounce Cointreau

¼ ounce lime juice or freshly squeezed lime

1 ounce cranberry juice

Lemon twist, orange twist, or lime wedge, for garnish

Pour all liquid ingredients into a shaker tin of ice. Shake and strain into a cocktail glass. Garnish with lemon twist, orange twist, or lime wedge.

Mango Heat Wave

2 ounces mandarin vodka

1 ounce Passoã passion fruit liqueur

2 ounces mango nectar

2 ounces sweet-and-sour mix

Tropical fruits, for garnish

1 paper parasol, for garnish

Put a cup of ice into a blender, then add all liquid ingredients. Blend. Pour into a tropical glass and garnish with fruits of your choice and a paper parasol.

Mango Seabreeze

1½ ounces mango vodka

Equal parts of cranberry and grapefruit juice to fill

Pour all the ingredients into a highball glass of ice and stir.

Melon Ball

1 ounce vodka

1 ounce melon liqueur

Freshly squeezed orange juice to fill

Pour ingredients into a mixing glass nearly filled with ice. Stir, then strain into a highball glass of ice.

Melon Baybreeze

1½ ounces melon vodka

Equal parts of cranberry and pineapple juice to fill

Pour all the ingredients into a highball glass of ice and stir.

Melon Cosmopolitan

1½ ounces melon vodka
½ ounce Cointreau
¼ ounce lime juice or freshly squeezed lime
1 ounce cranberry juice
Lemon twist, orange twist, or lime wedge, for garnish

Pour all liquid ingredients into a shaker tin of ice. Shake and strain into a cocktail glass. Garnish with lemon twist, orange twist, or lime wedge.

Melon Seabreeze

1½ ounces melon vodka
Equal parts of cranberry and grapefruit juice to fill

Pour all the ingredients into a highball glass of ice and stir.

Melonlicious Mistress

1 ounce melon liqueur
1 ounce lemon vodka or rum
7UP to fill
1 maraschino cherry

Pour melon liqueur and vodka or rum into a tall glass of ice. Fill with 7UP and stir. Garnish with maraschino cherry.

Metropolitan

1½ ounces vodka
½ ounce crème de framboise
1 ounce cranberry juice
¼ ounce fresh lime juice
1 raspberry

Pour liquid ingredients into a shaker full of ice. Shake, then strain into a chilled cocktail glass. Garnish with raspberry.

Moscow Mule

2 ounces Smirnoff vodka
1 ounce fresh lime juice
Ginger beer to fill

Pour ingredients into a highball glass nearly filled with ice. Stir well.

Mudslide

1 ounce vodka
½ ounce coffee liqueur
½ ounce Irish cream
Half-and-half to fill
Chocolate syrup and whipped cream (if frozen), for garnish

This drink can be made on the rocks or frozen. If making on the rocks, pour vodka, coffee liqueur, Irish cream, and half-and-half into a short glass of ice. Pour into a shaker. Shake and pour back into the glass. If making frozen, pour the same ingredients into a blender with a cup of ice. Blend, then pour into a tall chocolate-swirled glass and top off with whipped cream.

Orange White Russian

1 ounce orange vodka

1 ounce coffee liqueur

2 ounces cream

Shake all ingredients and pour into a short glass of ice.

Passion Cup

2 ounces vodka

1/2 ounce coconut cream

1 ounce passion fruit juice

2 ounces orange juice

1 maraschino cherry

Combine liquid ingredients in a shaker half filled with ice. Shake well. Strain into a large wine glass. Top with a cherry.

Peach Baybreeze

1½ ounces peach vodka

Equal parts of cranberry and pineapple juice to fill

Pour all the ingredients into a highball glass of ice and stir.

Peach Cosmopolitan

1½ ounces peach vodka

1/2 ounce Cointreau

1/4 ounce lime juice or freshly squeezed lime

1 ounce cranberry juice

Lemon twist, orange twist, or lime wedge, for garnish

Pour all liquid ingredients into a shaker tin of ice. Shake and strain into a cocktail glass. Garnish with lemon twist, orange twist, or lime wedge.

Peach Seabreeze

1½ ounces peach vodka

Equal parts of cranberry and grapefruit juice to fill

Pour all the ingredients into a highball glass of ice and stir.

Peaches and Creamtini

1½ ounces orange vodka

1½ ounces peach schnapps

2 ounces orange juice

Splash cream

Pour all ingredients into a shaker tin of ice. Shake, then strain into a martini glass.

Maraschino Cherries

Only infuse alcohol with cherries that do not contain artificial flavorings or colorings. The bright red cherries in a jar are made by taking real cherries, pitting them, and bleaching them white. The cherries are then dyed with red color #40. Use fresh cherries or look for the jarred dark red cherries. Check the label for any artificial ingredients.

Pear Baybreeze

1½ ounces pear vodka

Equal parts of cranberry and pineapple juice to fill

Pour all the ingredients into a highball glass of ice and stir.

Pear Cosmopolitan

1½ ounces pear vodka

½ ounce Cointreau

¼ ounce lime juice or freshly squeezed lime

1 ounce cranberry juice

Lemon twist, orange twist, or lime wedge, for garnish

Pour all liquid ingredients into a shaker tin of ice. Shake and strain into a cocktail glass. Garnish with lemon twist, orange twist, or lime wedge.

Pear Seabreeze

1½ ounces pear vodka

Equal parts of cranberry and grapefruit juice to fill

Pour all the ingredients into a highball glass of ice and stir.

Pearl Harbor

1½ ounces vodka

½ ounce melon liqueur

Pineapple juice to fill

Pour the vodka and melon liqueur into a highball glass of ice. Fill with pineapple juice.

Pineapple Baybreeze

1½ ounces pineapple vodka

Equal parts of cranberry and pineapple juice to fill

Pour all the ingredients into a highball glass of ice and stir.

Pineapple Seabreeze

1½ ounces pineapple vodka

Equal parts of cranberry and grapefruit juice to fill

Pour all the ingredients into a highball glass of ice and stir.

Pink Cadillactini

1 ounce vanilla vodka

½ ounce Galliano

½ ounce white crème de cacao

⅛ ounce grenadine

3 ounces cream or milk

Pour all ingredients into a shaker tin of ice and shake until cold and frothy. Strain into a martini glass.

Pink Lemonade

2 ounces lemon vodka

5 ounces lemonade

½ ounce grenadine

Fill a tall glass of your choice with ice. Add all the ingredients and stir.

Pizza Bloody Mary

Parmesan cheese and red pepper flakes, for rimming

2 ounces vodka

5 ounces Bloody Mary mix

1 pepperoni slice

1 cube of mozzarella cheese

1 green olive

Rim a tall glass with a mixture of parmesan cheese and red pepper flakes. Fill with ice and add the liquid ingredients. Skewer the pepperoni slice, cubed cheese, and olive to garnish the drink.

Pomegranate Baybreeze

1½ ounces pomegranate vodka

Equal parts of cranberry and pineapple juice to fill

Pour all the ingredients into a highball glass of ice and stir.

Pomegranate Cosmopolitan

1½ ounces pomegranate vodka

½ ounce Cointreau

¼ ounce lime juice or freshly squeezed lime

1 ounce cranberry juice

Lemon twist, orange twist, or lime wedge, for garnish

Pour all liquid ingredients into a shaker tin of ice. Shake and strain into a cocktail glass. Garnish with lemon twist, orange twist, or lime wedge.

Pomegranate Martini

2 ounces citrus vodka

1 ounce pomegranate juice

½ ounce simple syrup

Shake all ingredients well with ice and strain into a chilled martini glass.

Pomegranate Seabreeze

1½ ounces pomegranate vodka

Equal parts of cranberry and grapefruit juice to fill

Pour all the ingredients into a highball glass of ice and stir.

Pop Star

1 packet of strawberry Pop Rocks

2 ounces strawberry vodka

1 ounce fresh lemon juice

1 ounce simple syrup

1 star fruit slice

Rim a cocktail glass with Pop Rocks. Shake the liquid ingredients in a shaker with ice and strain into the cocktail glass. Garnish with the star fruit slice.

Raspberry Baybreeze

1½ ounces raspberry vodka

Equal parts of cranberry and pineapple juice to fill

Pour all the ingredients into a highball glass of ice and stir.

Raspberry Cosmopolitan

1½ ounces raspberry vodka
½ ounce Cointreau
¼ ounce lime juice or freshly squeezed lime
1 ounce cranberry juice
Lemon twist, orange twist, or lime wedge, for garnish

Pour all liquid ingredients into a shaker tin of ice. Shake and strain into a cocktail glass. Garnish with lemon twist, orange twist, or lime wedge.

Raspberry Seabreeze

2 ounces raspberry vodka
Equal parts of cranberry and grapefruit juice to fill

Fill a highball glass with ice. Pour in all the ingredients and stir.

Match Trick

Challenge someone to drop a paper match on the bar top or table top so that it lands on its side. They will try many times. To get it to work, bend the match a little before dropping it. It will land on its side.

Raspberry White Russian

1 ounce raspberry vodka
1 ounce coffee liqueur
2 ounces cream

Shake all ingredients and pour into a short glass of ice.

Russian Spring Punch

2 ounces vodka
¾ ounce crème de cassis
¾ ounce fresh lemon juice
½ ounce simple syrup
Sparkling wine to fill
1 lemon wedge and 2 raspberries

Build vodka, crème de cassis, lemon juice, and simple syrup over ice in a tall glass. Top with sparkling wine. Stir gently. Garnish with lemon wedge and raspberries.

Salty Dog

Salt for rimming
1½ ounces vodka
Grapefruit juice to fill
1 lime wedge

Rim a highball glass with salt. Fill with ice. Pour in the vodka and fill with grapefruit juice. Garnish with lime wedge.

Screwdriver

1½ ounces vodka
2½ ounces freshly squeezed orange juice

Fill a glass with ice. Add the ingredients and stir.

Seabreeze

1½ ounces vodka
Cranberry and grapefruit juice to fill
1 lime wedge

Pour into a highball glass over ice. Garnish with lime wedge.

Sex in Front of the Fireplace

1 ounce raspberry liqueur

1 ounce orange vodka

1 ounce peach schnapps

White (clear) cranberry juice and orange juice to fill

3 miniature Tootsie Rolls

1/2 ounce Grand Marnier

1 long fireplace match

Pour raspberry liqueur in a tall glass, then fill with ice. Mix vodka and peach schnapps and slowly pour into glass. Gently fill with equal parts of white (clear) cranberry and orange juice. Garnish with the Tootsie Rolls, pour the Grand Marnier on top, and light.

Wine from an Empty Bottle Trick

After you finish the last drop from a bottle of wine, announce to your friends that you can drink another shot of wine from the bottle. Your friends will think it's impossible, but you can prove them wrong. Simply turn the bottle upside down, pour some wine from your glass into the punt (the indention on the bottom of the bottle), then drink. You have just drunk a shot of wine from the empty bottle.

Sex on the Beach

1 1/2 ounces vodka

1 ounce peach schnapps

2 ounces orange juice

2 ounces cranberry juice

Combine all ingredients in a highball glass almost filled with ice. Stir.

Sloe Screw

1 ounce vodka

1 ounce sloe gin

2 ounces fresh orange juice

Pour all ingredients into a tall glass of ice and stir.

Smiling Tiger

1 ounce black vodka

1/2 ounce black sambuca

1/4 ounce vanilla extract

1 3/4 ounces orange juice

Cream to fill

Pour black vodka, black sambuca, and vanilla extract into a tall glass (black). Fill to the top with ice and slowly fill a little more than three-quarters with orange juice (orange). To make the white stripe, slowly fill the rest of the way with cream.

Sour Appletini

1 ounce citrus-flavored vodka

1 ounce sour apple liqueur

2 ounces sour mix

Pour all ingredients into a shaker. Shake and strain into a martini glass.

Strawberry Baybreeze

1½ ounces strawberry vodka

Equal parts of cranberry and pineapple juice to fill

Pour all the ingredients into a highball glass of ice and stir.

Strawberry Cosmopolitan

1½ ounces strawberry vodka

½ ounce Cointreau

¼ ounce lime juice or freshly squeezed lime

1 ounce cranberry juice

Lemon twist, orange twist, or lime wedge, for garnish

Pour all liquid ingredients into a shaker tin of ice. Shake and strain into a cocktail glass. Garnish with lemon twist, orange twist, or lime wedge.

Strawberry Seabreeze

1½ ounces strawberry vodka

Equal parts of cranberry and grapefruit juice to fill

Pour all the ingredients into a highball glass of ice and stir.

Strawberry White Russian

1 ounce strawberry vodka

1 ounce coffee liqueur

2 ounces cream

Shake all ingredients together and pour into a short glass of ice.

Stupid Cupid

2 ounces pear vodka

1 ounce sloe gin

1 ounce fresh lemon juice

Pour ingredients into a mixing glass nearly filled with ice. Stir, then strain into a cocktail glass.

Tangerine Baybreeze

1½ ounces tangerine vodka

Equal parts of cranberry and pineapple juice to fill

Pour all the ingredients into a highball glass of ice and stir.

Tangerine Cosmopolitan

1½ ounces tangerine vodka

½ ounce Cointreau

¼ ounce lime juice or freshly squeezed lime

1 ounce cranberry juice

Lemon twist, orange twist, or lime wedge, for garnish

Pour all liquid ingredients into a shaker tin of ice. Shake and strain into a cocktail glass. Garnish with lemon twist, orange twist, or lime wedge.

Tangerine Seabreeze

1½ ounces tangerine vodka

Equal parts of cranberry and grapefruit juice to fill

Pour all the ingredients into a highball glass of ice and stir.

Upside-Down Pineapple Martini

¼ ounce grenadine

1 ounce vanilla vodka

1 ounce Irish cream

1 ounce butterscotch schnapps

2 ounces pineapple juice

1 maraschino cherry

Pour the grenadine into a martini glass. Pour the rest of the liquid ingredients into a shaker tin of ice. Shake, then strain into the martini glass. Drop in the cherry.

Vanilla Baybreeze

1½ ounces vanilla vodka

Equal parts of cranberry and pineapple juice to fill

Pour all the ingredients into a highball glass of ice and stir.

Vanilla Seabreeze

1½ ounces vanilla vodka

Equal parts of cranberry and grapefruit juice to fill

Pour all the ingredients into a highball glass of ice and stir.

Vanilla White Russian

1 ounce vanilla vodka

1 ounce coffee liqueur

2 ounces cream

Shake all ingredients and pour into a short glass of ice.

Vodka and Tonic

2 ounces vodka

Tonic water to fill

1 lime wedge

Pour the vodka and tonic into a highball glass of ice, then stir. Add the garnish.

Vodka Collins

2 ounces vodka

1 ounce fresh lemon juice

¼ ounce simple syrup

Club soda to fill

1 orange slice and 1 cherry

Shake the first three ingredients with ice. Strain into a tall 12-ounce glass. Fill with club soda and garnish with orange slice and cherry.

Vodka Gimlet

2 ounces vodka

½ ounce Rose's lime juice (or ¼ ounce fresh lime juice and ¼ ounce simple syrup)

1 lime wedge

Add the liquid ingredients to a mixing glass half filled with ice. Shake and strain into a rocks glass of ice. Garnish with lime wedge.

Vodka Martini

½ ounce dry vermouth

2 ounces vodka

2 olives or 1 lemon twist

In a mixing glass half filled with ice, add the vermouth first, then the vodka. Stir, then strain into a martini glass. Serve with olives or a twist of lemon.

Vodka on the Rocks

2 ounces vodka

1 lemon twist

Place a few ice cubes in a rocks glass and add vodka. Garnish with lemon twist.

Vodka Red Bull

2 ounces vodka

Red Bull to fill

Pour the vodka into a highball glass of ice. Fill with Red Bull.

Vodka Sour

2 ounces vodka

1 ounce fresh lemon juice

¼ ounce simple syrup

1 orange slice and 1 cherry

Fill a shaker glass two-thirds with ice. Add liquid ingredients and shake. Strain into a highball glass or over a short glass of ice. Garnish with orange slice and cherry.

Watermelon Baybreeze

1½ ounces watermelon vodka

Equal parts of cranberry and pineapple juice to fill

Pour all the ingredients into a highball glass of ice and stir.

Watermelon Cosmopolitan

1½ ounces watermelon vodka

½ ounce Cointreau

¼ ounce lime juice or freshly squeezed lime

1 ounce cranberry juice

Lemon twist, orange twist, or lime wedge, for garnish

Pour all liquid ingredients into a shaker tin of ice. Shake and strain into a cocktail glass. Garnish with lemon twist, orange twist, or lime wedge.

Watermelon Seabreeze

1½ ounces watermelon vodka

Equal parts of cranberry and grapefruit juice to fill

Pour all the ingredients into a highball glass of ice and stir.

White Blueberry Cosmo

1½ ounces blueberry vodka

½ ounce Cointreau

¼ ounce lime juice or freshly squeezed lime

1 ounce white (clear) cranberry juice

1 lime wedge

Pour liquid ingredients into a shaker of ice and shake. Strain into a chilled cocktail glass. Garnish with lime wedge.

White Chocolatini

1½ ounces vanilla vodka
1 ounce Godiva White Chocolate
Liqueur
2 ounces cream
White chocolate shavings, for garnish

Pour the liquid ingredients into a shaker tin of ice. Shake, then strain into a martini glass. Sprinkle white chocolate shavings on top.

White Mango Cosmo

1½ ounces mango vodka
½ ounce Cointreau
¼ ounce lime juice or freshly squeezed lime
1 ounce white (clear) cranberry juice
1 lime wedge

Pour all liquid ingredients into a shaker of ice and shake. Strain into a chilled cocktail glass. Garnish with lime wedge.

White Melon Cosmo

1½ ounces melon vodka
½ ounce Cointreau
¼ ounce lime juice or freshly squeezed lime
1 ounce white (clear) cranberry juice
1 lime wedge

Pour all liquid ingredients into a shaker of ice and shake. Strain into a chilled cocktail glass. Garnish with lime wedge.

White Pineapple Cosmo

1½ ounces pineapple vodka
½ ounce Cointreau
¼ ounce lime juice or freshly squeezed lime
1 ounce white (clear) cranberry juice
1 lime wedge

Pour all liquid ingredients into a shaker of ice and shake. Strain into a chilled cocktail glass. Garnish with lime wedge.

White Raspberry Cosmo

1½ ounces raspberry vodka
½ ounce Cointreau
¼ ounce lime juice or freshly squeezed lime
1 ounce white (clear) cranberry juice
1 lime wedge

Pour all liquid ingredients into a shaker of ice and shake. Strain into a chilled cocktail glass. Garnish with lime wedge.

White Russian ♈

1 ounce vodka
1 ounce coffee liqueur
2 ounces cream

Shake all ingredients and pour into a short glass of ice.

White Russian Jolt

1 ounce espresso vodka
1 ounce coffee liqueur
2 ounces cream

Shake all ingredients and pour into a short glass of ice.

White Strawberry Cosmo

1½ ounces strawberry vodka

½ ounce Cointreau

¼ ounce lime juice or freshly squeezed lime

1 ounce white (clear) cranberry juice

1 lime wedge

Pour all liquid ingredients into a shaker of ice and shake. Strain into a chilled cocktail glass. Garnish with lime wedge.

Wildberry Baybreeze

1½ ounces wildberry vodka

Equal parts of cranberry and pineapple juice to fill

Pour all the ingredients into a highball glass of ice and stir.

Wildberry Cosmopolitan

1½ ounces wildberry vodka

½ ounce Cointreau

¼ ounce lime juice or freshly squeezed lime

1 ounce cranberry juice

Lemon twist, orange twist, or lime wedge, for garnish

Pour all liquid ingredients into a shaker tin of ice. Shake and strain into a cocktail glass. Garnish with lemon twist, orange twist, or lime wedge.

Wildberry Seabreeze

1½ ounces wildberry vodka

Equal parts of cranberry and grapefruit juice to fill

Pour all the ingredients into a highball glass of ice and stir.

Woo Woo 🍸

1 ounce vodka

1 ounce peach schnapps

Cranberry juice to fill

Pour the vodka and peach schnapps into a highball glass. Fill with cranberry juice.

gin: gin is in

In its basic form, gin is vodka that has been redistilled with herbs and botanicals. Gin-makers use citrus peels, coriander, ginger, rose petals, nutmeg, and cassia bark, but the most prominent is the juniper berry. Dr. Sylvius, a Dutch professor and physician, is credited with making gin as a cure-all tonic in the 1650s. Today, many alcohol historians debate this claim because the juniper berry was quite plentiful in Italy, which leads them to believe that Italian monks were the first to make gin.

Gin Classifications

The four main categories of gin are London dry gin, Plymouth English gin, genever (also spelled jenever), and New Western. The word *genever* is Dutch for juniper, and the word *gin* is a shortening of the Dutch term. Holland and Belgium make genever, which is considered the original style of gin made in pot stills. It's sweeter than London dry gin. London dry gin is the most popular because it mixes well. It doesn't have to be made in England (the United States, Germany, and Spain make gin as well). Plymouth English gin can only be made in Plymouth, England—and it was the first gin used in a printed recipe of the Martini. The New Western gins use less juniper and more ingredients like rose petals and cucumber. Examples of these are Hendrick's, Aviation, and Martin Miller's.

Alaska

1½ ounces gin
½ ounce yellow Chartreuse
2 dashes orange bitters
1 cherry

Shake the liquid ingredients in a shaker tin of ice. Strain into a martini glass. Garnish with the cherry.

Alexander

1 ounce gin
1 ounce crème de cacao
1 ounce sweet cream

Shake ingredients in a shaker of ice. Strain into a martini glass.

Kitty Cat Gin

Old Tom Gin is the only produced example we have today of what sweeter gin used to taste like. It got its name from a cat-shaped plaque that was mounted on the outside of some English pubs in the 18th century. One could deposit money in the cat's mouth and then place their mouth on a tube between the cats paws. A barman inside would pour a dram of gin into the tube. How about that for an ancient vending machine!

Apple Ginger Gin

2 ounces London dry gin
2 ounces apple juice
Ginger beer to fill

Pour the gin and apple juice into a tall glass. Fill with ginger beer. Stir.

Aviation

2 ounces gin
1 ounce maraschino liqueur
1 ounce fresh lemon juice
1 lemon twist

Shake all liquid ingredients in a shaker tin of ice. Strain into a martini glass. Garnish with lemon twist.

Maraschino Liqueur

Maraschino liqueur is made from crushed Dalmatian marasca cherries. The pits, stems, and seeds are also used. It's clear and has a neutral grain spirit base.

Barnum Cocktail

2 ounces gin
1 ounce apricot brandy
½ ounce fresh lemon juice
2 dashes Angostura bitters
1 lemon twist

Shake all the liquid ingredients in a shaker tin with ice, then strain into a chilled cocktail glass. Garnish with lemon twist.

Bee's Knees

2 ounces gin
¾ ounce honey
½ ounce fresh lemon juice

Shake all ingredients in a shaker tin of ice. Strain into a martini glass.

Belgian Brownie

1 ounce genever
1 ounce white crème de cacao
½ ounce cognac
Cream to fill

Pour the first three ingredients into a highball glass. Fill with cream. Stir.

Bermuda Rose

1¼ ounces dry gin
¼ ounce apricot nectar liqueur
¼ ounce grenadine

Shake ingredients in a shaker of ice. Strain into a martini glass.

Bijou

1 ounce Plymouth gin
1 ounce green Chartreuse
1 ounce sweet vermouth
Dash orange bitters

Shake all ingredients in a shaker tin of ice. Strain into a martini glass.

Bird of Violet Paradise

2 ounces gin
1 ounce violet liqueur
1/2 ounce fresh lime juice
1/2 ounce fresh grapefruit juice

Shake all the ingredients with ice and strain into a chilled cocktail glass.

Blooming Gin

2 ounces London dry gin
1 ounce elderflower liqueur
Perrier to fill

Pour gin and elderflower liqueur into a highball glass. Fill with Perrier. Stir.

The Blue Moon

2 ounces gin
1 ounce violet liqueur
1/2 ounce fresh lemon juice
1 lemon twist

Shake all the liquid ingredients in a shaker tin with ice, then strain into a chilled cocktail glass. Garnish with lemon twist.

A Businessman Walks Into a Bar and Orders a Martini

A businessman walks into a bar and orders a Martini. After he finishes the drink, he peeks inside his shirt pocket and orders another Martini. After he finishes that one, he again peeks inside his shirt pocket and orders yet another Martini. The bartender finally asks the man why he keeps looking inside his shirt. The man says, "I'm peeking at a photo of my wife. When she starts to look good, then I know it's time to go home."

Bolero Blood

2 ounces gin
1/2 ounce blood orange liqueur
1/4 ounce Fernet Branca
1 ounce simple syrup
1 ounce fresh grapefruit juice
1 ounce fresh lime juice

Shake all the ingredients with ice. Strain into a highball glass of ice.

Boxcar

2 ounces gin
1/2 ounce Cointreau
1/2 ounce fresh lime juice
1 organic egg white

Shake all the ingredients in a shaker tin with ice, then strain into a chilled cocktail glass.

Bramble

1½ ounces gin
1 ounce fresh lime juice
½ ounce simple syrup
½ ounce crème de mûre
2 blackberries

Shake the gin, fresh lime juice, and simple syrup in a shaker half filled with ice. Strain into a rocks glass filled with crushed ice. Float the crème de mûre on top. Garnish with 2 blackberries.

Bronx

1 ounce dry gin
1 ounce French dry vermouth
1 ounce fresh orange juice

Shake all ingredients in a shaker tin of ice. Strain into a martini glass.

Bull Dog

1½ ounces gin
2 ounces fresh orange juice
Ginger ale to fill

Pour the gin and orange juice into a highball glass. Fill with ginger ale. Stir.

Cabaret Cocktail

½ ounce gin
1 ounce absinthe
2 ounces cold espresso
1 lemon twist

Shake all liquid ingredients in a shaker tin of ice. Strain into a martini glass. Garnish with lemon twist.

Clover Club

2 ounces Plymouth gin
1 ounce fresh lemon juice
½ ounce grenadine
1 organic egg white

Shake all ingredients in a shaker tin of ice. Strain into a martini glass.

Colonial Cocktail

2 ounces gin
1 ounce grapefruit juice
½ ounce maraschino liqueur

Shake ingredients in a shaker of ice. Strain into a martini glass.

Cotton Gin

2 ounces London dry gin
1 ounce sambuca

Shake ingredients in a shaker tin of ice. Strain into a martini glass. The water from the ice will turn this drink white.

Cowboy Martini

3 ounces Plymouth gin
¼ ounce simple syrup
2 dashes orange bitters
4 or 5 mint leaves (partially torn)
1 orange twist

Shake all liquid ingredients and the mint in a shaker tin of ice. Strain into a martini glass. Garnish with orange twist.

Cucumber Gimlet

2 ounces fresh cucumber meat

2 ounces gin

1 ounce fresh lime juice

1 ounce simple syrup

Drop the fresh cucumber into the bottom of a short glass and muddle. Add ice and the rest of the ingredients. Stir.

Derby Cocktail

1/2 fresh peach, chopped

Several mint leaves (save one sprig for a garnish)

1/2 ounce peach liqueur

2 1/2 ounces Beefeater gin

Muddle together peach pieces, mint, and peach liqueur in a mixing glass or shaker tin. Add gin and ice, shake, then strain into a small martini glass. Garnish with sprig of mint.

Dirty Martini

2 ounces London dry gin

1/2 ounce olive juice

Olives, for garnish

Shake liquid ingredients in a shaker tin of ice. Strain into a martini glass. Garnish with olives.

Distressed Damson

1 fresh lime, peeled and chopped

Loose handful of blueberries

1 1/2 ounces damson gin

Muddle the chopped fresh lime and blueberries in a rocks glass. Add the damson gin, stir, and top up with crushed ice.

Damson Gin

Damson gin is made from damson juice (a type of plum), gin, and cane sugar. The fruit is grown in the orchards of the Lyth Valley, Cumbria, in the United Kingdom. Walking through a damson orchard is breathtaking because of the rich purple color of the fruit.

Dry Tea

2 ounces dry gin

2 ounces cold tea

Sprite or 7UP to fill

1 lemon wedge

Pour the gin and tea into a highball glass. Fill with Sprite or 7UP. Garnish with lemon wedge.

Dutch Breakfast

1 ounce gin
1/4 ounce Galliano
1 ounce advocaat
1/2 ounce fresh lime juice
1/2 ounce fresh lemon juice
1/2 ounce simple syrup

Pour all ingredients into a high-ball glass of ice. Stir.

Dutch Trade Winds

2 ounces genever
1/2 ounce curaçao
1/2 ounce lemon juice
1 teaspoon simple syrup

Pour all ingredients into a cocktail shaker half filled with ice. Shake. Strain into a martini glass.

Fallen Angel

1 1/2 ounces gin
1/2 ounce white crème de menthe
1/2 ounce fresh lemon juice
Dash bitters
1 cherry

Shake liquid ingredients in a shaker tin with ice, then strain into a chilled cocktail glass. Garnish with cherry.

Floradora

1 1/2 ounces gin
1/2 ounce fresh lime juice
1/2 ounce framboise liqueur or raspberry syrup
Ginger ale to fill
1 lime wedge

Pour the first three ingredients into a highball glass. Fill with ginger ale. Garnish with lime wedge.

French 75 🍸

1 ounce gin
1 ounce lemon juice
1/2 ounce simple syrup
Chilled champagne to fill
1 lemon twist

Build gin, lemon juice, and simple syrup into a champagne flute and top with chilled champagne. Garnish with lemon twist.

French 75

The French 75 is believed to have been invented by legendary bartender Harry MacElhone in honor of the famous French 75 light field gun. The artillery piece was a major weapon in World War I, and the cocktail debuted in Paris after the Great War.

French Martini

2 ounces dry gin
¼ ounce raspberry liqueur
1 ounce pineapple juice

Shake all ingredients in a shaker tin of ice. Strain into a martini glass.

Gibson

1½ ounces dry gin
½ ounce French vermouth
3 pearl onions
1 lemon twist

Shake gin and vermouth in a shaker tin of ice. Strain into a martini glass. Garnish with onions and a lemon twist.

Gimlet

2 ounces gin
¾ ounce sweetened lime juice (or fresh lime juice and simple syrup)
1 lime wedge

Shake the gin and lime juice in a shaker of ice. Strain into a rocks glass of ice. Garnish with lime wedge.

Gin and It

2 ounces gin
¾ ounce sweet vermouth

Pour ingredients into a mixing glass of ice and stir. Strain into a martini glass.

Gin and Juice

1½ ounces gin
Orange juice to fill

Pour the gin into a highball glass of ice. Fill with orange juice. Stir.

Gin and Sin

2 ounces gin
¼ ounce fresh lemon juice
¼ ounce orange juice
¼ ounce grenadine

Shake all ingredients in a shaker of ice. Strain into a martini glass.

Gin and Tonic

1½ ounces gin
Tonic to fill
1 lime wedge

Pour the gin into a highball glass of ice. Fill with tonic. Garnish with lime wedge.

Gin Daisy

2 ounces gin
¼ ounce Grand Marnier
¼ ounce simple syrup
Juice from ½ lemon
Club soda to fill

Combine first four ingredients in a shaker of ice and shake well. Strain into large wine glass. Fill with club soda.

Gin Fizz

2 ounces genever
1/2 ounce fresh lemon juice
1/2 ounce simple syrup
1/2 egg white
Soda water to fill
1 lemon wedge

Combine genever, lemon juice, syrup, and egg white in a shaker of ice. Shake well and strain into a tall glass of ice. Fill with soda water and garnish with lemon wedge.

Gin-Gin Mule

1 1/2 ounces gin
3/4 ounce fresh lime juice
1 ounce simple syrup
6 sprigs of fresh mint
1 ounce ginger beer

Put the first four ingredients into a shaker tin of ice. Shake hard and strain into a highball glass of fresh ice. Top with ginger beer.

Gin Rickey

2 ounces gin
Juice from 1 lime
Club soda to fill

Shake the gin and lime juice in a shaker of ice. Strain into a highball glass of ice. Fill with club soda.

Gin Sour

2 ounces gin
1 ounce fresh lemon juice
1/2 ounce simple syrup
1/2 egg white

Shake the ingredients in a shaker of ice. Strain into a highball glass of ice.

Huckleberry Finn Gin

3 ounces huckleberry-infused genever
1 huckleberry bloom

Shake the huckleberry genever in a shaker tin of ice and strain into a martini glass. Garnish with huckleberry bloom.

Homemade Infused Huckleberry Gin

Buy a bottle of genever and 2 pints of huckleberries (the season is mid- to late summer in the United States). Next, obtain a large-mouthed glass container to make your infusion. Place the washed huckleberries in the jar, then add the genever. Close the lid tightly, remove from direct sunlight, and let sit from 4 days to 2 weeks. Strain and bottle when finished.

Jasmine

1½ ounces gin
¼ ounce Cointreau
¾ ounce freshly squeezed lemon juice
¼ ounce Campari

Shake all ingredients in a shaker of ice. Strain into a martini glass.

Jupiter Cocktail

1½ ounces Plymouth gin
½ ounce dry vermouth
¼ ounce fresh orange juice
¼ ounce Parfait d'Amour

Shake all ingredients in a shaker of ice. Strain into a martini glass.

Looney Bin Gin

3 ounces Seagram's Orange Twisted Gin

Shake the gin in a shaker of ice. Strain into a martini glass.

Magnolia Blossom

1½ ounces gin
½ ounce cream
½ ounce fresh lemon juice
¼ ounce grenadine

Shake all the ingredients in a shaker tin with ice. Strain into a chilled cocktail glass.

Martinez

2 ounces Martini Rosso (red vermouth)
1 ounce Tanqueray No. 10 gin
2 dashes Luxardo maraschino liqueur
Dash Angostura bitters

Stir all ingredients in a mixing glass of ice. Strain into a martini glass.

Martini

2 ounces gin
⅛ ounce dry vermouth
2 large pimiento-stuffed green olives

Shake gin and vermouth in a shaker of ice. Strain into a martini glass. Garnish with the olives. Some people pour the dry vermouth into a mister and mist the top of the martini.

King of Cocktails

By far, the Martini is the king of cocktails. It is the icon of the cocktail culture and whole books have been written about its simplicity—with a dash of controversy. You should know that no one knows when, where, or by whom the first Martini was created. What we do know is that Jerry Thomas published a cocktail recipe called a Martinez in his *Bar-Tenders Guide* in 1887.

Million-Dollar Cocktail

1½ ounces gin

1 ounce sweet vermouth

1½ ounces pineapple juice

½ ounce fresh lemon juice

1 ounce cream

¼ ounce simple syrup

¼ ounce grenadine

Shake all ingredients with ice and strain into a martini glass.

Monkey Gland

2 ounces gin

1 ounce orange juice

Dash Pernod

¼ ounce grenadine

1 orange twist

Shake all liquid ingredients with ice and strain into a martini glass. Garnish with orange twist.

Negroni

1 ounce gin

1 ounce sweet vermouth

1 ounce Campari

1 orange twist

Pour liquid ingredients into a shaker. Shake and strain into a rocks glass of ice. Garnish with orange twist.

Ninja Turtle

1 ounce gin

½ ounce blue curaçao

Fresh orange juice to fill

Pour the gin and curaçao into a highball glass of ice. Fill with orange juice.

Park Avenue

1½ ounces gin

¼ ounce dry vermouth

¼ ounce sweet vermouth

¼ ounce pineapple juice

Shake all the ingredients in a shaker tin with ice, then strain into a chilled cocktail glass.

Pegu Club

2 ounces dry gin

1 ounce curaçao

Dash Angostura bitters

Dash orange bitters

¼ ounce lime juice

Pour the ingredients into a shaker with ice. Shake, then strain into a martini glass.

The Pegu Club

The original Pegu Club entertained British colonial officers stationed in Burma. It was renowned for its cocktails, and its house drink gained worldwide popularity by the 1930s. The club has closed, but master bartender Audrey Saunders has introduced a Pegu Club in New York City. The new Pegu Club strives to make cocktails the way they were supposed to be made, with fresh ingredients and a commitment to superior mixology.

Pink Gin

2–3 ounces gin
3 or 4 dashes Angostura bitters

Pour the ingredients into a shaker with ice. Shake, then strain into a martini glass.

Pink Lady

1½ ounces gin
¼ ounce grenadine
1 organic egg white
¼ ounce sweet cream

Pour the ingredients into a shaker with ice and shake well. Strain into a martini glass.

Pink Peony

1 ounce gin
1 ounce elderflower liqueur
½ ounce fresh lemon juice
½ ounce simple syrup
½ ounce pomegranate juice

Shake all the ingredients in a shaker tin with ice, then strain into a chilled cocktail glass.

Pirate's Sour

2 ounces dry gin
1½ ounces sour mix
3 dashes Angostura bitters
Float (½ ounce) of Goldschläger

Shake the first three ingredients with ice. Strain into a rocks glass and float the Goldschläger on top.

Poet's Dream

2 ounces dry gin
1 ounce Luxardo maraschino liqueur
½ ounce Noilly Prat Original Dry
¼ ounce Cynar

Shake all the ingredients with ice and strain into a chilled cocktail glass.

Ramos Gin Fizz

1½ ounces gin
½ ounce fresh lemon juice
½ ounce fresh lime juice
1¼ ounces simple syrup
2 ounces milk
1 egg white
2 drops orange flower water
Club soda to fill

Shake all ingredients except the club soda with ice. Strain into a highball glass without ice. Fill with club soda.

The Ramos Gin Fizz

The Ramos Gin Fizz proudly traces its roots to New Orleans, where it was created in the 1880s by Henry C. Ramos. It uses milk and egg white to complement the traditional gin/juice/syrup base. The orange flower water gives the drink its unique exotic taste. You can find orange flower water at specialty grocery stores and online retail sites.

Raspberry Collins

2 ounces Plymouth gin

¾ ounce raspberry liqueur

1 ounce fresh lemon juice

½ ounce simple syrup

½ ounce raspberry purée

Club soda to fill

1 lemon slice and 2 raspberries

Shake all the liquid ingredients except the club soda with ice. Strain into a tall glass of ice. Fill with club soda. Garnish with lemon slice and raspberries.

Red Snapper (Original Recipe) 🍸

2 ounces gin

Bloody Mary mix to fill

1 celery stalk or 1 lime slice

Pour the gin into a tall glass and fill with the Bloody Mary mix. Gently roll into another glass and back again. Garnish with celery, lime, or whatever you desire.

Rusty Windmill

1 ounce genever

1 ounce Drambuie

Pour the ingredients into a rocks glass of ice.

Seventh Heaven

1¾ ounces gin

½ ounce maraschino liqueur

¼ ounce fresh grapefruit juice

1 sprig of mint

Shake the liquid ingredients in a shaker tin with ice, then strain into a chilled cocktail glass. Garnish with sprig of mint.

Shangri-Las

1½ ounces gin

½ ounce apricot brandy

½ ounce fresh orange juice

¼ ounce grenadine

4 ounces sparkling wine

Fill a wine glass with ice and add all the ingredients. Stir.

Shore Breeze

1½ ounces gin

2 ounces grapefruit juice

Tonic to fill

Pour the gin and grapefruit juice into a highball glass of ice. Fill with tonic.

Singapore Sling #1 🍸

1½ ounces gin

Club soda to fill

2 ounces sour mix

½ ounce cherry brandy

Shake the gin and sour mix with ice. Strain into a tall glass of ice. Fill with club soda. Float the cherry brandy.

Singapore Sling #2 Y

1½ ounces gin
½ ounce Cherry Heering
½ ounce Cointreau
½ ounce Bénédictine
½ ounce pineapple juice
½ ounce fresh lime juice
½ ounce grenadine
Dash bitters

Pour all ingredients into a shaker of ice. Shake. Strain into a tall glass of ice.

Skip and Go Naked

½ ounce gin
½ ounce sweet-and-sour mix
Beer to fill

Shake the gin and sweet-and-sour mix with ice. Pour into a highball glass of ice. Fill with beer.

Stork Club Cocktail

1½ ounces gin
½ ounce Cointreau
¼ ounce fresh lime juice
1 ounce fresh orange juice
Dash Angostura bitters
1 orange twist

Shake all liquid ingredients with ice. Strain into a martini glass. Garnish with orange twist.

Liquid Beauty
Some homemade shampoo and conditioner recipes call for common alcohols such as gin, rum, and vodka. If you look at the ingredients in your current shampoo and conditioner, you'll almost certainly find alcohol—although not the kind you'd like to drink!

Straits Sling

2 ounces Plymouth gin
¼ ounce kirschwasser
¼ ounce Bénédictine
1 ounce fresh lemon juice
2 dashes Angostura bitters
2 dashes orange bitters
Soda water to top
1 orange slice

Build first six ingredients over ice in a tall glass. Top with soda water. Garnish with orange slice.

Strike's On

2 ounces genever
½ ounce lemon juice
⅓ ounce pineapple syrup
1½ ounces sparkling apple juice
1 lemon slice

Shake all liquid ingredients except sparkling apple juice and strain into an old-fashioned glass filled with broken ice. Add sparkling apple juice and slice of lemon and serve.

Thin Gin

2 ounces dry gin

Diet ginger ale to fill

Pour the gin into a highball glass of ice. Fill with diet ginger ale.

Tom Collins

1½ ounces gin

2 ounces sweet-and-sour mix (or fresh lime juice and simple syrup)

Club soda to fill

1 orange slice and 1 cherry

Combine gin and sweet-and-sour mix in a shaker. Shake and strain into a Collins glass of ice. Fill with club soda. Garnish with orange slice and cherry.

The Wet Spot

1½ ounces Plymouth gin

½ ounce apricot brandy

1 ounce apple juice

½ ounce elderflower syrup

¾ ounce lemon juice

1 lemon twist

Shake this award-winning cocktail by Will Shine and Aisha Sharpe with ice. Strain into a martini glass. Garnish with lemon twist.

NASCAR

During Prohibition, bootleggers carrying moonshine would soup up their car engines in order to outrun the police. After Prohibition, they raced each other on country roads for the fun of it. These were the humble offshoot beginnings of NASCAR. A legendary moonshiner of the 1940s and 1950s named Junior Johnson was one of NASCAR's first drivers.

White Lady

1½ ounces Plymouth gin

¾ ounce Cointreau

¾ ounce fresh lemon juice

1 lemon twist

Shake all liquid ingredients with ice and strain into a chilled martini glass. Garnish with lemon twist.

rum: how sweet it is

Rum is a spirit distilled from sugar cane and its by-products—sugar cane juice or molasses. It's produced in hot climates. It comes in three styles: white (light), gold (aged), and dark.

Rum History

Beginning in the 1600s, members of the British Royal Navy received a half pint of rum a day to ward off scurvy. It didn't work (scurvy is caused by a vitamin C deficiency), but Britannia did rule the oceans for many years. The rum the British soldiers drank was a crude alcohol that bears little resemblance to the spirit we enjoy today. We owe the transformation to a family by the name of Bacardí. In the 1800s, a Spanish wine merchant named Don Facundo Bacardí Massó moved with his family to Cuba. He and his brother José opened a small store and developed a passion for making rum. They were determined to create the first smooth rum. The result was Bacardi rum, and today it's the most popular rum in the world.

Ace of Clubs

2 ounces gold rum

½ ounce white crème de cacao

½ ounce fresh lime juice

½ ounce simple syrup

Shake all the ingredients in a shaker tin with ice, then strain into a chilled cocktail glass.

Admiral Nelson's Brew

1 ounce spiced rum

½ ounce applejack

Hot apple cider to fill

Pour the rum and applejack into a coffee mug and fill with hot apple cider.

Almond Joytini

1 ounce coconut rum

1 ounce amaretto

1 ounce crème de cacao

2 ounces cream

Pour all ingredients into a shaker tin of ice. Shake, then strain into a martini glass.

The Real McCoy

In rum-running times, captains would add water to the rum bottles to stretch their profits. Captain McCoy was one captain who did not cut his rum, and one theory states that's where we get the phrase "the real McCoy."

Apple Mojito

3 sprigs of mint (1 for garnish)
½ fresh lime, chopped
1 ounce simple syrup
1½ ounces apple rum
Club soda to fill

Muddle 2 sprigs of mint, lime, and simple syrup in a mixing glass. Add the rum. Shake in a shaker tin of ice. Strain into a highball glass of cracked ice. Fill with club soda. Garnish with mint sprig.

Bacardi Cocktail

1½ ounces Bacardi light rum
¾ ounce fresh lemon juice
1 ounce simple syrup
2 dashes grenadine

Shake all ingredients with ice. Strain into a cocktail glass.

Bahama Mama

1 ounce light rum
1 ounce dark rum
2 ounces Piña Colada mix
2 ounces bar punch mix (a mix of orange juice, pineapple juice, sour mix, and grenadine)
1 pineapple slice and 1 cherry

Pour the rums and mixes into a blender with a cup of ice. Blend, then pour into a tropical glass. Garnish with pineapple slice and cherry.

Banana Boat

1 ounce light rum
1 ounce white crème de cacao
1 ounce crème de banana
2 scoops vanilla ice cream

Blend ingredients in a blender. Pour into a tropical glass.

Banana Daiquiri

1½ ounces banana rum
1 ounce simple syrup
¾ ounce fresh lime juice

Shake all ingredients with ice. Strain into a chilled cocktail glass.

Banana Mojito

3 sprigs of mint (1 for garnish)
½ fresh lime, chopped
1 ounce simple syrup
1½ ounces banana rum
Club soda to fill

Muddle 2 sprigs of mint, lime, and simple syrup in a mixing glass. Add the rum. Shake in a shaker tin of ice. Strain into a highball glass of cracked ice. Fill with club soda and garnish with mint sprig.

Banana Piña Colada

1½ ounces banana rum

1 ounce Coco Lopez

3 ounces pineapple juice

1 pineapple slice

Put the liquid ingredients into a blender with some ice. Blend and pour into a tropical glass. Garnish with pineapple slice.

Banana Popsicle

1 ounce Cabana Boy banana rum

1 ounce crème de banana

1 ounce simple syrup

1 ounce water

Paper parasol, for garnish

Blend liquid ingredients in a blender. Pour into a tropical glass. Garnish with paper parasol.

Batiste

2 ounces light rum

1 ounce Grand Marnier

Shake ingredients in a shaker tin with ice, then strain into a chilled cocktail glass.

Beachbum

2 ounces lemon rum

3 ounces cranberry juice

Sprite or 7UP to fill

Fill a tall glass of your choice with ice. Pour in all the ingredients and stir.

The Beauty Beneath

2 ounces Appleton Estate rum

1 ounce Vergano Americano chinato

½ ounce Cointreau

Dash Fee Brothers' Old Fashion Aromatic Bitters

Pour ingredients into a mixing glass nearly filled with ice. Stir and strain into a chilled cocktail glass.

Benzocolada

2 ounces coconut rum

½ ounce triple sec

1¾ ounces strawberry-kiwi juice

¼ ounce simple syrup

¼ ounce maraschino cherry juice

½ ounce fresh lime juice

Fill a highball glass with ice. Shake and strain all the ingredients in a shaker tin with ice and strain into the glass.

Bermuda Triangle Tea

2 ounces Gosling's Black Seal rum

2 ounces Bacardi light rum

Equal amounts of Florida orange juice and sweet-and-sour mix to fill

Paper parasol, for garnish

Fill a tall glass with ice and pour in all the liquid ingredients. Garnish with paper parasol.

Between the Sheets

¾ ounce light rum
½ ounce lemon juice
¾ ounce triple sec
1 lemon twist
¾ ounce brandy

Shake liquid ingredients with ice. Strain into a martini glass. Garnish with lemon twist.

Mind Your P's and Q's
We get the phrase "mind your P's and Q's" from old English pubs. In old England, patrons ordered ale in pints and quarts. When they got unruly, the bartender would yell at them to mind their own pints and quarts and settle down.

Blackberry Mojito

5 blackberries
3 sprigs of mint (1 for a garnish)
½ fresh lime, chopped
1 ounce simple syrup
1½ ounces light rum
Club soda to fill

Muddle the blackberries, 2 sprigs of mint, lime, and simple syrup in a mixing glass. Add the rum. Shake in a shaker tin of ice. Strain into a highball glass of cracked ice. Fill with club soda and garnish with mint sprig.

Blue Hawaiian

1 ounce light rum
1 ounce blue curaçao
Pineapple juice to fill
1 pineapple slice

Pour the liquid ingredients into a highball glass of ice. Stir and garnish with pineapple slice.

Bolo

2 ounces light rum
1 ounce lime juice or juice from ½ lime
1 ounce orange juice
1 teaspoon fine sugar

Combine ingredients in a shaker nearly filled with ice. Strain into a cocktail glass.

Bon Bon

Capful vanilla extract
¼ ounce fresh lemon juice
¼ ounce simple syrup
3 strawberries
1½ ounces cherry rum
½ ounce dark chocolate liqueur
Club soda to fill

Muddle the vanilla extract, lemon juice, simple syrup, and strawberries in a mixing glass. Add the rum, chocolate liqueur, and some ice. Shake and strain into a highball glass of ice. Fill with club soda.

Brazilian Breakfast

1½ ounces cachaça
½ ounce peach brandy
1 teaspoon brown sugar
1 ounce fresh grapefruit juice
1 ounce apple juice

Shake all ingredients with ice. Strain into a short glass of ice.

Cachaça

Cachaça (cuh-SHA-suh) is Brazilian rum made from sugar cane juice. Portuguese settlers of Brazil began making it in the 1500s. There are around 4,000 brands of cachaça in Brazil.

Brown Derby

1½ ounces dark rum
1 ounce fresh lime juice
¼ ounce maple syrup

Shake all the ingredients in a shaker tin with ice, then strain into a chilled cocktail glass.

Bushwacker

2 ounces dark rum
1 ounce coffee liqueur
4 ounces Piña Colada mix

Blend all ingredients in a blender with 1 cup of ice. Pour into a tall glass.

Caipirinha

½ lime, chopped
1 teaspoon granulated sugar
2 ounces cachaça

Muddle the lime and sugar in a mixing glass. Add the cachaça and ice. Shake, then strain into a rocks glass of cracked ice.

Captain's Blood

1½ ounces dark rum
¼ ounce lime juice
¼ ounce simple syrup
2 dashes Angostura bitters
1 lemon peel spiral

Shake all liquid ingredients with ice. Strain into a short glass of ice. Garnish with spiral of lemon peel.

Caribbean Eclipse

2 ounces Mount Gay Eclipse rum
1 ounce dark crème de cacao
1 ounce fresh lime juice
½ ounce simple syrup

Shake all ingredients with ice. Strain into a martini glass.

Castaway

1 ounce coconut rum
1 ounce mango rum
Pineapple juice to fill
Tropical fruit and paper parasol, for garnish

Pour the liquid ingredients into a tall glass of ice. Stir. Garnish with tropical fruit of your choice and a paper parasol.

Cherry Daiquiri

1½ ounces cherry rum

1 ounce simple syrup

¾ ounce fresh lime juice

Shake all ingredients with ice. Strain into a chilled cocktail glass.

Cherry Mojito

3 sprigs of mint (1 for garnish)

½ fresh lime, chopped

1 ounce simple syrup

1½ ounces cherry rum

Club soda to fill

Muddle 2 sprigs of mint, lime, and simple syrup in a mixing glass. Add the rum. Shake in a shaker tin of ice. Strain into a highball glass of cracked ice. Fill with club soda. Garnish with mint sprig.

Cherry Piña Colada

1½ ounces cherry rum

1 ounce Coco Lopez

3 ounces pineapple juice

1 pineapple slice

Put the liquid ingredients into a blender with ice. Blend and pour into a tropical glass. Garnish with pineapple slice.

Chicago Fizz

1 ounce dark rum

1 ounce ruby port

½ ounce lemon juice

½ ounce simple syrup

1 organic egg white

Fill a highball glass with ice. Shake all the ingredients in a shaker tin with ice, then strain into the highball glass.

Chocolate Coco

2 ounces Bacardi Coco

1 ounce white crème de cacao

1 ounce cream

Shake all ingredients with ice. Strain into a martini glass.

Chocolate Piña Colada

1½ ounces chocolate rum

1 ounce Coco Lopez

3 ounces pineapple juice

1 pineapple slice

Put the liquid ingredients into a blender with ice. Blend and pour into a tropical glass. Garnish with pineapple slice.

Coconut Mojito

3 sprigs of mint (1 for garnish)
1/2 fresh lime, chopped
1 ounce simple syrup
1 1/2 ounces coconut rum
Club soda to fill

Muddle 2 sprigs of mint, lime, and simple syrup in a mixing glass. Add the rum. Shake in a shaker tin of ice. Strain into a highball glass of cracked ice. Fill with club soda. Garnish with mint sprig.

Cuba Libre (Rum and Coke)

2 lime wedges
2 ounces Cuban rum
Cola to fill

Fill a highball glass with ice. Squeeze the juice of one of the lime wedges over the ice and discard the wedge. Pour in the rum and fill with cola. Squeeze the second lime wedge into the drink. Swipe the rim with the lime and drop it into the drink.

Daiquiri

1 1/2 ounces light rum
1 ounce simple syrup
3/4 ounce fresh lime juice

Shake all ingredients with ice. Strain into a martini glass.

Dark 'n' Stormy

2 ounces Gosling's Black Seal rum
Ginger beer to fill
1 lime wedge

Pour the rum over ice in a high-ball glass and fill with ginger beer. Squeeze in a lime wedge.

Dragon Berry Mojito

3 sprigs of mint (1 for garnish)
1/2 fresh lime, chopped
1 ounce simple syrup
1 1/2 ounces Bacardi Dragon Berry rum
Club soda to fill

Muddle 2 sprigs of mint, lime, and simple syrup in a mixing glass. Add the rum. Shake in a shaker tin of ice. Strain into a highball glass of cracked ice. Fill with club soda and garnish with mint sprig.

Dragon Daiquiri

1 1/2 ounces Bacardi Dragon Berry rum
1 ounce simple syrup
3/4 ounce fresh lime juice

Shake ingredients with ice. Strain into a chilled cocktail glass.

Dragon Lily

2 ounces Bacardi Dragon Berry rum
1 ounce elderflower liqueur
4 ounces white (clear) cranberry juice
Nontoxic flower petals, for garnish

Fill a tall glass with ice and add the liquid ingredients. Stir, then garnish with nontoxic flower petals.

Dragon Piña Colada

1½ ounces Bacardi Dragon Berry rum
1 ounce Coco Lopez
3 ounces pineapple juice
1 pineapple slice

Add the liquid ingredients into a blender with ice. Blend and pour into a tropical glass. Garnish with pineapple slice.

Eggnog Grog

1½ ounces dark rum
Eggnog to fill
Nutmeg, for garnish

Pour the dark rum into a tall or short glass of your choice and fill with eggnog. The amount of eggnog you use depends on whether you want the drink to taste strong or weak. If the eggnog is cold, you won't need to add ice. Garnish with pinch of nutmeg on top.

Gosling's

Gosling's has been making rum in Bermuda since the 1800s. In Bermuda, it's a tradition to use rum to christen all new buildings.

First Kiss

1½ ounces coconut rum
1½ ounces pineapple juice
1 ounce milk
¼ ounce grenadine

Shake ingredients with ice. Strain into a chilled martini glass.

Flamingo

1½ ounces light rum
1½ ounces pineapple juice
¼ ounce fresh lime juice
¼ ounce grenadine

Shake ingredients well with ice. Serve in a martini glass.

Forbidden Fruit

1 ounce spiced rum
1 ounce apple schnapps
¼ ounce cinnamon schnapps
7UP to fill

Pour the first three ingredients into a glass of ice. Fill with 7UP.

Gingered Apple

1½ ounces apple rum
1 ounce pear purée
1 ounce fresh lemon juice
Ginger beer to fill

Pour the first three ingredients into a tall glass of ice. Fill with ginger beer.

Bar Palindromes

Palindromes are words or phrases that read the same in both directions. Here are some bar-related ones: evil olive; red rum, sir, is murder; Sela Ward did draw ales; no pinot noir on Orion to nip on; campus motto: bottoms up, Mac.

Goin' Coconutini

1 teaspoon corn syrup

Shredded coconut

2 ounces coconut rum

3 ounces white (clear) cranberry juice

Pour the corn syrup onto one saucer and shredded coconut onto another. Turn your martini glass upside down and dip the rim into the syrup, then into the coconut. Shake rum and juice, then strain into the glass.

Green Apple Daiquiri

1½ ounces green apple rum

1 ounce simple syrup

¾ ounce fresh lime juice

Shake all ingredients with ice. Strain into a chilled cocktail glass.

Green Apple Piña Colada

1½ ounces green apple rum

1 ounce Coco Lopez

3 ounces pineapple juice

1 pineapple slice

Put the liquid ingredients into a blender with ice. Blend and pour into a tropical glass. Garnish with pineapple slice.

Hanging Chad

2 ounces golden rum

2 ounces pineapple juice

2 dashes Angostura bitters

Dash absinthe

Ginger ale to fill

½ ounce 151 rum to float

Fill a highball glass with ice and add the ingredients, saving the 151 last to float on top.

Hawaiian Volcano

1 ounce dark rum

½ ounce 151 rum

2 ounces Passoã passion fruit liqueur

4 ounces Piña Colada mix

Blend all ingredients with ice. Pour into a tropical glass.

Hemingway Daiquiri

1 ounce light rum

¼ ounce maraschino liqueur

½ ounce grapefruit juice

¾ ounce simple syrup

¾ ounce fresh lime juice

Shake all ingredients well with ice. Serve in a martini glass.

Hot Buttered Rum

1 ounce dark rum or spiced rum
1 tablespoon Hot Buttered Rum Mix
(see recipe Chapter 14)
Hot water to fill

Pour all ingredients in an Irish
coffee mug. Stir.

Hot Buttered Sugarplum Rum

1 ounce dark rum
1/2 ounce plum liqueur
2 tablespoons Hot Buttered Rum Mix
(see recipe in Chapter 14)
Hot water to fill

Pour all ingredients in an Irish
coffee mug. Stir.

Hot Gingerbread Toddy

1/2 cup water
1" knob ginger, thinly sliced
1/8 cup sugar
1 ounce light rum
1 cup hot apple cider

Combine the water and ginger in
a saucepan and bring to a boil.
Remove from heat. Cover and
steep 30 minutes. Add the sugar
and boil again, stirring until the
sugar dissolves. Strain 1/4 cup
into a mug, then add the rum.
Fill with hot apple cider.

Hurricane

1 ounce light rum
1 ounce dark rum
1 ounce passion fruit juice
Bar punch to fill
1 orange slice and cherry

Combine the liquid ingredients
in a shaker. Shake and strain into
a tall glass or a hurricane glass of
ice. Garnish with orange slice
and cherry.

In the Mood

1 tablespoon hot chocolate mix
1 ounce dark rum
1 ounce dark crème de cacao
3 ounces cream or milk

Dip the rim of a martini glass in
water, then dip it into the powdered hot chocolate mix. Pour
the rum, crème de cacao, and
cream or milk into a shaker tin of
ice. Shake and strain into the
rimmed martini glass.

Pat O'Brien's

The most famous bar in New
Orleans, Pat O'Brien's, invented the Hurricane. During
World War II, whiskey was
in low supply but there was
plenty of rum. The hurricane
glass is modeled after a hurricane lamp.

Italian Breeze

1 ounce light rum

1 ounce Disaronno amaretto

1/2 ounce pineapple juice

1/2 ounce cranberry juice

Shake all ingredients. Strain into a chilled martini glass.

Jamaican Me Crazy

1 ounce light rum

1 ounce coconut rum

1 ounce banana liqueur

1/2 ounce cranberry juice

1/2 ounce pineapple juice

1 cherry

Combine and shake the liquid ingredients. Strain into a tall glass of ice. Garnish with the cherry.

Jolly Roger

2 ounces light rum

2 ounces Drambuie

1 ounce fresh lime juice

Club soda to fill

Combine the first three ingredients and shake well with ice. Strain into a highball glass of ice. Fill with club soda.

Knickerbocker

2 ounces Appleton rum

1/2 ounce orange curaçao

1/2 ounce raspberry syrup

3/4 ounce fresh lemon juice

1 lemon wedge

Stir liquid ingredients with ice in a mixing glass. Strain into a chilled martini glass. Garnish with lemon wedge.

Hollywood Knickerbocker

In the 1934 film *The Thin Man*, William Powell and Myrna Loy drink Knickerbockers.

Latitude Attitude Adjuster

1/2 glass any beer

1/2 glass orange juice

1/2 ounce 151 rum

1/2 ounce amaretto

Fill a tall glass with beer and orange juice. Set aside. Pour the 151 rum and amaretto into a shot glass. Hold the shot glass in one hand and the tall glass in the other, drop the shot into the glass, and chug the entire drink.

Lava Colada

1 ounce raspberry rum
4 ounces Piña Colada mix
1 ounce raspberry syrup

Blend the rum and Piña Colada mix with 1 cup of ice. Pour the raspberry syrup in the bottom of a tropical glass. Pour the blended mixture on top. The syrup will ooze up the sides.

Lemon Chiffon Pie

1 ounce light rum
1 ounce white crème de cacao
2 scoops vanilla ice cream
1 ounce fresh lemon juice

Blend all ingredients with ice. Pour into a tropical glass.

Lounge Lizard

1½ ounces dark rum
½ ounce amaretto
Cola to fill

Pour the rum and amaretto in a highball glass of ice. Fill with cola.

Mai Tai Me Up

1 ounce dark rum
½ ounce light rum
1 ounce pineapple juice
1 ounce fresh lemon juice
½ ounce simple syrup
1 slice canned pineapple
1 maraschino cherry

Shake liquid ingredients in a cocktail shaker with ice. Strain in a martini glass. Garnish with pineapple and cherry.

A Man Walked Into a Bar

A man walked into a bar and ordered Martini after Martini, each time removing the olives and placing them in a jar. When the jar was filled with olives, the man started to leave. The bartender asked him what that was all about, and he said, "My wife just sent me out for a jar of olives."

Mango Daiquiri

1½ ounces mango rum
1 ounce simple syrup
¾ ounce fresh lime juice

Shake all ingredients with ice. Strain into a chilled cocktail glass.

Mango Mojito

3 sprigs of mint (1 for garnish)
½ fresh lime, chopped
1 ounce simple syrup
1½ ounces mango rum
Club soda to fill

Muddle 2 sprigs of mint, lime, and simple syrup in a mixing glass. Add the rum. Shake in a shaker tin of ice. Strain into a highball glass of cracked ice. Fill with club soda and garnish with mint sprig.

Mango Piña Colada

1½ ounces mango rum
1 ounce Coco Lopez
3 ounces pineapple juice
1 pineapple slice

Put the liquid ingredients into a blender with ice. Blend and pour into a tropical glass. Garnish with pineapple slice.

Mary Pickford

2 ounces light rum
1½ ounces pineapple juice
¼ ounce grenadine
¼ ounce maraschino liqueur

Shake all ingredients with ice. Strain into a chilled martini glass.

Melon Mojito

3 sprigs of mint (1 for garnish)
½ fresh lime, chopped
1 ounce simple syrup
1½ ounces melon rum
Club soda to fill

Muddle 2 sprigs of mint, lime, and simple syrup in a mixing glass. Add the rum. Shake in a shaker tin of ice. Strain into a highball glass of cracked ice. Fill with club soda and garnish with mint sprig.

Mojito

3 sprigs mint (1 for a garnish)
½ lime, cut
2 teaspoons of sugar
1½ ounces light rum
Club soda to fill

Muddle 2 sprigs of mint, lime, and sugar in a mixing glass. Add the rum. Shake in a shaker tin with ice, then strain into a highball glass of cracked ice. Fill with club soda and garnish with mint sprig.

007 Does It Again

In the film *Die Another Day* (2002), James Bond drinks Bollinger champagne, Havana rum, two vodka martinis (one with an olive), and a Mojito. The Mojito's popularity exploded soon after.

Navy Grog

1½ ounces Mount Gay Eclipse rum
1½ ounces orange curaçao
¾ ounce fresh lime juice
2 ounces fresh orange juice
Dash Angostura bitters

Combine all ingredients and shake well with ice. Strain into a chilled martini glass.

Olympia

3 ounces dark rum

1 ounce cherry brandy

1 ounce fresh lime juice

Shake all ingredients with ice. Strain into a chilled martini glass.

Painkiller

2 ounces Pusser's rum

4 ounces Piña Colada mix

1 ounce fresh orange juice

Sprinkle of nutmeg

Blend all liquid ingredients with ice. Pour into a tropical glass. Sprinkle with nutmeg.

Paradise under a Coconut Tree

1 coconut

2 ounces coconut rum

1 ounce light rum

3 ounces Coco Lopez

3 ounces pineapple juice

2 ounces cream

¼ ounce vanilla extract

Paper parasol, for garnish

In advance, carefully cut a coconut in half to make a coconut cup. There is no need to chip out the white coconut meat. Reserve for when you are ready to serve the drink. Pour the liquid ingredients into a blender and blend with a cup of ice. Pour into the coconut cup and garnish with paper parasol.

Passion Daiquiri

1½ ounces passion fruit rum

1 ounce simple syrup

¾ ounce fresh lime juice

Shake all ingredients with ice. Strain into a chilled cocktail glass.

Passion Mojito

3 sprigs of mint (1 for garnish)

½ fresh lime, chopped

1 ounce simple syrup

1½ ounces passion fruit rum

Club soda to fill

Muddle 2 sprigs of mint, lime, and simple syrup in a mixing glass. Add the rum. Shake in a shaker tin of ice. Strain into a highball glass of cracked ice. Fill with club soda and garnish with mint sprig.

Passion Piña Colada

1½ ounces passion fruit rum

1 ounce Coco Lopez

3 ounces pineapple juice

1 pineapple slice

Put the liquid ingredients into a blender with some ice. Blend and pour into a tropical glass. Garnish with pineapple slice.

Peaches at the Beaches

2 ounces peach schnapps

1 ounce light rum

1/4 ounce grenadine

Orange juice to fill

Paper parasol, for garnish

Pour the peach schnapps, light rum, and grenadine into a tall glass of ice. Fill with orange juice. Garnish with paper parasol.

Peach Mojito

3 sprigs of mint (1 for garnish)

1/2 fresh lime, chopped

1 ounce simple syrup

1 1/2 ounces peach rum

Club soda to fill

Muddle 2 sprigs of mint, lime, and simple syrup in a mixing glass. Add the rum. Shake in a shaker tin of ice. Strain into a highball glass of cracked ice. Fill with club soda and garnish with mint sprig.

Piña Colada

1 1/2 ounces light rum

3 ounces pineapple juice

1 ounce Coco Lopez

1 pineapple slice

Put the liquid ingredients into a blender with some ice. Blend and pour into a tropical glass. Garnish with pineapple slice.

Pineapple Mist

2 ounces light rum

3 ounces pineapple juice

1 maraschino cherry

Combine rum and juice in a blender with ice. Blend thoroughly. Pour into a cocktail glass and serve with a cherry.

Pineapple Mojito

3 sprigs of mint (1 for garnish)

1/2 lime, chopped

2 pieces fresh pineapple

2 teaspoons sugar

1 1/2 ounces light rum

Club soda to fill

Muddle 2 sprigs of mint, lime, pineapple, and sugar in a mixing glass. Add the rum. Shake in a shaker tin of ice, then strain into a highball glass of cracked ice. Fill with club soda and garnish with mint sprig.

A Man Walks Into a Bar

A man walks into a bar and sits down next to a lady and a dog. The man asks, "Does your dog bite?" The lady answers, "Never!" The man reaches out to pet the dog and the dog bites him. The man says, "I thought you said your dog doesn't bite!" The woman replies, "He doesn't. This isn't my dog."

Planter's Punch

2 ounces dark rum
Bar punch mix to fill
1 orange slice and 1 cherry

Combine liquid ingredients and shake, then strain into a tall glass of ice. Garnish with orange slice and cherry.

Raspberry Daiquiri

1½ ounces raspberry rum
1 ounce simple syrup
¾ ounce fresh lime juice

Shake all ingredients with ice. Strain into a chilled cocktail glass.

Raspberry Mojito

3 sprigs of mint (1 for garnish)
½ fresh lime, chopped
1 ounce simple syrup
1½ ounces raspberry rum
Club soda to fill

Muddle 2 sprigs of mint, lime, and simple syrup in a mixing glass. Add the rum. Shake in a shaker tin of ice. Strain into a highball glass of cracked ice. Fill with club soda. Garnish with mint sprig.

Raspberry Piña Colada

1½ ounces raspberry rum
1 ounce Coco Lopez
3 ounces pineapple juice
1 pineapple slice

Put the liquid ingredients into a blender with ice. Blend and pour into a tropical glass. Garnish with pineapple slice.

Red Leather String Bikini

1 red licorice string
2 ounces coconut rum
5 ounces white (clear) cranberry juice

Lower the licorice string into a tall glass. Slowly add ice and spiral string at the same time. Add the liquid ingredients.

Rockapolitan

1 ounce Cruzan citrus rum
1 ounce Cruzan orange rum
¼ ounce fresh lime juice
¼ ounce cranberry juice

Shake all ingredients in a cocktail shaker with ice. Strain into a martini glass.

Rum Runner

1 ounce dark rum
½ ounce 151 rum
½ ounce crème de banana
½ ounce blackberry brandy
½ ounce grenadine
½ ounce Rose's lime juice
1 cherry

Put all liquid ingredients into a blender with ice. Blend and pour into a tropical glass. Garnish with cherry.

Scorpion

1 ounce light rum
1 ounce brandy
1/2 ounce amaretto
3/4 ounce fresh lemon juice
1/2 ounce simple syrup
1 ounce fresh orange juice
1 pineapple slice and 1 cherry

Combine all liquid ingredients and shake with ice. Strain into a tall glass of ice. Garnish with pineapple slice and cherry.

Sex with the Captain

1 1/2 ounces Captain Morgan spiced rum
1/2 ounce peach schnapps
Cranberry and orange juice to fill

Fill a tall glass with ice. Pour in the Captain Morgan and peach schnapps. Fill with equal parts of cranberry and orange juice. Stir.

Sonora

1 1/2 ounces light rum
1/2 ounce applejack
1/2 ounce apricot-flavored brandy
1 ounce fresh lemon juice

Shake ingredients with ice. Strain into a martini glass.

Spiced Mojito

3 sprigs of mint (1 for garnish)
1/2 fresh lime, chopped
1 ounce simple syrup
1 1/2 ounces spiced rum
Club soda to fill

Muddle 2 sprigs of mint, lime, and simple syrup in a mixing glass. Add the rum. Shake in a shaker tin of ice. Strain into a highball glass of cracked ice. Fill with club soda and garnish with mint sprig.

Spicy Pear

1 1/2 ounces Captain Morgan spiced rum
1/2 ounce Goldschläger
1 ounce pear purée
1 ounce apple juice
5 thin slices of fresh ginger

Combine all ingredients in a shaker with ice. Shake hard, then strain into a highball glass of crushed ice.

Spicy Piña Colada

1 1/2 ounces spiced rum
1 ounce Coco Lopez
3 ounces pineapple juice
1 pineapple slice

Put the liquid ingredients into a blender with ice. Blend and pour into a tropical glass. Garnish with pineapple slice.

Strawberry Daiquiri

1½ ounces light rum
4 ounces strawberry mix
Strawberry, lime wedge, sugared rim, or whipped cream with a cherry on top, for garnish

Put the liquid ingredients into a blender with some ice. Blend and pour into a tropical glass. Garnish as desired.

Strawberry Mix

Most bars have a strawberry mix, but they are usually just sweetened strawberry-flavored liquids. Bars in tropical locations tend to bump it up a notch and stock better and meatier brands, but the very best is a blend of fresh crushed strawberries, fresh lime juice, and simple syrup to make a pourable strawberry mix. At home you can buy the frozen strawberries that are packed in sugar to help bulk up the mixture. Lime juice is an essential part of a good strawberry mix, and the reason why a lime wedge makes a good garnish for strawberry drinks.

Swinging Chad

2 ounces golden rum
2 ounces pineapple juice
2 dashes Angostura bitters
Dash absinthe
Ginger ale to fill

Fill a highball glass with ice and add the ingredients.

Think Pink

1½ ounces raspberry rum
½ ounce Passoã passion fruit liqueur
Sprite or 7UP to fill

Pour the rum and Passoã into a highball glass of ice. Fill with Sprite or 7UP. Stir.

Truffle

1½ ounces Gosling's Black Seal rum
½ ounce Cherry Heering
½ ounce maple syrup
1 ounce cold espresso

Shake all ingredients in a cocktail shaker with ice. Strain into a martini glass.

Vanilla Daiquiri

1½ ounces vanilla rum
1 ounce simple syrup
¾ ounce fresh lime juice

Shake all ingredients with ice. Strain into a chilled cocktail glass.

Vanilla Mojito

3 sprigs of mint (1 for garnish)
1/2 fresh lime, chopped
1 ounce simple syrup
1 1/2 ounces vanilla rum
Club soda to fill

Muddle 2 sprigs of mint, lime, and simple syrup in a mixing glass. Add the rum. Shake in a shaker tin of ice. Strain into a highball glass of cracked ice. Fill with club soda and garnish with mint sprig.

Vanilla Piña Colada

1 1/2 ounces vanilla rum
1 ounce Coco Lopez
3 ounces pineapple juice
1 pineapple slice

Put the liquid ingredients into a blender with some ice. Blend and pour into a tropical glass. Garnish with pineapple slice.

White Lion

2 ounces light rum
1/4 ounce raspberry liqueur
3/4 ounce fresh lime juice
1/2 ounce simple syrup
1/2 ounce curaçao
Berries and lime wedge, for garnish

Combine all liquid ingredients and shake with ice. Strain into a white wine glass filled with crushed ice. Garnish with berries and a lime wedge.

Wonderland Green Mint Tea

5 mint leaves
1/2 ounce simple syrup
2 lime wedges
1 ounce light rum
Hot green tea to fill
1 tablespoon honey

In a mug, muddle the mint in simple syrup with the lime wedges. Add the rum. Pour steaming green tea on top. Sweeten with honey to taste.

Yellow Bird 𝒴

2 ounces light rum
1/2 ounce banana liqueur
1/2 ounce Galliano
3/4 ounce fresh lime juice

Combine all ingredients and shake with ice. Strain into a tall glass of ice.

Zombie 𝒴

1 ounce light rum
1 ounce dark rum
1 ounce apricot brandy
Bar punch mix to fill
1/2 ounce 151 rum to float
1 orange slice and 1 cherry

Combine liquid ingredients except the 151 rum and shake with ice. Strain into a tall glass of ice. Float the 151 rum on top. Garnish with orange slice and cherry.

tequila: mexican beauty

Tequila is North America's first distilled spirit. The name comes from a Mexican town of the same name in the state of Jalisco. Tequila is made from the hearts of the agave plant. By law, for a liquor to be called and labeled tequila, 51 percent of it must be made from the blue agave plant grown near the town of Tequila.

Tequila History

Legend has it that the Aztec ruler Montezuma welcomed the Spanish explorer Hernando Cortés with a wine made from the agave plant. Poor man. The ungrateful Cortés became Montezuma's conqueror, took the agave wine, and distilled it to make tequila. This all took place around the early 1500s, and by the 1600s tequila was being mass-produced. Jose Cuervo tequila was introduced in 1795.

Tequila Today

With its distinctive dry taste, tequila is the basis for marvelous drinks, not the least of which is the Margarita. There are five types of tequila: blanco (not aged, and also called white or silver), joven (blanco that is colored to look gold), reposado (gold from aging), anejo (aged the longest in oak barrels where it acquires its mellow color of gold), and maduro (mature, vintage, or ultra aged). Maduro tequilas were first introduced in 2006. This tequila is aged a minimum of three years in oak barrels from France and Canada and produces a smooth, superior spirit that is often called the cognac of tequila.

Acapulco Clam Digger

1½ ounces blanco tequila
¼ ounce fresh lemon juice
3 ounces clam juice
Splash Tabasco
Splash Worcestershire sauce
3 ounces tomato juice
1 tablespoon horseradish
1 lemon wedge

Put liquid ingredients and horseradish into a highball glass. Stir and garnish with lemon wedge.

Adios Amigos

1 ounce mango tequila
1 ounce coconut tequila
1 ounce passion fruit tequila
Equal parts of orange and pineapple juice to fill

Fill a tall glass with ice and add all the ingredients. Stir.

Alamo

1 ounce aged tequila
1 ounce fresh orange juice
1 ounce pineapple juice
Sprite or 7UP to fill

Pour the first three ingredients into a highball glass of ice. Fill with Sprite or 7UP.

Alamo PowWow

1 ounce blanco tequila
1 ounce DeKuyper Hot Damn! cinnamon schnapps
Club soda to fill

Pour the tequila and schnapps into a highball glass of ice. Fill with club soda.

Anita Rita Now

1½ ounces blanco tequila
¾ ounce triple sec
½ ounce lime juice
3 ounces limeade

Pour the tequila in a shot glass. Pour the triple sec and the lime juice in another shot glass. Pour the limeade in a rocks glass. Then drink each one right after the other. That is the fastest Rita when you need a Rita now!

Astronaut Sunrise

1½ ounces tequila
½ ounce grenadine
Tang to fill

Fill a highball glass with ice, then pour in all the ingredients.

Avocado Margarita

¼ of an avocado, mashed
Kosher salt, for rimming
1½ ounces aged tequila
½ ounce triple sec
3 ounces margarita mix
1 lime wheel or 1 avocado slice

Rim a margarita glass with mashed avocado and then with salt. Put the liquid ingredients in a blender with a cup of ice and blend. Pour into the avocado salt-rimmed glass and garnish with the lime wheel or avocado slice.

Aztec Gold

1 ounce aged tequila
½ ounce crème de banana
¼ ounce amaretto
½ ounce Galliano

Shake all ingredients with ice. Strain into a martini glass.

Beer Belly Margarita

Kosher salt, for rimming
1½ ounces blanco tequila
2 ounces Mexican beer
Juice from 1 lime
2 ounces simple syrup
1 lime wheel

Rim a margarita glass with salt. Pour the tequila, beer, lime juice, and syrup in a blender with a cup of ice and blend. Pour into the glass and garnish with the lime wheel.

Between the Hotel Sheets Margarita

Kosher salt, for rimming
2 ounces aged tequila
1 ounce Grand Marnier
Juice from 1 lime
1 ounce simple syrup
1 lime wheel

Rim a margarita glass with salt. Pour the tequila, Grand Marnier, lime juice, and syrup in a blender with a cup of ice and blend. Pour into the glass and garnish with the lime wheel.

Bird of Paradise

1 ounce tequila
1 ounce white crème do cacao
1 ounce amaretto
1 ounce cream

Shake all ingredients with ice. Strain into a martini glass.

Bloody Maria

2 ounces aged tequila
Bloody Mary mix to fill
1 celery stalk and lime wedge

Pour the tequila into a tall glass of ice. Fill with Bloody Mary mix. Stir. Garnish with celery and lime wedge.

Blue Voodoo Doll

1¼ ounces Voodoo Tiki Blue Dragon Kiwi tequila
½ ounce blue curaçao
2 ounces sour mix
¼ ounce cranberry juice
Sugar, for rimming

Shake all liquid ingredients with ice. Strain into a sugar-rimmed martini glass.

Brave Bull

2 ounces blanco tequila
1 ounce coffee liqueur

Pour ingredients into an old-fashioned glass almost filled with ice. Stir well.

Cactus Bite

2 ounces aged tequila
¼ ounce triple sec
¼ ounce Drambuie
2 ounces lemon juice
½ teaspoon sugar
Dash bitters

Shake all ingredients with ice. Strain into a martini glass.

Chalino Special

3 ounces blanco tequila

¼ ounce crème de cassis

½ ounce fresh lemon juice

½ ounce fresh lime juice

¼ ounce simple syrup

1 lemon twist

Shake all the liquid ingredients in a shaker tin with ice, then strain into a chilled cocktail glass. Garnish with lemon twist.

Charro Negro

1 ounce Herradura blanco tequila

Juice from ½ lemon

Cola to fill

Pour the tequila and lemon juice into a highball glass of ice. Fill with cola.

Coconut Tequila Sunrise

2 ounces coconut tequila

½ ounce grenadine

Fresh orange juice to fill

Pour the tequila and grenadine into a highball glass of ice. Fill with fresh orange juice.

Compadre

1½ ounces blanco tequila

½ teaspoon maraschino liqueur

1 teaspoon grenadine syrup

2 dashes orange bitters

Shake all ingredients with ice. Strain into a martini glass.

Cranberry Cosmorita

Kosher salt, for rimming

1½ ounces blanco tequila

½ ounce triple sec

Juice from ½ lime

2 ounces cranberry juice

2 ounces sweet-and-sour mix

1 lime wheel

Rim a margarita glass with salt. Blend all ingredients in a blender with a cup of ice. Pour into the glass and garnish with lime.

Downsider

1½ ounces blanco tequila

½ ounce crème de banana

½ ounce Galliano

1 ounce cream

¼ ounce grenadine

Shake all ingredients with ice. Strain into a martini glass.

Dynamite

Kosher salt, for rimming

1 ounce reposado tequila

1 ounce blanco tequila

1 ounce Clamato juice

1 ounce fresh lime juice

¼ ounce Tabasco

Rim a short glass with kosher salt. Fill the glass with ice and pour all ingredients in.

El Diablo

2 ounces aged tequila

¾ ounce crème de cassis

Ginger ale to fill

1 lime wedge

Pour the tequila and crème de cassis into a highball glass of ice. Fill with ginger ale. Garnish with lime wedge.

El Niño

¾ ounce aged tequila

¾ ounce Alizé Gold

¾ ounce grenadine

Prepare this layered drink in a rocks glass three-quarters full of ice, using a layering spoon on the rim of the glass. Pour slowly and carefully to prevent the layers from mixing. Pour the ingredients in the order they are listed.

Flat Tire at the Border

2 ounces blanco tequila

1 ounce black sambuca

Shake the tequila and sambuca over ice. Strain into a rocks glass of ice.

Freddy Fudpucker

1 ounce blanco tequila

Orange juice to fill

½ ounce Galliano to float

Pour the tequila into a highball glass filled with ice and fill with orange juice. Stir. Float the Galliano on top.

God Bless Texastini

1 ounce aged tequila

1 ounce Tequila Rose

1 ounce orange juice

1 ounce pineapple juice

Shake all ingredients with ice. Strain into a martini glass.

Green Iguana

Kosher salt, for rimming

1½ ounces aged tequila

1 ounce melon liqueur

3 ounces sweet-and-sour mix

1 lime wheel

Rim a margarita glass with salt. Pour the tequila, melon liqueur, and sweet-and-sour mix in a blender with 1 cup of ice and blend. Pour into the glass and garnish with the lime wheel.

Habla Español Fly

1½ ounces blanco tequila
1½ ounces coffee liqueur
2 ounces cold black coffee
Cream to fill

Pour the tequila, coffee liqueur, and the cold coffee into a highball glass of ice, then fill with cream. Stir.

Horny Margarita

Kosher salt, for rimming
1½ ounces Sauza Hornitos reposado tequila
1 ounce Cointreau
Juice from ½ lime
3 ounces sweet-and-sour mix
1 lime wheel

Rim a margarita glass with salt. Pour the tequila, Cointreau, lime juice, and sweet-and-sour mix into a blender with 1 cup of ice and blend. Pour into the glass and garnish with the lime wheel.

Hypnotizing Margarita

Kosher salt, for rimming
1½ ounces aged tequila
1 ounce Hpnotiq
Juice from ½ lime
3 ounces sweet-and-sour mix
1 lime wheel

Rim a margarita glass with salt. Pour the tequila, Hpnotiq, lime juice, and sweet-and-sour mix in a blender with 1 cup of ice and blend. Pour into the glass and garnish with lime wheel.

Jalapeño Marmalade Margarita

1½ ounces aged tequila
½ ounce triple sec
3 ounces margarita mix
¼ of a fresh jalapeño
1 ounce orange marmalade
1 lime wheel or 1 jalapeño

Put the first five ingredients in a blender with a cup of ice and blend. Pour into a margarita glass and garnish with the lime wheel or jalapeño.

Jalisco Smash

3 sprigs from mint (1 for garnish)
½ fresh peach, chopped
2 teaspoons sugar
1 ounce fresh lime juice
2 ounces aged tequila

Muddle 2 sprigs of mint, peach pieces, sugar, and lime juice in a mixer glass. Add the tequila. Shake in a shaker tin of ice. Strain over a short glass of crushed ice. Garnish with mint sprig.

Jumping Beans

1½ ounces aged tequila
½ ounce sambuca
3 coffee beans

Pour the tequila and sambuca into a brandy snifter and drop in the coffee beans.

Key Lime Pie Margarita

1 crushed graham cracker, for rimming

1½ ounces aged tequila

½ ounce key lime crème liqueur

3 ounces key lime yogurt

Juice from ½ lime

1 lime wheel

Rim a margarita glass with crushed graham cracker. Put the remaining ingredients, except lime wheel, in a blender with 1 cup of ice and blend. Pour into the glass and garnish with lime wheel.

Kiss from a Rosarita

Kosher salt, for rimming

1½ ounces aged tequila

1 ounce Tequila Rose

3 ounces sweet-and-sour mix

3 strawberries

1 lime wheel

Rim a margarita glass with salt. Put the liquid ingredients and the strawberries in a blender with 1 cup of ice and blend. Pour into the glass and garnish with lime wheel.

Word Meanings

Agave comes from a Greek word that means "noble." *Tequila* means "the rock that cuts." Most believe the name originated from the sharp rocks created by lava that surround the town of Tequila.

La Bomba

1½ ounces blanco tequila

½ ounce Cointreau

1 ounce pineapple juice

1 ounce orange juice

¼ ounce grenadine

Combine and shake all ingredients with ice. Strain into a martini glass.

Lemon Raspberry Rita

1½ ounces aged tequila

½ ounce Chambord raspberry liqueur

Juice from ½ lemon

Lemonade to fill

1 lemon wheel

Fill a margarita glass with ice. Pour the tequila, Chambord, and lemon juice into a shaker. Shake and strain into the margarita glass. Fill with lemonade. Garnish with lemon wheel.

Lolita

2 ounces blanco tequila
1 banana, chopped (save ½ for garnish)
1 mango, chopped (save ½ for garnish)
1 papaya, chopped (save ½ for garnish)
2 ounces orange juice

Blend the tequila, half the banana, half the mango, half the papaya, and the orange juice in a blender with 1 cup of ice. Pour into a margarita glass, then sprinkle the chopped garnishes on top.

Mango Tequila Sunrise

2 ounces mango tequila
½ ounce grenadine
Fresh orange juice to fill

Pour the tequila and grenadine into a highball glass of ice. Fill with fresh orange juice.

Margarita Name

There are many stories of how the Margarita got its name. One is that it was named after a Mexican bartender's girlfriend, Margarita. What we know for sure is that the Margarita is by far the most popular drink in the entire world.

Margarita

Kosher salt, for rimming
1½ ounces aged tequila
½ ounce Cointreau
1 ounce freshly squeezed lime juice
½ ounce simple syrup
1 lime wedge or wheel

Rim a margarita glass with salt. Add ice to the glass. In a shaker tin of ice, shake liquid ingredients and strain into the glass. Garnish with lime wedge or wheel.

Mexican Headhunter

1 ounce blanco tequila
1 ounce ginger liqueur
1 ounce pineapple juice
1 ounce fresh lime juice
1 ounce agave nectar
1 pineapple slice

Shake all the liquid ingredients with ice, then strain into a tall glass of ice. Garnish with pineapple slice.

Mexican Madras

1 ounce blanco tequila
1 ounce orange juice
3 ounces cranberry juice
¼ ounce lime juice

Combine all ingredients in a shaker half filled with ice. Shake well. Strain into a highball glass of ice.

Mexican Moonlight

1 ounce black tequila

1 ounce black vodka

1 ounce lime juice

1 ounce simple syrup

Combine and shake all ingredients with ice. Strain into a martini glass.

Montezuma

2 ounces blanco tequila

1 ounce Madeira

1 egg yolk

Blend all ingredients with ½ cup crushed ice in a blender on low speed. Pour into a champagne flute and serve.

Muy Bonita Rita

Crushed graham crackers, for rimming

1½ ounces aged tequila

1½ ounces Licor 43

1 ounce sweet-and-sour mix

1 ounce cream

1 lime wheel

Rim a martini glass with crushed graham crackers. Shake the tequila, Licor 43, sweet-and-sour mix, and cream with ice. Strain into the glass. Garnish with lime wheel.

Passion Tequila Sunrise

2 ounces passion fruit tequila

½ ounce grenadine

Fresh orange juice to fill

Pour the tequila and grenadine into a highball glass of ice. Fill with fresh orange juice.

Pepper Tequila Sunrise

2 ounces pepper tequila

½ ounce grenadine

Fresh orange juice to fill

Pour the tequila and grenadine into a highball glass of ice. Fill with fresh orange juice.

Petroleo

1 serrano chili, halved lengthwise and seeded (wash hands and kitchen tools immediately after seeding to avoid irritation)

2 ounces aged tequila

1 ounce fresh lime juice

Dash salt and pepper

Splash Worcestershire sauce

Splash Maggi seasoning sauce

Drop one of the chili halves into a rocks glass. Fill the glass with ice. Put the rest of the ingredients into a shaker of ice (including the remaining chili half) and shake. Strain over the rocks glass of ice.

Piñata

1½ ounces blanco tequila
½ ounce blue curaçao
Citrus soda (such as Fresca) to fill
Handful of multicolored gummy bears

Pour the tequila and curaçao into a tall glass of ice. Fill with citrus soda. Garnish with the gummy bears on top.

Pink Tequila Sour

Kosher salt, for rimming
2 ounces gold tequila
1 ounce triple sec
1 ounce fresh lime juice
¼ ounce fresh orange juice
½ ounce simple syrup
¼ ounce grenadine

Rim a margarita glass with kosher salt and fill with ice. Shake all ingredients in a shaker tin of ice, then strain into the glass.

Pomegranate Tequila Sunrise

2 ounces pomegranate tequila
½ ounce grenadine
Fresh orange juice to fill

Pour the tequila and grenadine into a highball glass of ice. Fill with fresh orange juice.

Salma Hayek

Sugar, for rimming
2 ounces aged tequila
½ ounce vanilla schnapps
2 ounces pomegranate juice

Combine and shake all liquid ingredients with ice. Strain into a sugar-rimmed martini glass.

Selena

2 ounces aged tequila
1 ounce fresh lime juice
1 ounce honey
2 dashes Regans' orange bitters

Combine and shake all ingredients with ice. Strain into a martini glass.

Shady Lady

1 ounce blanco tequila
1 ounce melon liqueur
Fresh pink grapefruit juice to fill

Pour the tequila and melon liqueur into a highball glass of ice. Fill with grapefruit juice.

Silk Stocking

2 ounces aged tequila
1 ounce Chambord raspberry liqueur
1 ounce crème de cacao
1 ounce cream

Combine and shake all ingredients with ice. Strain into a martini glass.

South of the Peachy Border Rita

Kosher salt, for rimming

1½ ounces blanco tequila

1 ounce peach schnapps

⅛ ounce grenadine

3 ounces sweet-and-sour mix

1 lime wheel

Rim a margarita glass with salt. Pour the liquid ingredients into a blender with 1 cup of ice and blend. Pour into the glass and garnish with lime wheel.

Spanish Moss

1 ounce blanco tequila

1 ounce coffee liqueur

1 ounce crème de menthe

Combine and shake all ingredients with ice. Strain into a rocks glass of ice.

Strawberry Mojitorita

½ lime, chopped

3 sprigs of mint (1 for garnish)

4 large strawberries (1 for garnish)

1½ ounces blanco tequila

½ ounce triple sec

1 ounce simple syrup

1 ounce fresh lime juice

Muddle the lime, 2 mint sprigs, and 3 strawberries in a shaker. Add the remaining liquid ingredients and ice to fill. Shake and strain into a margarita glass of ice. Garnish with remaining mint sprig and strawberry.

Sunbathing on a Mexican Beach

1 ounce blanco tequila

1 ounce coconut rum

Pineapple juice to fill

Pour the tequila and coconut rum into a tall glass of ice. Fill with pineapple juice.

Swim-Up Bar Margarita

Kosher salt, for rimming

1½ ounces blanco tequila

1 ounce blue curaçao

Juice from ½ lime

3 ounces sweet-and-sour mix

1 lime wheel

Rim a margarita glass with salt. Pour liquid ingredients into a blender with 1 cup of ice and blend. Pour into the glass and garnish with lime wheel.

Tangerine Tequila Sunrise

2 ounces tangerine tequila

½ ounce grenadine

Fresh orange juice to fill

Pour the tequila and grenadine into a highball glass of ice. Fill with fresh orange juice.

Tasting Away in Margaritaville

Kosher salt, for rimming
1½ ounces blanco tequila
½ ounce triple sec
2 ounces mango nectar
1 ounce sweet-and-sour mix
1 lime wheel

Rim a margarita glass with salt. Pour the liquid ingredients into a blender with 1 cup of ice and blend. Pour into the glass and garnish with lime wheel.

Tequila Mockingbird Margarita

Kosher salt, for rimming
1½ ounces aged tequila
½ ounce green crème de menthe
Juice from ½ lime
3 ounces sweet-and-sour mix
1 lime wheel

Rim a margarita glass with salt. Pour the liquid ingredients into a blender with 1 cup of ice and blend. Pour into the glass and garnish with lime wheel.

Tequila Sunrise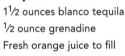

1½ ounces blanco tequila
½ ounce grenadine
Fresh orange juice to fill

Pour the tequila and grenadine into a highball glass of ice. Fill with fresh orange juice.

Tequila Sunrise Margarita

Kosher salt, for rimming
1½ ounces blanco tequila
½ ounce grenadine
½ ounce triple sec
1 ounce sweet-and-sour mix
1 ounce orange juice
1 lime wheel

Rim a margarita glass with salt. Pour liquid ingredients into a blender with 1 cup of ice and blend. Pour into the glass and garnish with lime wheel.

Tequila Sunset

1½ ounces tequila
½ ounce blackberry brandy
Fresh orange juice to fill

Fill a highball glass with ice and pour in all the ingredients.

The Tequila Sunrise

The Tequila Sunrise was created in Mexico in the 1950s to welcome tourists to Acapulco and Cancun. The drink gained popularity again in the 1970s.

Tezón Caramel Apple Pie

1½ ounces Tezón tequila

½ ounce butterscotch schnapps

1 ounce apple cider

½ ounce fresh lemon juice

Shake all ingredients with ice. Strain into a martini glass.

Thorny Mexican

1 ounce aged tequila

2 ounces Tequila Rose strawberry cream liqueur

1 rose petal

Shake liquid ingredients with ice, then strain into a martini glass. Garnish by dropping the rose petal on top.

Toreador

2 ounces blanco tequila

1 ounce crème de cacao

1 ounce cream

¼ teaspoon cocoa powder

Shake all ingredients with ice. Strain into a martini glass.

Jose Antonio de Cuervo

In 1758, Jose Antonio de Cuervo founded a distillery in the village of Tequila. Thirty-seven years later, his son Jose Guadalupe was granted the first license by the king of Spain to produce what was then called "wine of the earth."

White Sangriarita

Kosher salt, for rimming

1½ ounces blanco tequila

1 ounce white wine

4 ounces sweet-and-sour mix

Lime wheel, orange wheel, lemon wheel, and cherry, for garnish

Rim a margarita glass with salt. Pour the tequila, white wine, and sweet-and-sour mix into a blender with a cup of ice and blend. Pour into the glass and float the citrus wheels and cherry on top.

CHAPTER 10

whiskey:
amber waves of grain

Four prominent countries—Scotland, Ireland, Canada, and the United States—produce whiskey, an alcohol distilled from fermented barley and other grains. Ireland and Scotland still argue over who made it first. Ireland and the United States spell whiskey with an "e," while Canada and Scotland do not. Each country makes different types of whiskey.

Types of Whiskey

Whiskeys from different regions have strikingly different tastes. Local grains go through an arduous process of distillation, fermentation, blending, and aging. Each whiskey region has its own techniques and traditions, which accounts for the vast difference in taste between Johnnie Walker and Jack Daniel's.

Scotland produces blended Scotch whisky and single malt whisky. For a bottle to bear the "Scotch" label, it must be made in Scotland. The single malt is made from a single distillation of malted barley, while the blended contains a combination of single malts and grain whiskys.

Ireland produces Irish whiskey, and there are only 10 distilleries in operation or under construction. Irish whiskey comes in three types—pure pot still whiskey, single malt whiskey, and blended whiskey.

Canada produces blended whisky and rye whisky. Blended versions may combine many whiskys together to create a smooth-tasting final product.

America produces bourbon whiskey, corn whiskey, rye whiskey, blended whiskey, and Tennessee whiskey. High-end bourbon breaks down into two other categories called small batch bourbon and single barrel bourbon. By law, bourbon can only be made in America, and a label can only say "Kentucky bourbon" if it's made in Kentucky.

Scotch

The different and distinctive tastes of Scotches are caused by the air quality, peat bogs, and water where the liquor is made, a fact that should make ardent environmentalists out of all Scotch drinkers. There are eight regions of single malt producers in Scotland, and the product of each is unique. Admirers of single malts are usually devotees of a particular brand. Enthusiasts of a blended label maintain that the art is in the blending. But few would deny the supremacy of Scotch in the domain of whisky.

Affinity

2 ounces blended Scotch whisky
1 ounce sweet vermouth
1 ounce dry vermouth
3 dashes bitters

Pour ingredients into a shaker with ice. Shake and strain into a cocktail glass.

Aggravation

2 ounces blended Scotch whisky
1 ounce coffee liqueur

Pour ingredients into a short glass of ice and stir.

Arnaud's Special Cocktail

2 ounces Scotch
1 ounce Dubonnet Rouge
3 dashes orange bitters
1 orange twist

Shake all the liquid ingredients in a shaker tin with ice, then strain into a chilled cocktail glass. Garnish with orange twist.

Balmoral

2 ounces blended Scotch whisky
1/2 ounce sweet vermouth
1/2 ounce dry vermouth
2 dashes bitters

Combine all ingredients in a mixing glass half filled with ice. Stir and strain into a cocktail glass.

Blinder

2 ounces blended Scotch whisky
5 ounces grapefruit juice
1 teaspoon grenadine

Pour Scotch and grapefruit juice into an ice-filled highball glass. Add grenadine and stir slightly.

Blue Blazer

1 1/2 ounces boiling water
1/4 ounce simple syrup
1 lemon twist
1/2 ounce blended Scotch whisky

You will be pouring hot flaming Scotch back and forth (chemistry-set style) so you'll need 2 mugs with handles that won't get hot. Some bartenders use silver-plated or metal mugs to stay authentic to the original recipe of the 1800s. Fill both mugs with hot water and let them warm up while you boil the water. Further prep by putting the simple syrup and lemon twist into an Irish coffee mug. When the water boils, dump the hot water out of the mugs. Pour the Scotch and 1 1/2 ounces of boiling water into one of the mugs and ignite with a match. Carefully pour the liquid stream of fire into the other mug and back again 3 or 4 times. Pour the drink into the Irish coffee mug.

Bobby Burns

1½ ounces blended Scotch whisky
1½ ounces sweet vermouth
1 teaspoon Bénédictine

Pour ingredients into a mixing glass nearly filled with ice. Stir and strain into a cocktail glass.

Borden Chase

2 ounces Scotch
½ ounce dry vermouth
¼ ounce absinthe
2 dashes orange bitters

Shake all the ingredients in a shaker tin with ice, then strain into a chilled cocktail glass.

Godfather

2 ounces blended Scotch whisky
¾ ounce amaretto

Pour Scotch and amaretto into an old-fashioned glass over ice.

Johnnie Bee Good

2 ounces Johnnie Walker Scotch
1 ounce honey
1 lemon twist

Pour Scotch and honey into a rocks glass and stir until the honey is dissolved. Add ice, then garnish with lemon twist.

Knock on Wood

2 ounces Scotch
½ ounce peach schnapps
½ ounce Madeira
3 dashes peach bitters

Shake all the ingredients with ice and strain into a short glass of ice.

Mamie Taylor

2 ounces Scotch
¾ ounce fresh lime juice
Ginger beer to fill

Fill a highball glass with ice and add all the ingredients. Stir.

Modern Cocktail

1½ ounces blended Scotch whisky
1 teaspoon dark rum
½ teaspoon anisette
½ teaspoon lemon juice
2 dashes orange bitters

Pour all ingredients into a shaker half filled with ice. Shake well and strain into a cocktail glass.

Perfect Rob Roy

2 ounces blended Scotch whisky
1 teaspoon sweet vermouth
1 teaspoon dry vermouth
1 lemon twist

Pour liquid ingredients into a mixing glass nearly filled with ice. Stir and strain into a cocktail glass. Garnish with lemon.

Rob Roy

1½ ounces blended Scotch whisky
½ ounce sweet vermouth
Dash orange bitters
1 lemon twist

Combine the liquid ingredients in a mixing glass. Stir well. Strain into a cocktail glass. Garnish with lemon twist.

Rusty Nail

1½ ounces Scotch
½ ounce Drambuie

Pour ingredients into a short glass of ice.

Scotch and Milk

2 ounces blended Scotch whisky
Milk to fill

Pour ingredients into a short glass of ice.

Scotch and Soda

2 ounces blended Scotch whisky
Club soda to fill

Pour ingredients into a short glass of ice.

Scotch Holiday Sour

1½ ounces blended Scotch whisky
1 ounce cherry brandy
½ ounce sweet vermouth
1 ounce lemon juice

Combine ingredients in a shaker half filled with ice. Shake well. Strain into a short glass of ice.

Scotch Mist

2 ounces blended Scotch whisky

Pour Scotch into a short glass of crushed ice.

Scotch on the Rocks

2 ounces blended Scotch whisky

Pour Scotch into a short glass of ice.

Scotch Sour

1½ ounces blended Scotch whisky
1 ounce lemon juice

Combine ingredients in a shaker half filled with ice. Shake well. Strain into a short glass of ice.

Smoke and Mirrors

2 ounces Scotch
1 ounce absinthe
½ ounce simple syrup
½ ounce fresh lime juice

Shake all the ingredients with ice and strain into a short glass of ice.

Ireland: Whiskey in the Jar

Irish whiskey comes in several forms. There is a single malt whiskey made from 100 percent malted barley distilled in a pot still, and a grain whiskey made from grains distilled in a column still. Grain whiskey is much lighter and more neutral in flavor than single malt whiskey and is almost never bottled as a single grain. It is instead used to blend with single malts to produce a lighter blended whiskey. Unique to Irish whiskey is pure pot still whiskey (100 percent barley, both malted and unmalted, distilled in a pot still). The green, unmalted barley gives pure pot still whiskey a spicy, uniquely Irish quality. Like single malt, pure pot still is sold alone or blended with grain whiskey. Usually no real distinction is made between blended whiskeys made from single malt or pure pot still.

Black Thorn

1 ounce Irish whiskey

1 ounce dry vermouth

3 dashes Pernod

3 dashes bitters

Pour ingredients into a shaker with ice. Stir and strain into a short glass of ice.

Blarney Stone

2 ounces Irish whiskey

1/2 teaspoon anisette

1/2 teaspoon Cointreau

1/2 teaspoon maraschino syrup

Dash bitters

Pour all ingredients into a short glass of ice and stir.

Brainstorm

2 ounces Irish whiskey

1/4 ounce sweet vermouth

1/4 ounce Bénédictine

Dash Angostura bitters

Shake all the ingredients in a shaker tin with ice, then strain into a chilled cocktail glass.

Irish Coffee

Coffee to fill
1½ ounces Irish whiskey
1 teaspoon brown sugar
Whipped cream, for garnish

Preheat an Irish coffee mug with hot water. Pour out the water and add coffee until the mug is three-quarters full. Add the whiskey and brown sugar and stir. Fill to the top with whipped cream.

Irish Coffee Cake
Add some kick to a brunch staple by soaking a coffee cake in a syrup made of Irish whiskey, coffee, and sugar.

Irish Magic

1 ounce Irish whiskey
¼ ounce white crème de cacao
5 ounces orange juice

Pour all ingredients over ice in a tall glass and stir.

Irish Rickey

1½ ounces Irish whiskey
Juice from ½ lime
Club soda to fill

Pour the Irish whiskey and lime juice into a highball glass of ice. Top with club soda.

Irish Shillelagh

1½ ounces Irish whiskey
Juice from ½ lemon
1 teaspoon powdered sugar
1 tablespoon sloe gin
1 tablespoon light rum

Combine all ingredients in a shaker with ice. Shake and strain into a short glass of ice.

Paddy Cocktail

2 ounces Irish whiskey
2 or 3 dashes Angostura bitters
¾ ounce sweet vermouth

Pour all ingredients into a short glass of ice and stir.

Shamrock

1½ ounces Irish whiskey
¾ ounce dry vermouth
1 teaspoon green Chartreuse
1 teaspoon green crème de menthe

Pour all ingredients into a short glass of ice and stir.

The First Whiskey?
Irish whiskey is believed to be one of the earliest distilled beverages in Europe, dating to the mid-twelfth century. The Old Bushmills Distillery lays claim to being the oldest licensed distillery in the world. James I awarded the distillery its license in 1608.

North American Whiskey/Whisky

It's no surprise that the Mint Julep and bourbon have the same home territory—Bourbon County, Kentucky. Bourbon whiskey, born in the late 1700s, is America's original native brew. Like most liquors, its ingredients are humble—corn and wood. But bourbon's distinctive flavor emerges from its 51 percent corn mash and the charred oak barrels in which the liquor ages. A *mash*, the source of all whiskeys and beers, is milled cereal cooked in water. The quality of that water is all-important. Eighty percent of the world's bourbon is produced in America because of the clear limestone spring water of the Kentucky hills. People think that Jack Daniel's Tennessee whiskey gets its flavor from being a sour mash. Wrong! Many whiskeys are made from a sour mash. JD gets its flavor from dripping through ten feet of sugar maple charcoal before it's put into charred barrels.

Canadian whisky production grew tremendously because of the American Prohibition. Windsor, Ontario, supplied its upriver neighbors in Detroit, Michigan, with alcohol, and the porous United States–Canadian border allowed for a steady trade between the two countries. Today, the most popular Canadian whiskys are Crown Royal, Canadian Club, Seagram's V.O., and Black Velvet.

Ace of Royal Spades

1 ounce Crown Royal Canadian whisky

1 ounce amaretto

Cola to fill

Pour Crown Royal and amaretto into a highball glass of ice. Fill with cola.

Agent Orange

1 ounce Tennessee whiskey

1 ounce Southern Comfort

Orange juice to fill

Pour the whiskey and Southern Comfort into a highball glass of ice. Fill with orange juice.

Algonquin

1½ ounces rye whiskey
1 ounce dry vermouth
1 ounce pineapple juice

Combine ingredients in a shaker half filled with ice. Shake well. Strain into a short glass of ice.

The Algonquin Cocktail

1½ ounces rye whiskey
¾ ounce dry vermouth
¾ ounce pineapple juice

Shake all the ingredients in a shaker tin with ice. Strain into a chilled cocktail glass.

All American

1 ounce bourbon
1 ounce Southern Comfort
2 ounces cola

Pour all ingredients in an old-fashioned glass and stir.

Americana

1 ounce Tennessee whiskey
1 teaspoon fine sugar
Dash bitters
Chilled champagne to fill

Pour the first three ingredients into a champagne glass. Fill with champagne.

Kentucky Whisky

America spells whiskey with the "e." However, Kentucky spells it without the "e." This is because Kentucky whisky is made Scottish style using cold winter wheat instead of the summer wheat. By doing this, Kentucky honors the Scottish ways and uses the Scottish spelling as well.

American Cobbler

1 ounce bourbon
1 ounce Southern Comfort
¼ ounce peach brandy
4 dashes lemon juice
Simple syrup (to taste)
Club soda to fill
1 peach slice and 1 mint leaf (optional)

Pour the first five ingredients into an ice-filled shaker. Shake and strain into a highball glass of ice. Fill with club soda. Garnish with peach slice and mint leaf if desired.

Bourbon and Branch

2 ounces bourbon
Still mineral water to fill

Pour the bourbon into a short glass of ice. Fill with water.

Bourbon Daisy

1½ ounces bourbon
½ ounce lemon juice
1 teaspoon grenadine
Club soda to fill
¼ ounce Southern Comfort, to float
1 orange slice and 1 pineapple stick

Shake the bourbon, lemon juice, and grenadine with ice. Strain into a highball glass of ice. Fill with club soda and float the Southern Comfort. Garnish with the orange slice and pineapple stick.

Bourbon on the Rocks

2 ounces bourbon

Pour bourbon into a short glass of ice and stir.

Bourbon Satin

2 ounces bourbon
1 ounce white crème de menthe
1 ounce light cream

Combine ingredients in a shaker half filled with ice. Shake, then strain into a cocktail glass.

Bull and Bear

2 ounces bourbon
1 ounce orange curaçao
¼ ounce grenadine
1 ounce lime juice
1 cherry

Combine liquid ingredients in a shaker half filled with ice. Shake and strain into a cocktail glass. Garnish with cherry.

Elijah Craig

Elijah Craig, a Baptist preacher, was the first to discover that aging whiskey in charred barrels changed the flavor and color. The only barrels he could afford in the beginning were used herring barrels, so he'd torch the insides to burn the fish smell out of them. Today, all whiskey factories char their oak barrels.

California Lemonade

2 ounces blended whiskey
1 tablespoon sugar
1 ounce lemon juice
1 ounce lime juice
Club soda to fill
1 lemon wedge

Pour the first four ingredients into a shaker half filled with ice. Shake well. Strain into a highball glass of ice. Fill with club soda and garnish with lemon wedge.

Canadian Cherry

2 ounces Canadian whisky
1/2 ounce cherry-flavored brandy
1 teaspoon lemon juice
2 teaspoons orange juice
1 cherry

Shake liquid ingredients in a shaker half filled with ice. Strain into a highball glass of ice. Garnish with cherry.

Canadian Cocktail

1 1/2 ounces Canadian whisky
1/2 ounce Cointreau
1 teaspoon sugar
Dash bitters

Combine ingredients in a shaker half filled with ice. Shake, then strain into a cocktail glass.

Commodore

2 ounces rye whiskey
1 ounce fresh lemon juice
1 ounce simple syrup
2 dashes orange bitters

Shake all ingredients in a shaker tin with ice. Strain into a chilled cocktail glass.

Country Gentleman

2 ounces Gentleman Jack whiskey
1 ounce lemon juice
1 ounce simple syrup

Shake all the ingredients with ice, then strain into a short glass of ice.

Dixie Spice

2 ounces bourbon
1 ounce ginger liqueur

Shake ingredients with ice and strain into a short glass of ice.

Esquire

2 ounces bourbon
1/2 ounce Grand Marnier
1/2 ounce fresh orange juice
1/4 ounce fresh lemon juice
2 dashes Angostura bitters
1 lemon twist

Shake all the liquid ingredients in a shaker tin with ice, then strain into a chilled cocktail glass. Garnish with lemon twist.

Gentleman's Cocktail

2 ounces bourbon
1/2 ounce brandy
1/2 ounce crème de menthe
Club soda to fill
1 lemon twist

Pour liquors into a highball glass of ice. Fill with club soda. Garnish with lemon twist.

Jack Be Nimble Java

1 ounce Jack Daniel's
1 ounce amaretto
Hot coffee to fill
Whipped cream, for garnish (optional)

Pour Jack Daniel's and amaretto into a mug. Fill with coffee. Top with whipped cream if desired.

John Collins

2 ounces rye whiskey
Juice from 1/2 lemon
1/2 ounce simple syrup
Club soda to fill
1 orange slice and 1 cherry

Shake the first three ingredients.
Strain into a Collins glass of ice.
Fill with club soda and garnish
with orange and cherry.

J.R.'s Godfather

2 ounces bourbon
1/2 ounce amaretto

Pour bourbon and amaretto into
a short glass of ice. Stir well.

Kentucky Colonel

1 1/2 ounces bourbon
1/2 ounce Bénédictine
1 lemon twist

Combine bourbon and
Bénédictine in a mixing glass
half filled with ice. Stir, then
strain into a cocktail glass. Serve
with a lemon twist.

Lady's Cocktail

2 ounces blended whiskey
1/2 ounce anisette
Dash bitters

Add to a shaker half filled with
ice; shake and strain into a glass.

Leatherneck

2 ounces blended whiskey
3/4 ounce blue curaçao
1/2 ounce fresh lime juice
1 lime wheel

Shake all the liquid ingredients in
a shaker tin with ice, then strain
into a chilled cocktail glass.
Garnish with lime wheel.

Lynchburg Lemonade

1 1/2 ounces Jack Daniel's
1/2 ounce triple sec
2 ounces sweet-and-sour mix
Sprite or 7UP to fill
1 lemon wedge

Pour the first three ingredients
into a tall glass of ice. Fill with
Sprite or 7UP. Garnish with
lemon wedge.

Mahogany

2 ounces bourbon
1/2 ounce cherry brandy
1/2 ounce black walnut liqueur
2 dashes bitters

Shake all the ingredients with ice
and strain into a short glass of
ice.

Manhattan

2 ounces rye whiskey
1/2 ounce sweet vermouth
2 dashes Angostura bitters
1 cherry

Pour liquid ingredients into a shaker. Shake and strain into a cocktail glass. Garnish with cherry. Manhattans can also be served on the rocks.

Manhattan

It is believed that a bartender at a party hosted by Winston Churchill's mother invented the Manhattan. The party was at the Manhattan Club in New York City.

Man O' War

2 ounces bourbon
1 ounce orange curaçao
1/2 ounce sweet vermouth
Juice from 1/2 lime

Shake all ingredients. Strain into a cocktail glass.

Millionaire Sour

2 ounces rye bourbon
1 ounce orange curaçao
1 ounce lemon juice
1 teaspoon grenadine
1 teaspoon framboise
1 egg white

Shake all ingredients. Strain into a cocktail glass.

Mint Julep

5 sprigs of spearmint leaves (1 for garnish)
1 tablespoon sugar
2 ounces bourbon

Muddle 4 spearmint sprigs and the sugar in a highball glass. Fill with ice. Add the bourbon and stir until glass gets very cold. Add more ice if needed. Garnish with remaining sprig.

The Mint Julep

The Mint Julep is the official drink of the Kentucky Derby. The cocktail, served in a traditional silver cup and garnished with bourbon-infused mint, should be stirred until frost forms on the outside of the cup.

Old-Fashioned

1 tablespoon sugar
1 orange slice
1 cherry
2 dashes Angostura bitters
2 ounces rye, bourbon, or whiskey

Muddle the sugar, orange slice, cherry, and bitters in an old-fashioned glass. Fill with ice. Add the whiskey.

Original Old-Fashioned

The original Old-Fashioned is built with a spoon of sugar, two dashes of bitters, a spoon of water, ice, rye whiskey, and a lemon peel garnish. Adding club soda or more water is incorrect.

Old Pal

1 ounce Canadian whisky
1 ounce dry vermouth
1 ounce Campari

Pour ingredients into a short glass of ice and stir.

The Queen Stinger

2 ounces Crown Royal Canadian whisky
1 ounce white crème de menthe

Pour the Crown Royal and the white crème de menthe into a short glass of ice and stir.

Rye and Ginger

2 ounces rye whiskey
Ginger ale to fill

Pour rye into a highball glass of ice and fill with ginger ale. Stir.

Sazerac

2 ounces rye whiskey
½ ounce simple syrup
2 dashes Peychaud's bitters
½ teaspoon absinthe
1 lemon peel

Fill an old-fashioned glass with ice and water to chill the glass. Pour the rye whiskey, simple syrup, and Peychaud's bitters into a mixing glass, then add ice and stir for 10 seconds. Dump the ice out of the glass and coat the glass with absinthe by swirling it around. Pour out most of what remains. Strain the cocktail into the chilled absinthe-rinsed glass, then twist a lemon peel and run it around the rim of the glass, colored side out, then discard peel. You can also pour the absinthe in a small spray bottle and spray the inside of the glass.

The Sazerac

This is one of the first cocktails on record. It was invented in New Orleans by Antoine Amedie Peychaud (pay-SHOWD).

The Scofflaw

1½ ounces rye whiskey
¾ ounce pomegranate grenadine
¾ ounce fresh lemon juice
1 ounce dry vermouth
1 lemon twist

Shake all the liquid ingredients in a shaker tin with ice, then strain into a chilled cocktail glass. Garnish with lemon twist.

Seven and Seven

2 ounces Seagram's 7
Sprite or 7UP to fill

Pour liquor into a highball glass of ice. Fill with Sprite or 7UP.

Southern Lady

2 ounces bourbon
1 ounce Southern Comfort
1 ounce amaretto
3 ounces pineapple juice
Sprite or 7UP to fill

Pour the first four ingredients into a tall glass of ice. Fill with Sprite or 7UP.

T-Bird

1½ ounces Canadian whisky
½ ounce amaretto
2 ounces pineapple juice
1 ounce orange juice

Pour all ingredients into a tall glass of ice. Stir.

SoCo

Many believe that Southern Comfort (Cuff and Buttons was its first name) is a whiskey-based liqueur. While it is a liqueur, it does not have whiskey in it. It's made from crushed peaches, apricots, and honey with a neutral grain spirit base.

Ward 8

1½ ounces bourbon
½ ounce lemon juice
½ ounce orange juice
1 teaspoon grenadine

Shake all ingredients with ice. Strain into a cocktail glass.

Whiskey Sour

2 ounces bourbon or whiskey
1 ounce lemon juice
1 ounce simple syrup

Shake all ingredients, then strain into a short glass of ice.

CHAPTER 11

shots and shooters

Shots and shooters are meant to be drunk very quickly in one gulp. They can measure from 1 ounce up to almost 4 ounces and are served in shot glasses, cordial glasses, shooter glasses, or rocks glasses. The difference between a shot and a shooter is based on the alcohol content. For example, a shot of tequila and a Liquid Cocaine are both pure alcohol, so they are *shots*. A Purple Hooter and a Red Snapper have a nonalcoholic mix to them, so they are *shooters*.

Shot History

A classic image of downing shots comes from old western movies when a cowboy would stroll into the local saloon. Things were simple—just beer and shots. Ancient diggings reveal that shots have been around a lot longer than that. In 1982, a Tang Dynasty (C.E. 618–907) vessel used for drinking games was unearthed in Dantu county in Jiangsu province. It has a tortoise-shaped pedestal and a barrel to hold liquor. It's inscribed with a quotation from the *Analects* of Confucius—an instruction to drink, persuade others to drink, punish, or let go. It's believed to be a drinking game relic.

Types of Shots and Shooters

Shots and shooters can be prepared one of three ways: neat, layered, and chilled straight up. Types and names for shots and shooters can be *shot, shooter, drop, bomb,* and *slammer.* Drops and bombs refer to a shot of something being dropped into a glass of something else and then chugged. A slammer is slammed down on the table, and you drink it while it fizzes. Shots and shooters can also be layered or flamed (both of which are exactly what they sound like).

Know that you can take practically any popular drink and make a shooter from it by reducing the amount of mixer. When ordering shooters at a club, be sure to watch the bartender make them because you can get ripped off. Some bartenders only put 1 ounce of alcohol for six shooters, filling it up with mixer to make it look like they are giving you a large shooter.

Shots

Shots are 100 percent alcohol. There are many sizes of shot glasses, so adjust the amounts to fit your glassware.

Alabama Slammer Shot

1/3 ounce Southern Comfort

1/3 ounce amaretto

1/3 ounce sloe gin

Shake and strain into a shot glass.

Banana Jack

3/4 ounce Jack Daniel's

3/4 ounce banana liqueur

Shake and strain into a shot glass.

Bazooka Joe

1/3 ounce Irish cream

1/3 ounce blue curaçao

1/3 ounce banana liqueur

Shake and strain into a shot glass.

Beam Me Up, Scotty

1/2 ounce coffee liqueur

1/2 ounce crème de banana

1/2 ounce Irish cream

Shake and strain into a shot glass.

Black Death

1/2 ounce black vodka

1/2 ounce black sambuca

1/2 ounce Jägermeister

Shake and strain into a shot glass.

Homemade Ice Shot Glasses

You'll need small Dixie cups, snow cone cups, and duct tape. Strengthen the tips of the snow cone cups with duct tape. Fill the Dixie cups three-quarters full with water; then stick the snow cone cups in, point side down, until the water level reaches the top. Duct-tape the cups in place and freeze. Rip off the duct tape and cups, and you'll have ice shot glasses.

Blue Balls

1/2 ounce blue curaçao

1/2 ounce coconut rum

1/2 ounce peach schnapps

Squeeze of a lemon wedge

Shake and strain into a shot glass.

Chocolate Cake

1/2 ounce citrus vodka

1/2 ounce Frangelico

1 lemon wedge

Shake and strain the vodka and Frangelico into a shot glass. Drink the shot, then bite into the lemon. For some reason, it tastes like chocolate cake.

Falling Star

1 ounce bourbon
1 ounce sambuca

Shake the ingredients in a shaker tin with ice, then strain into a shot glass.

Happy Buddha

1 ounce Buddha's Hand Citron Vodka
1 ounce green tea liqueur

Shake all the ingredients in a shaker tin with ice, then strain into a shot glass.

Jelly Bean

½ ounce blackberry brandy
½ ounce anisette or sambuca

Shake and strain into a shot glass.

Lemon Drop Shot

1½ ounces citrus vodka
Sugar, for rimming

Shake and strain into a sugar-rimmed shot glass.

Liquid Cocaine

⅓ ounce Jägermeister
⅓ ounce Goldschläger
⅓ ounce Rumple Minze

Shake with ice and strain into a shot glass if ingredients are room temperature. If liqueur is already chilled, just pour into a shot glass.

Moon Pie

½ ounce chocolate liqueur
½ ounce banana liqueur
½ ounce Irish cream

Shake all the ingredients in a shaker tin with ice, then strain into a shot glass.

Oatmeal Cookie

1½ ounces Kahlúa
1½ ounces Baileys
1½ ounces Goldschläger

Shake and strain into a shot glass.

Orgasm Shot

⅓ ounce amaretto
⅓ ounce coffee liqueur
⅓ ounce Irish cream

Shake and strain into a large shot, shooter, or rocks glass.

Peanut Butter and Jelly

¾ ounce Frangelico
¾ ounce Chambord raspberry liqueur

Shake and strain into a shot glass.

Poison Ivy

1 ounce cinnamon schnapps
1 ounce coffee liqueur

Shake in a shaker tin with ice, then strain into a shot glass.

Polar Bear

1/2 ounce white crème de cacao

1/2 ounce peppermint schnapps

Shake and strain into a shot glass.

Homemade Chocolate Shot Glasses

You'll need baking chocolate, a double boiler or mock double boiler, 2-ounce plastic cups and 1-ounce plastic cups (found in restaurant supply stores), unflavored cooking spray (like PAM), and a cookie sheet. Melt the chocolate in the double boiler. Spray the insides of the 2-ounce portion cups and the outsides of the 1-ounce portion cups with the cooking spray to prevent sticking. Pour chocolate three-quarters of the way up the 2-ounce cups, then place the 1-ounce cups inside until the chocolate oozes up to the top. This molds the shot glass. Place on a cookie sheet and put in the freezer for about 10 minutes to set up. Remove from the freezer and pop off the portion cups.

Prairie Fire Shooter

1 1/2 ounces tequila

3 dashes Tabasco

Pour tequila into a shot glass and add the Tabasco.

Rat Pack

1/2 ounce Jack Daniel's whiskey

1/2 ounce Johnnie Walker Scotch

1/2 ounce coffee liqueur

Shake all ingredients in a shaker tin with ice, then strain into a shot glass.

Russian Quaalude

1/3 ounce vodka

1/3 ounce Irish cream

1/3 ounce Frangelico

Shake and strain into a shot glass.

Sammy Jäger

1 ounce sambuca

1 ounce Jägermeister

Shake and strain into a shot glass.

Screaming Orgasm

1/4 ounce vodka

1/4 ounce amaretto

1/4 ounce coffee liqueur

1/4 ounce Irish cream

Shake and strain into a large shot, shooter, or rocks glass.

Three Wise Men

1/2 ounce Johnnie Walker Scotch whisky

1/2 ounce Jim Beam bourbon whiskey

1/2 ounce Jack Daniel's Tennessee whiskey

Shake and strain into a shot glass.

Three Wise Men Go Hunting

1/2 ounce Johnnie Walker Scotch whisky

1/2 ounce Jim Beam bourbon whiskey

1/2 ounce Jack Daniel's Tennessee whiskey

1/2 ounce Wild Turkey bourbon whiskey

Shake and strain into a shot glass.

Three Wise Men Visit Mexico

1/2 ounce Johnnie Walker Scotch whisky

1/2 ounce Jim Beam bourbon whiskey

1/2 ounce Jack Daniel's Tennessee whiskey

1/2 ounce Jose Cuervo Gold tequila

Shake and strain into a shot glass.

Vampire's Embrace

2 ounces Jack Daniel's

1 ounce red cinnamon schnapps

Shake all the ingredients in a shaker tin with ice then strain into a shot glass.

Shooters

Shooters have a mix to them, so you need a larger shot glass, shooter glass, or rocks glass to hold them.

Blue Marlin Shooter

1 ounce light rum

1/2 ounce blue curaçao

1 ounce lime juice

Pour ingredients into a mixing glass half filled with ice. Stir. Strain into a large shot, shooter, or rocks glass.

Blueberry Kamikaze

1 1/2 ounces blueberry vodka

1/2 ounce triple sec

1/4 ounce Rose's lime juice

Shake all the ingredients in a shaker tin with ice, then strain into a rocks glass.

Brain Hemorrhage

1 ounce peach schnapps
1/4 ounce Irish cream
1/4 ounce grenadine syrup

First, pour the peach schnapps into a shot glass. Slowly add the Irish cream, and it will clump and settle at the bottom. Next, slowly pour grenadine to give it a bloody, disgusting brain-hemorrhage look.

Broken-Down Golf Cart

3/4 ounce melon liqueur
3/4 ounce amaretto
1/4 ounce cranberry juice
1/4 ounce lime juice

Shake and strain into a large shot, shooter, or rocks glass.

Cement Mixer

1 1/2 ounces Irish cream
1/4 ounce Rose's lime juice

This is a gag shooter. Pour the ingredients into a shot glass and drink. It curdles in your mouth.

Cherry Kamikaze

1 1/2 ounces cherry vodka
1/2 ounce triple sec
1/4 ounce Rose's lime juice

Shake all the ingredients in a shaker tin with ice, then strain into a rocks glass.

Coconut Kamikaze

1 1/2 ounces coconut vodka
1/2 ounce triple sec
1/4 ounce Rose's lime juice

Shake all the ingredients in a shaker tin with ice, then strain into a rocks glass.

Grape Kamikaze

1 1/2 ounces grape vodka
1/2 ounce triple sec
1/4 ounce Rose's lime juice

Shake all the ingredients in a shaker tin with ice, then strain into a rocks glass.

Kamikaze

1 1/2 ounces vodka
1/2 ounce triple sec
1/4 ounce lime juice

Shake and strain into a large shot, shooter, or rocks glass.

Shooters of Yesterday

Today anything poured into a martini glass is called a Martini. Just know that the chugged shooters of yesterday are really just the flavored Martinis you sip today. A real Martini is gin and dry vermouth. Period.

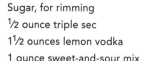

Lemon Drop Shooter

Sugar, for rimming
1/2 ounce triple sec
11/2 ounces lemon vodka
1 ounce sweet-and-sour mix

Rim a shooter or rocks glass with sugar. Shake and strain ingredients into a glass.

Mandarin Kamikaze

11/2 ounces mandarin vodka
1/2 ounce triple sec
1/4 ounce Rose's lime juice

Shake all the ingredients in a shaker tin with ice, then strain into a rocks glass.

Mango Kamikaze

11/2 ounces mango vodka
1/2 ounce triple sec
1/4 ounce Rose's lime juice

Shake all the ingredients in a shaker tin with ice, then strain into a rocks glass.

Melon Kamikaze

11/2 ounces melon vodka
1/2 ounce triple sec
1/4 ounce Rose's lime juice

Shake all the ingredients in a shaker tin with ice, then strain into a rocks glass.

Mind Eraser

1 ounce vodka
1 ounce coffee liqueur
Club soda to fill

Pour the first two ingredients into a short glass of ice. Fill with club soda. Stick in a straw and drink all at once.

Quarter and Shot Glass Trick

Set a glass on top of a bill. Then balance a coin on the rim of the glass. The challenge is to get the bill out from underneath the glass without jerking it quickly or shimmying it around. The answer? Roll the bill and it will push the glass off.

Monkey's Lunch

1 ounce banana liqueur
1 ounce coffee liqueur
1 ounce milk or cream

Shake and strain into a large shot, shooter, or rocks glass.

Peach Kamikaze

11/2 ounces peach vodka
1/2 ounce triple sec
1/4 ounce Rose's lime juice

Shake all the ingredients in a shaker tin with ice, then strain into a rocks glass.

Pear Kamikaze

1½ ounces pear vodka

½ ounce triple sec

¼ ounce Rose's lime juice

Shake all the ingredients in a shaker tin with ice, then strain into a rocks glass.

Pomegranate Kamikaze

1½ ounces pomegranate vodka

½ ounce triple sec

¼ ounce Rose's lime juice

Shake all the ingredients in a shaker tin with ice, then strain into a rocks glass.

Purple Hooter

1½ ounces vodka

1 ounce raspberry liqueur

1 ounce pineapple juice

1 ounce sweet-and-sour mix

Shake and strain into a large shot, shooter, or rocks glass.

Raspberry Kamikaze

1½ ounces raspberry vodka

½ ounce triple sec

¼ ounce Rose's lime juice

Shake all the ingredients in a shaker tin with ice, then strain into a rocks glass.

Raspberry Lemon Drop

Sugar, for rimming

1½ ounces raspberry vodka

½ ounce triple sec

1 ounce sweet-and-sour mix

Rim a rocks glass with sugar. Shake liquid ingredients in a shaker with ice and strain into the glass.

Jell-O Shots

To make Jell-O shots, simply replace the cold water portion of a Jell-O recipe with alcohol. Use small plastic cups (1- to 2-ounce cups) found at bulk restaurant supply stores or online. You can also buy lids to make them portable. The paper cups are sometimes called nut cups. You'll have to make some space in your fridge to set the Jell-O shots. The cheapest method is to measure the space in your fridge and cut out cardboard or foam board squares to create a stacking system of cardboard and layers of shots.

Redheaded Slut

1 ounce Jägermeister

1 ounce peach schnapps

2 ounces cranberry juice

Shake and strain into a large shot, shooter, or rocks glass.

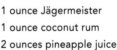
Red Snapper

1 ounce Crown Royal
1 ounce amaretto
2 ounces cranberry juice

Shake and strain into a large shot, shooter, or rocks glass.

Sexy Alligator

1 ounce melon liqueur
1 ounce amaretto
½ ounce Jägermeister
1 ounce pineapple juice

Shake and strain into a large shot, shooter, or rocks glass.

Snake Bite

2 ounces Yukon Jack
½ ounce Rose's lime juice

Shake and strain into a large shot, shooter, or rocks glass.

Snowshoe

¾ ounce Wild Turkey
¾ ounce peppermint schnapps

Shake and strain into a large shot, shooter, or rocks glass.

SoCo and Lime

2 ounces Southern Comfort
½ ounce Rose's lime juice

Shake and strain into a large shot, shooter, or rocks glass.

Stop Light

3 shots vodka
Splash melon liqueur
Splash cranberry juice
Splash orange juice

Line up three shot glasses and pour 1 shot of vodka into each glass. Add a splash of melon liqueur to one, a splash of orange juice to another, and a splash of cranberry juice to the third. Drink them down red, yellow, green.

Strawberry Kamikaze

1½ ounces strawberry vodka
½ ounce triple sec
¼ ounce Rose's lime juice

Shake all the ingredients in a shaker tin with ice then strain into a rocks glass.

Surfer on Acid

1 ounce Jägermeister
1 ounce coconut rum
2 ounces pineapple juice

Shake and strain into a large shot, shooter, or rocks glass.

Tangerine Kamikaze

1½ ounces tangerine vodka
½ ounce triple sec
¼ ounce Rose's lime juice

Shake all the ingredients in a shaker tin with ice, then strain into a rocks glass.

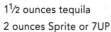

Tequila Slammer

1½ ounces tequila

2 ounces Sprite or 7UP

Pour the ingredients into a rocks glass, place a napkin over the glass, and slam glass on the table or bar top so that it fizzes. Drink.

Tootsie Roll Shooter

1 ounce coffee liqueur

1 ounce crème de cacao

1 ounce orange juice

Shake and strain into a large shot, shooter, or rocks glass.

Washington Apple

1 ounce Crown Royal

1 ounce sour apple schnapps

1 ounce cranberry juice

Shake and strain into a large shot, shooter, or rocks glass.

Shooter Pyramid

Why not make a shooter pyramid out of six shooters? Three glasses will be on the bottom, two balanced on top of the space between those, and then one on top. You have to curve the pattern in order to strain into all the glasses.

Woo Woo

1 ounce vodka

1 ounce peach schnapps

1 ounce cranberry juice

Shake and strain into a large shot, shooter, or rocks glass.

Layered Shots

Liqueurs have different densities, so it's possible to *carefully* layer them to create a rainbow or striped effect. The official name for this technique is *pousse-café*.

Astro Pop

¼ ounce grenadine

¼ ounce crème de banana

¼ ounce melon liqueur

¼ ounce vodka

Into a shot glass, layer each ingredient in order with a spoon.

B-52

½ ounce coffee liqueur

½ ounce Irish cream

½ ounce Grand Marnier

Into a shot glass, layer each ingredient in order with a spoon.

Black Rose

¾ ounce Tequila Rose
¾ ounce black vodka

Into a shot glass, layer each ingredient in order with a spoon.

Black Slippery Nipple

¾ ounce black sambuca
¾ ounce Irish cream

Into a shot glass, layer each ingredient in order with a spoon.

Blow Job

½ ounce coffee liqueur
½ ounce Irish cream
Whipped cream

Into a shot glass, layer the coffee liqueur and the Irish cream in that order with a spoon. Top with whipped cream. The novelty of this shot is that the drinker sucks up the whipped cream and then wraps his mouth around the glass and drinks with his hands behind his back.

Buttery Nipple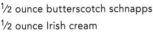

½ ounce butterscotch schnapps
½ ounce Irish cream

Into a shot glass, layer each ingredient in order with a spoon.

Candy Corn

⅓ ounce Galliano
⅓ ounce orange curaçao
⅓ ounce cream

Into a shot glass, layer each ingredient in order with a spoon.

Captain's Stripes

¼ ounce coffee liqueur
¼ ounce Galliano
¼ ounce Irish cream
¼ ounce Captain Morgan rum

Into a shot glass, layer each ingredient in order with a spoon.

Drink Two Beers Faster Than One Shot

Set up two draft beers in pint glasses and a shot of your choice. Challenge a friend that you can drink two beers before he or she can drink one shot. The rules are that you get a one-beer head start, you can't touch each other's glasses, and he or she can't drink until your glass is set down on the table. The trick is that you drink your first beer and turn your glass over the shot. Then drink your second beer.

Cigar Band

½ ounce amaretto

½ ounce Irish cream

½ ounce cognac

Into a shot glass, layer each ingredient in order with a spoon.

Coral Snake Bite

⅓ ounce coffee liqueur

⅓ ounce Galliano

⅓ ounce cherry brandy

Into a shot glass, layer each ingredient in order with a spoon.

Easter Egg

¼ ounce raspberry liqueur

¼ ounce Parfait d'Amour

¼ ounce crème de banana

¼ ounce cream

Into a shot glass, layer each ingredient in order with a spoon.

Green-Eyed Irish Blonde

⅓ ounce melon liqueur

⅓ ounce crème de banana

⅓ ounce Irish cream

Into a shot glass, layer each ingredient in order with a spoon.

Jack Black

¾ ounce black sambuca

¾ ounce Jack Daniel's

Into a shot glass, layer each ingredient in order with a spoon.

Mexican Flag

⅓ ounce green crème de menthe

⅓ ounce peppermint schnapps

⅓ ounce sloe gin

Into a shot glass, layer each ingredient in order with a spoon.

Salt and Pepper Shot Glasses

You'll need salt, pepper, and two shot glasses. Sprinkle some salt and pepper into the first glass and challenge someone to separate the salt and pepper by using only one item found at the bar. The answer is to pour water into the other shot glass and then pour the salt and pepper into that glass. The salt will sink to the bottom and the pepper will float on top.

Pirate's Treasure

½ ounce chilled Goldschläger

½ ounce chilled Captain Morgan spiced rum

Into a shot glass, layer each ingredient in order with a spoon. The gold at the bottom is the pirate's treasure.

Rhinestone Dallas Cowboy

½ ounce Goldschläger
½ ounce blue curaçao

Into a shot glass, layer each ingredient in order with a spoon.

Silk Panty

¾ ounce black sambuca
¾ ounce peach schnapps

Into a shot glass, layer each ingredient in order with a spoon.

Kahlúa and Cream Trick

You need two shot glasses, one filled with Kahlúa and the other with cream. Ask your challenger to put the contents of one glass into the other without pouring any out (or pouring one in their mouth). He or she is allowed one tool—a driver's license. The answer? Lay the license over the shot glass that contains the Kahlúa, then turn it upside down on top of the cream without spilling. Slowly remove the license and the Kahlúa and cream will switch glasses. This works because the Kahlúa is heavier than the cream.

Tequila Passion Shot

You'll need salt, lime, a shot of tequila, and a willing partner. To prep the shot: Lick a part of your partner's body, sprinkle the salt on the wet spot, and place the lime, meat side out, between your partner's lips or teeth. To take the shot, lick the salt, drink the tequila, and take a bite of the lime.

Slippery Dick

¾ ounce banana liqueur
¾ ounce Irish cream

Into a shot glass, layer each ingredient in order with a spoon.

Slippery Nipple

¾ ounce sambuca
¾ ounce Irish cream

Into a shot glass, layer each ingredient in order with a spoon.

Wicked Witch's Socks

⅓ ounce coffee liqueur
⅓ ounce white crème de cacao
⅓ ounce black vodka

Into a shot glass, layer each ingredient in order with a spoon.

Flaming Shots and Shooters

Flamed shots and shooters are set on fire, and much precaution should always be taken when playing with fire. Always make sure everything in the area around and above you is nonflammable. Flames should be blown out before the shot ever reaches your mouth. And always light the shot with a match as opposed to a lighter. With a lighter, you risk contaminating your shot with lighter fluid.

Baileys Comet

1½ ounces Baileys Irish Cream
⅛ ounce 151 rum
Several pinches cinnamon

Pour the Baileys Irish Cream into a shot glass. Slowly layer the 151 rum on top of the Baileys, then light with a match. When you see the flame, sprinkle cinnamon on the flame and it will make tiny fireworks-type sparkles, creating a comet effect. After the flame burns out, drink.

Dragon's Breath

½ ounce green crème de menthe
½ ounce gold tequila
⅛ ounce Grand Marnier

Into a shot glass, carefully layer each ingredient in order with a spoon. Light the Grand Marnier with a match; allow the flame to die out, then drink.

Eternal Flame

½ ounce Dooley's toffee liqueur
½ ounce coffee liqueur
¾ ounce Grand Marnier
1 Reese's Peanut Butter Cup

Pour the toffee liqueur, coffee liqueur, and ½ ounce of Grand Marnier in a shot glass. Take a spoon and scoop out a little of the middle of the Reese's Peanut Butter Cup, leaving the entire chocolate bottom intact. Eat the middle and set the rest of the peanut butter cup on top of the shot glass. Pour the remaining ¼ ounce of Grand Marnier into the scooped out area and light. When the flame dies, drink the shot and eat the candy.

Hot Apple Pie

¼ ounce sour apple schnapps

¼ ounce cinnamon schnapps

¼ ounce Irish cream

¼ ounce Captain Morgan spiced rum

⅛ ounce 151 rum

Squirt of whipped cream

Pour the apple schnapps, cinnamon schnapps, Irish cream, and Captain Morgan rum in a shot glass. Carefully float the 151 rum on top and light. Put out the flame by squirting whipped cream on top. Eat the whipped cream and drink the shot.

Hot Blooded

1½ ounces tequila

Several dashes Tabasco

⅛ ounce 151 rum

Pour the tequila into a shot glass and add several dashes of Tabasco. Gently layer the 151 rum on top, then light. Allow the flame to die out, then drink.

S'mores

½ ounce dark crème de cacao

¼ ounce butterscotch schnapps

¼ ounce Irish cream

⅛ ounce 151 rum

Toothpick stuck with 2 miniature marshmallows

Pour the first three ingredients in a shot glass. Float the 151 rum on top. Light the rum, roast the marshmallows, then drink the shot after the fire has died down.

Statue of Liberty

⅓ ounce grenadine

⅓ ounce blue curaçao

⅓ ounce white crème de cacao

⅛ ounce 151 rum

Into a shot glass, carefully layer each ingredient in order with a spoon. Light, hold up like the Statue of Liberty, blow out the flame, and drink. It will taste like a chocolate-covered cherry.

Wish Upon a Burning Star

1 star fruit slice

1 teaspoon raw sugar

Pinch cinnamon

1½ ounces Goldschläger

⅛ ounce 151 rum

1 bamboo skewer

Dip the star fruit into the raw sugar and cinnamon. Into a shot glass, pour the Goldschläger and half of the rum on top. Skewer the star fruit, pour on the remaining rum, and hold over the flame to light. Make a wish, blow out the flames, drink the shot, then eat the star fruit.

Drops and Bombs

The original name for drops and bombs is a *Boilermaker* (shot of whiskey dropped into a beer). The words *drops* and *bombs* gained popularity about a decade ago.

Boilermaker

1½ ounces whiskey

Half glass beer

Pour a shot of whiskey into the shot glass and fill a glass halfway with beer. Drop the shot into the beer and chug.

Burning Busch

1 bottle Busch beer

1 ounce Southern Comfort

⅛ ounce 151 rum

Pour a bottle of Busch beer into a beer glass. In a shot glass, pour in the Southern Comfort and carefully layer the 151 rum on top. Light the shot and let it burn for a bit to burn most of the rum away. Drop into the beer and chug.

Flaming Dr. Pepper

⅛ ounce grenadine

1 ounce amaretto

¼ ounce 151 rum

½ glass light beer

Pour the first three ingredients into a shot glass and half-fill a glass with beer. Light the shot and drop the shot glass into the beer. Chug.

Irish Car Bomb

½ ounce Irish whiskey

½ ounce Irish cream

8 ounces Guinness stout

Pour Irish whiskey and Irish cream into a shot glass. Drop it into a glass of Guinness. Chug before the drink curdles.

Jäger Bomb

1 can Red Bull

1 ounce Jägermeister

Pour a can of Red Bull into a glass and drop a shot of Jägermeister in. Drink.

Red Bull

Red Bull may seem like a new product, but it has been around since the early 1960s in Asia. It was very popular among blue-collar workers. By the early 1990s it reached Europe, and then the United States in the late 1990s. Now you see it everywhere.

Lunch Box

3½ ounces orange juice
1½ ounces beer
1½ ounces amaretto
1½ ounces Southern Comfort

Pour the orange juice and beer into a highball glass. Then take a shot glass and pour in the amaretto and Southern Comfort. Drop the shot glass into the highball glass, then chug.

Walk-Into-a-Bar Jokes

A guy walks into a bar and says, "Ouch!" Two peanuts walk into a bar and one was a salted. Four fonts walk into a bar and the barman says, "Get out! We don't want your TYPE in here!"

Sake to Me

1¼ ounces sake
¼ ounce 151 rum
½ glass beer
1 pair chopsticks

Pour the sake into a shot glass and float the rum on top. Pour beer into a glass until it is half full. Lay the chopsticks on top of the glass, and balance the shot glass on top of the chopsticks. Light the shot and karate-chop the bar top—the shot will drop into the beer. Chug.

multi-spirited specialty drinks

When a Long Island Iced Tea recipe calls for vodka, gin, rum, tequila, and triple sec, which chapter should it be in? You see the dilemma. These recipes are multi-spirited. Some are frozen, while others are on the rocks or served chilled straight up. You'll find classic, tropical, hot, juicy, creamy, and sour recipes all living together here.

Multi-Spirited Drink History

Popular lore says that one of the first cocktails was a multi-spirited drink, mixed in New Orleans in the early 1800s. The Sazerac was made with rye whiskey, absinthe, bitters, and sugar. There have been many punches and sangrias since then, but it's believed that the multi-spirited froufrou seed was planted when TGI Fridays opened the first casual bar and grill in New York City in 1965. Fridays was first to create a cocktail menu to go alongside the food menu, a tradition it proudly carries on today.

By the late 1970s, hundreds of imitative bar and grills opened nationwide, and all had menus advertising multi-spirited drinks full of the flavors of the time: coffee liqueur; Irish cream; amaretto; blue curaçao; crème de cacao, menthe, noyaux, and banana; flavored brandies; grenadine; and Midori. Between the 1980s and 2000s the menus exploded, thanks to a glut of new products flooding the market, including schnapps in all flavors, crème liqueurs in all flavors, and every category of spirit infused with every flavor imaginable. The results of these new tastes can be found in the drinks in this chapter.

57 Chevy

½ ounce vodka

1½ ounces Southern Comfort

½ ounce Grand Marnier

½ ounce amaretto

Orange juice to fill

Pour the first four ingredients into a tall glass of ice. Fill with orange juice.

57 Chevy with Hawaiian License Plates

½ ounce vodka

1½ ounces Southern Comfort

½ ounce Grand Marnier

½ ounce amaretto

Pineapple juice to fill

Pour the first four ingredients into a tall glass of ice. Fill with pineapple juice.

Acapulco Zombie

1 ounce tequila
1 ounce vodka
1 ounce rum
¼ ounce apricot brandy
Orange and grapefruit juice to fill

Pour the first four ingredients into a tall glass of ice. Fill with orange and grapefruit juice.

Ace Ventura

1 ounce vodka
¼ ounce tequila
¼ ounce rum
¼ ounce sambuca red
¼ ounce sambuca blue
¼ ounce sambuca green
¼ ounce sambuca black
¼ ounce sambuca white
¼ ounce sambuca gold
Sprite or 7UP to fill

Pour the vodka, tequila, rum, and sambucas into a tall glass of ice. Fill with Sprite or 7UP.

Adam and Eve

1 ounce Vicario Mirto Rosso Liqueur
½ ounce gin
½ ounce apple brandy
¼ ounce lemon juice

Shake all ingredients with ice. Strain into a martini glass.

Vicario Mirto Rosso Liqueur
Vicario Mirto Rosso Liqueur is made from myrtle berries. The myrtle berry is believed to come from the Garden of Eden in some religions. It has also been known to be used by the Romans and Egyptians for medicinal and decorative uses.

AK-47

¼ ounce brandy
¼ ounce whiskey
¼ ounce gin
¼ ounce vodka
¼ ounce rum
¼ ounce bourbon
¼ ounce Cointreau
1 ounce lime juice
Club soda to fill

Pour the liquors and lime juice into a tall glass of ice. Fill with club soda.

Alabama Slammer

½ ounce vodka
½ ounce Southern Comfort
½ ounce amaretto
½ ounce sloe gin
Orange juice to fill

Pour the first four ingredients into a tall glass of ice. Fill with orange juice.

Aloha

¼ ounce dark rum
¼ ounce dry vermouth
¼ ounce cognac
¼ ounce gin
1 ounce fresh lime juice

Shake all ingredients with ice.
Strain into a martini glass.

Alpine Lemonade

1 ounce vodka
1 ounce gin
1 ounce rum
Lemonade and cranberry juice to fill

Pour the vodka, gin, and rum
into a tall glass of ice. Fill with
equal parts of lemonade and
cranberry juice.

Alternatini

3 ounces vodka
¼ ounce white crème de cacao
¼ ounce sweet vermouth
¼ ounce dry vermouth

Shake all ingredients with ice.
Strain into a martini glass.

Angel's Fall

1 ounce amaretto
½ ounce gin
½ ounce vodka
½ ounce 151 rum
½ ounce dark rum
1 ounce grenadine
Cranberry, pineapple, and grapefruit
juice to fill

Pour the liquors and grenadine
into a tall glass of ice. Fill with
equal parts of cranberry, pineapple, and grapefruit juice.

Apple Pie ᵧ

1 ounce rum
½ ounce sweet vermouth
1 teaspoon apple brandy
1 ounce lemon juice
½ teaspoon grenadine

Combine all ingredients in a
shaker half filled with ice. Shake
well. Strain into a cocktail glass.

Around the World

½ ounce Russian vodka
½ ounce Caribbean rum
½ ounce Italian amaretto
½ ounce tequila
½ ounce Jägermeister
Hawaiian Punch to fill

Pour the first five ingredients into
a tall glass of ice. Fill with
Hawaiian Punch.

Asylum

1 ounce absinthe

1 ounce gin

¼ ounce grenadine

Pour all ingredients into a rocks glass of ice. Stir.

Barbary Coast

½ ounce Scotch

½ ounce gin

½ ounce rum

½ ounce white crème de cacao

½ ounce cream

Shake all ingredients with ice. Strain into a martini glass.

Big Banana!

1 ounce banana rum

1 ounce amaretto

1 ounce coconut rum

1 ounce crème de banana

Pineapple juice to fill

Pour the first four ingredients into a tall glass of ice. Fill with pineapple juice.

Bionic Tonic

1 ounce Chambord raspberry liqueur

1 ounce Alizé Gold Passion

1 ounce vodka

Club soda to fill

Pour each ingredient one by one into a short glass of ice. They will layer on top of one another.

Cocktails in the Sky

The first in-flight cocktails were served to paying passengers on the Zeppelin (airship) flying over Germany. The year was 1910.

Black Maria

2 ounces light rum

1 ounce coffee-flavored brandy

3 ounces cold strong black coffee

2 teaspoons fine sugar

Pour all ingredients into a brandy snifter and stir. Add ice.

The Blackthorn Cocktail

2 ounces gin

¾ ounce kirschwasser

¾ ounce Dubonnet Rouge

1 lemon twist

1 cherry

Shake the liquid ingredients in a shaker tin with ice, then strain into a chilled cocktail glass. Garnish with lemon twist and cherry.

Blue Knickers

1 ounce vodka

1 ounce blue curaçao

1 ounce Galliano

1 ounce pineapple juice

1¼ ounces cream

Shake the first four ingredients with ice. Strain into a martini glass. Slowly float the cream on top.

Blue Velvetini

Sugar, for rimming
A few drops blue food coloring
1 ounce light rum
1 ounce blue curaçao
1 ounce blueberry schnapps
2 ounces white (clear) cranberry juice

Mix the sugar and a few drops of blue food coloring on a saucer with a spoon. Wet the rim of a martini glass with water and dip the rim into the blue sugar. Shake the rum, curaçao, blueberry schnapps, and white (clear) cranberry juice with ice. Strain into the glass.

Bolero

1½ ounces light rum
¾ ounce calvados or apple brandy
1 teaspoon sweet vermouth

Combine ingredients in a mixing glass half filled with ice. Stir well. Pour into an old-fashioned glass with ice.

Boston Sidecar

1 ounce light rum
½ ounce brandy
¾ ounce triple sec
1 ounce lime juice or juice from ½ lime

Combine ingredients in a shaker nearly filled with ice. Strain into a cocktail glass.

Brass Monkey

1 ounce vodka
1 ounce rum
Fresh orange juice to fill

Pour vodka and rum into a highball glass of ice. Fill with orange juice.

The Brooklyn Cocktail

2 ounces rye whiskey
¾ ounce dry vermouth
¼ ounce maraschino liqueur
¼ ounce Amer Picon
1 cherry

Shake all the liquid ingredients in a shaker tin with ice, then strain into a chilled cocktail glass. Garnish with cherry.

A Guy Walks Into a Bar

A guy walks into a bar and asks for ten shots of the finest gin. The bartender sets him up, and the guy takes the first shot in the row and pours it on the floor. He then takes the last shot and does the same. The bartender asks, "Why did you do that?" And the guy replies, "Well the first shot always tastes like crap, and the last one always makes me sick!"

Chatham Hotel Special

1½ ounces brandy

½ ounce ruby port

¼ ounce dark crème de cacao

½ ounce cream

Shake all ingredients in a shaker tin with ice then strain into a chilled cocktail glass.

Cherry Blossom

5 pitted sour cherries

½ ounce lemon juice

½ ounce Cherry Heering liqueur

½ ounce curaçao

1½ ounces brandy

Muddle cherries with lemon juice and liqueurs in a mixing glass. Add brandy and ice. Shake, then strain into a cocktail glass.

Cherry Pink and Apple Blossom White

1 ounce cherry vodka

1 ounce green apple rum

5 ounces white (clear) cranberry juice

¼ ounce grenadine

Fill a tall glass with ice and add all the ingredients. Stir.

Continental

1½ ounces light rum

½ ounce green crème de menthe

½ teaspoon fine sugar

1 tablespoon lime juice

1 teaspoon lemon juice

1 lemon twist

Combine liquid ingredients in a shaker nearly filled with ice. Strain into a cocktail glass. Serve with a lemon twist.

Corkscrew

1½ ounces light rum

½ ounce peach-flavored brandy

½ ounce dry vermouth

1 lemon twist

Combine liquid ingredients in a shaker nearly filled with ice. Strain into a cocktail glass. Serve with a lemon twist.

Corpse Reviver

1 ounce gin

½ ounce Cointreau

½ ounce Lillet Blanc

¾ ounce fresh lemon juice

¼ ounce absinthe

Shake all ingredients with ice. Strain into a martini glass.

The Derby

1 ounce bourbon
¾ ounce fresh lime juice
½ ounce sweet vermouth
½ ounce orange curaçao
1 mint leaf

Shake all the liquid ingredients in a shaker tin with ice, then strain into a chilled cocktail glass. Garnish with mint leaf.

Dixie Whiskey

1½ ounces bourbon whiskey
½ ounce orange curaçao
¼ ounce white crème de menthe
2¼ ounces Angostura bitters
¾ ounce fresh lemon juice

Shake all ingredients with ice. Strain into a martini glass.

Dutchie

1 ounce cherry brandy
1 ounce crème de banana
1 ounce apricot brandy
Milk, as needed
1 ounce chilled advocaat

Pour the first three ingredients into a tall glass of ice. Fill three-quarters full with milk. Slowly pour the advocaat over the top of the milk and watch as the advocaat drips around the ice and through the milk.

El Chico

1½ ounces light rum
½ ounce sweet vermouth
¼ teaspoon grenadine
¼ teaspoon curaçao
1 cherry and 1 lemon twist

Combine liquid ingredients in a shaker nearly filled with ice. Strain into a cocktail glass. Serve with cherry and lemon twist.

A Guy Walks Into a Bar

A guy walks into a bar, sits down, and hears a small voice say, "You look nice today." A few minutes later, he again hears a small voice: "That's a nice shirt." The guy asks the bartender, "Who is that?" The bartender says, "Those are the peanuts. They're complimentary!"

El Presidente

1½ ounces light rum
¾ ounce curaçao
¾ ounce dry vermouth
¼ ounce grenadine

Shake all ingredients with ice. Strain into a martini glass.

Electric Iced Tea

1/2 ounce vodka
1/2 ounce gin
1/2 ounce rum
1/2 ounce tequila
1/2 ounce blue curaçao
1 ounce sour mix
Splash Sprite or 7UP

Pour all ingredients into a tall glass of ice. Stir.

Embassy Cocktail

3/4 ounce brandy
3/4 ounce Cointreau
3/4 ounce Appleton Jamaican rum
1/2 ounce fresh lime juice
1/4 ounce Angostura bitters

Shake all ingredients with ice. Strain into a martini glass.

Falling Leaves

1 ounce pear brandy
1 ounce Riesling
1/2 ounce orange curaçao
1/4 ounce honey
Dash Peychaud's bitters

Shake all the ingredients in a shaker tin with ice, then strain into a chilled cocktail glass.

Feliz Natal

1 ounce port
1 ounce amaretto
2 ounces crème de cacao
1 ounce cherry brandy

Pour all ingredients together in a short glass of ice. Stir.

Floridita

1 1/2 ounces rum
1/2 ounce sweet vermouth
1/8 ounce white crème de cacao
1/2 ounce lime juice
1/8 ounce grenadine

Shake all ingredients with ice. Strain into a martini glass.

Fog Cutter

2 ounces white rum
1/2 ounce gin
1 ounce brandy
1 ounce fresh orange juice
2 ounces fresh lemon juice
1/2 ounce orgeat syrup
1/2 ounce sweet sherry

Shake everything but the sherry with ice. Strain into a tall glass of ice. Float the sherry on top.

Foggy Afternoon

1 ounce vodka
1/2 ounce apricot brandy
1/2 ounce triple sec
1 1/4 ounces crème de banana
1 1/4 ounces fresh lemon juice

Shake all ingredients with ice. Strain into a martini glass.

Golden Friendship

1 ounce light rum
1 ounce sweet vermouth
1 ounce amaretto
4 ounces ginger ale
1 cherry

Pour rum, vermouth, and amaretto into a Collins glass with ice. Add ginger ale. Garnish with cherry.

Hand Grenade

1 ounce 151 rum
1 ounce vodka
1 ounce melon liqueur
1 ounce amaretto
Pineapple juice to fill

Pour the first four ingredients into a tall glass of ice. Fill with pineapple juice.

Hawaiian Iced Tea

1/2 ounce vodka
1/2 ounce gin
1/2 ounce light rum
1/2 ounce tequila
1/2 ounce triple sec
1 ounce sour mix
1 ounce pineapple juice

Pour all ingredients into a tall glass of ice. Stir.

Honeymoon Cocktail

2 ounces applejack
1/2 ounce Bénédictine
1/2 ounce curaçao
1/2 ounce fresh lemon juice
1 lemon twist

Shake all liquid ingredients with ice. Strain into a martini glass. Garnish with lemon twist.

The Honey Month

In ancient Babylon, for a month after a wedding, the bride's father supplied his new son-in-law with all the mead he could drink. Because the Babylonian calendar was lunar based, what they called the honey month is what we know today as the honeymoon.

Hyde Park

2 ounces orange vodka
1 ounce Aperol
1/2 ounce Galliano
1/4 ounce passion fruit syrup

Shake all the ingredients in a shaker tin with ice, then strain into a chilled cocktail glass.

Ice Palace

1 ounce light rum
½ ounce Galliano
½ ounce apricot brandy
2 ounces pineapple juice
¼ ounce fresh lemon juice

Pour all ingredients into a tall glass of ice. Stir.

Irish Shannigan

1½ ounces Irish whiskey
½ ounce light rum
½ ounce sloe gin
1 teaspoon powdered sugar
1 ounce fresh lemon juice
¼ cup fresh peaches
¼ cup fresh raspberries

Combine all ingredients in a blender with ice. Blend, then pour into a tall glass.

K.G.B.

½ ounce kirschwasser
½ ounce fresh lemon juice
¼ ounce apricot brandy
½ teaspoon sugar
1½ ounces gin
1 lemon twist

Shake liquids and sugar with ice. Strain into a martini glass and garnish with lemon twist.

Las Vegas, Baby!

½ ounce Seagram's 7
½ ounce Licor 43
½ ounce Pimm's No. 1
½ ounce 151 rum
Sprite or 7UP to fill

Pour the liquors into a tall glass of ice. Fill with Sprite or 7UP.

Long Beach Tea

½ ounce vodka
½ ounce gin
½ ounce light rum
½ ounce tequila
½ ounce triple sec
1 ounce sour mix
1 ounce cranberry juice

Pour all ingredients into a tall glass of ice. Stir.

Long Island Iced Tea

Some cocktail historians claim the LIIT was created during Prohibition as a way to disguise an alcoholic beverage as a nonalcoholic drink (iced tea). However, others say it was invented in the mid-1970s by a bartender from Long Island, New York. TGI Fridays says it was responsible for the classic drink. LIIT was a big hit during the disco years (and still is).

Long Island Iced Tea

½ ounce vodka
½ ounce light rum
½ ounce tequila
½ ounce triple sec
½ ounce gin
1 ounce sour mix
Splash of cola

Pour all ingredients into a tall glass of ice. Stir.

Magnum

1 ounce Goldschläger
1 ounce Jack Daniel's
1 ounce rum
1 ounce vodka
2 ounces fruit punch

Blend all ingredients with ice. Pour into a tall glass.

Man Hunting

1½ ounces Wild Turkey 101
1 ounce curaçao
½ ounce sweet vermouth
½ ounce fresh lemon juice

Shake all ingredients with ice. Strain into a martini glass.

Miami Iced Tea

½ ounce vodka
½ ounce gin
½ ounce light rum
½ ounce peach schnapps
½ ounce triple sec
1 ounce sour mix
1 ounce cranberry juice
Splash Sprite or 7UP

Pour all ingredients into a tall glass of ice. Stir.

Miami Vice

The Miami Iced Tea is not the same as a Miami Vice. A Miami Vice is half Strawberry Daiquiri and half Piña Colada.

The Millionaire

1½ ounces dark rum
¾ ounce sloe gin
¾ ounce apricot brandy
1 ounce fresh lime juice
1 lime wedge

Shake all the liquid ingredients in a shaker tin with ice, then strain into a chilled cocktail glass. Garnish with lime wedge.

Mojo

1 ounce light rum

1 ounce cherry brandy

3 ounces amber beer

Pineapple juice and Sprite to fill

Pour the first three ingredients into a tall glass of ice. Fill with equal parts of pineapple juice and Sprite.

Moonlight Drive

1 ounce vodka

1 ounce rum

1 ounce sloe gin

1 ounce coconut rum

½ ounce amaretto

Orange and pineapple juice to fill

Pour the liquors into a tall glass of ice. Fill with juices.

Mudslide Martini

1 ounce vodka

1 ounce Irish cream

1 ounce coffee liqueur

1 ounce cream

Shake all ingredients with ice, then strain into a martini glass.

Naked Twister

1 ounce melon liqueur

½ ounce vodka

½ ounce Tuaca

Pineapple juice to fill

Pour the first three ingredients into a tall glass of ice. Fill with pineapple juice.

Neapolitan Martini

1 ounce vanilla vodka

1 ounce orange vodka

½ ounce Grand Marnier

½ ounce Parfait d'Amour

Splash fresh lime juice

1 orange twist

Shake all liquid ingredients with ice. Strain into a martini glass. Garnish with orange twist.

Neapolitan History

Layering three colors or three flavors began in Naples, Italy. These days, the most common name for this layering in Italy is *spumoni*. The most common place to find this layering in America is in your local grocer's freezer. It's called *Neapolitan ice cream*.

PB&J

1 ounce Frangelico

1 ounce raspberry liqueur

1 ounce raspberry vodka

1 ounce cream

Shake all ingredients with ice. Strain into a martini glass.

PB&J with Bananas

1 ounce Frangelico
½ ounce raspberry liqueur
1 ounce raspberry vodka
1 ounce banana liqueur
1 ounce cream

Shake all ingredients with ice. Strain into a martini glass.

Port Authority

2 ounces port wine
1 ounce Grand Marnier
½ ounce amaretto

Pour all ingredients into an old-fashioned glass of ice and stir.

Punch and Judy

1 ounce cognac
¼ ounce rum
½ ounce gin
½ ounce triple sec
½ ounce fresh lime juice
½ ounce orange juice
½ ounce agave nectar
2 dashes Angostura bitters
4 mint leaves
1 lime wheel
Pinch nutmeg

Put the liquid ingredients and the mint leaves into a shaker tin of ice and shake hard. Strain into a tall glass of fresh ice. Float the lime wheel on top, then sprinkle with nutmeg.

Raspberry Long Island Ice Tea

½ ounce raspberry vodka
½ ounce gin
½ ounce raspberry rum
½ ounce tequila
½ ounce triple sec
1 ounce sour mix
Splash Sprite or 7UP

Pour all ingredients into a tall glass of ice. Stir.

Red Death

¾ ounce vodka
¾ ounce Southern Comfort
¼ ounce sloe gin
¼ ounce triple sec
¼ ounce Rose's lime juice
¼ ounce grenadine
Orange juice to fill

Pour liquors, lime juice, and grenadine into a tall glass of ice. Fill with orange juice.

Renaissance

2 ounces brandy
1½ ounces sweet vermouth
½ ounce limoncello
Dash peach bitters

Shake all the ingredients in a shaker tin with ice, then strain into a chilled cocktail glass.

Satan's Whiskers

3/4 ounce gin

3/4 ounce dry vermouth

3/4 ounce sweet vermouth

1/2 ounce Grand Marnier

1/2 ounce orange juice

2 dashes orange bitters

Shake all ingredients with ice. Strain into a martini glass.

Sex on the Farm

1 ounce Wild Turkey honey liqueur

1/2 ounce peach schnapps

1/2 ounce raspberry liqueur

1 ounce cranberry juice

1 ounce pineapple juice

Shake all ingredients with ice. Strain into a martini glass.

Shalom

1 1/2 ounces gin

1/2 ounce cherry brandy

1/2 ounce Madeira

1 ounce orange juice

Shake all ingredients with ice. Strain into a martini glass.

Sloe Comfortable Fuzzy Screw Against the Wall

1/2 ounce sloe gin

1/2 ounce Southern Comfort

1/2 ounce peach schnapps

1/2 ounce vodka

1/2 ounce Galliano

Orange juice to fill

Pour all ingredients into a highball glass filled with ice. Stir.

Sloe Comfortable Screw

1 ounce sloe gin

1 ounce Southern Comfort

1 ounce vodka

Orange juice to fill

Pour all ingredients into a highball glass filled with ice. Stir.

Sloe Comfortable Screw Against the Wall

1 ounce sloe gin

1 ounce Southern Comfort

1 ounce vodka

Orange juice to fill

1/2 ounce Galliano

Pour the first three ingredients into a highball glass filled with ice and stir. Fill with orange juice. Float Galliano on top.

Sloe Comfortable Screw Against the Wall in Mexico

1/2 ounce sloe gin

1/2 ounce Southern Comfort

1/2 ounce vodka

1/2 ounce tequila

Orange juice to fill

Pour all ingredients into a highball glass filled with ice. Stir.

Sloe Comfortable Screw Between the Sheets

½ ounce sloe gin
½ ounce Southern Comfort
½ ounce vodka
½ ounce rum
½ ounce brandy
Orange juice to fill

Pour all ingredients into a high-ball glass filled with ice. Stir.

Tango

½ ounce rum
½ ounce sweet vermouth
½ ounce dry vermouth
½ ounce Bénédictine
1 ounce orange juice

Shake all ingredients with ice. Strain into a martini glass.

Texas Ex's

½ ounce sherry
½ ounce brandy
½ ounce Tequila Rose
½ ounce strawberry vodka
1 ounce lemon juice
Cranberry juice to fill

Pour all ingredients into a tall glass filled with ice. Stir.

Texas Tea

½ ounce tequila
½ ounce vodka
½ ounce rum
½ ounce triple sec
1 ounce sour mix
Splash of cola

Pour all ingredients into a tall glass of ice. Stir.

Three Señoritas Margarita

½ ounce blanco tequila
Juice from ½ lime
5 ounces sweet-and-sour mix
3 plastic test tubes
¾ ounce brandy
¾ ounce Tequila Rose
¾ ounce sherry

Blend the tequila, lime juice, and sweet-and-sour mix with 1 cup of ice, then pour into a margarita glass. Fill the first test tube with brandy, the next with Tequila Rose, and the third with sherry. Stick the test tubes in the margarita.

Tropical Itch

1 ounce dark rum
1 ounce American whiskey
1 ounce triple sec
4 ounces orange juice
1 pineapple slice
1 cherry

Shake the liquid ingredients with ice and strain into a tall tropical glass of fresh ice. Garnish with the pineapple and cherry.

Tropical Rain Forest

½ ounce lemon vodka
½ ounce cherry rum
½ ounce white tequila
½ ounce blue curaçao
½ ounce melon liqueur
Cranberry, pineapple, and orange juice to fill
Paper parasol and fruit of your choice, for garnish

Pour the liquors into a tall glass of ice. Fill with equal amounts of cranberry, pineapple, and orange juice. Garnish with paper parasol and fruit of your choice.

Twelve Mile Limit

1 ounce light rum
½ ounce rye whiskey
½ ounce brandy
½ ounce grenadine
½ fresh lemon juice
1 lemon twist

Shake all the liquid ingredients in a shaker tin with ice, then strain into a chilled cocktail glass. Garnish with lemon twist.

Twentieth Century

1½ ounces gin
½ ounce white crème de cacao
½ ounce Lillet Blanc
¼ ounce fresh lemon juice

Shake all ingredients with ice. Strain into a martini glass.

Vesper

3 ounces gin
1 ounce vodka
½ ounce Lillet Blanc
1 lemon twist

Shake all liquid ingredients with ice. Strain into a martini glass. Garnish with lemon twist.

Vieux Carre

1 ounce rye whiskey
1 ounce cognac
¼ ounce Bénédictine D.O.M.
2 dashes Peychaud's bitters
2 dashes Angostura bitters

Fill an old-fashioned glass with ice and all the ingredients. Stir.

Waldorf

1½ ounces bourbon
¾ ounce Pernod
½ ounce sweet vermouth

Pour all ingredients into a shaker with ice. Shake very well and strain into a martini glass over ice.

The Widow's Kiss

1½ ounces calvados
¾ ounce green Chartreuse
¾ ounce Bénédictine
1 cherry

Shake all the liquid ingredients in a shaker tin with ice, then strain into a chilled cocktail glass. Garnish with cherry.

punches and party, holiday, and seasonal drinks

Punches and party, holiday, and seasonal drinks stir up a sense of social warmth and togetherness. Most are made in mass quantities and shared with dear friends, family, coworkers, and new acquaintances. They are celebratory by nature.

Punches and Party Drinks

The most important points to know about making and serving mass quantities of punch are these: You should start with everything cold, and you should invite guests to serve themselves by providing everything they need on a well-decorated table. Try to think outside the box. Visit discount stores in the summer to gather fun and inexpensive partyware. To keep punches cold, you can freeze molds made of the punch with some water to float in the punch, make punch bowls out of ice, or rent a cooling champagne fountain from a local party store. If drinks need to be shaken, then hire a local bartender, whip up a batch of what you want in mass quantities, and just have her shake and serve the drinks. Just make sure you set up your drink station at the opposite end—across the room—from the food station for crowd flow. Also, know that any single drink recipe in this chapter can be mass-produced.

Ace of Spades (Casino Party Martini)
Serves 1

2 ounces Blavod black vodka
2 ounces white (clear) crème de cacao

Shake the ingredients with ice, then strain into a martini glass.

Baby Shower Champagne
Serves 1

½ ounce pomegranate juice
Nonalcoholic sparkling apple cider or ginger ale
1 strawberry

Pour the pomegranate juice in a champagne flute. Add the sparkling apple cider or ginger ale. Garnish with the strawberry on the rim.

Bachelorette Strip and Go Naked Punch
Serves 12

1 bottle lime-flavored gin
3 ounces grenadine
12-pack light beer
2 (12-ounce) cans frozen limeade
Lime wheels and cherries, for garnish

Put the gin in the freezer and the grenadine and beer in the fridge; allow the limeade to thaw, then refrigerate. When ready, pour everything (add the beer slowly) into a punch bowl and add the garnishes. Ladle into tall glasses of ice and garnish with lime wheels and cherries. Search the Internet for naughty bachelorette drink items to accompany this punch.

Blinded by the Light Girly Birthday Drink

Serves 1

1½ ounces light rum

Crystal Light pink lemonade to fill

1 glow stick

⅛ ounce 151 rum

1 piece flash paper

This is a drink for the birthday person. Pour the light rum into a tall glass of ice and fill with the Crystal Light pink lemonade. Activate a glow stick and drop it in the drink. (Be careful not to break the glow stick.) Top the drink with 151 rum, then light. While the drink is flaming, hold and hide flash paper in your palms and light it with the flame.

Divorce Party Blues

Serves 1

½ ounce blue curaçao

¾ glass Sprite or 7UP

2 ounces Blavod black vodka

Celebrate the mourning (black vodka) of a divorce by getting the blues (blue curaçao)! Pack a tall glass with ice and pour in the blue curaçao. Fill three-quarters of the glass with Sprite or 7UP, then float the black vodka on top.

Garden Party Sangria

Serves 8

2 cups water

1 cup sugar

12 cinnamon sticks

2 bottles nondry white wine

2 cups sparkling water

2 cups apple juice

1 cup white (clear) cranberry juice

Pitcher of roses and rose petals

3 apples cut in chunks

Cherries, for garnish

Heat the water, sugar, and cinnamon sticks to a simmer. Simmer for 5 minutes, then remove from heat. Cool to room temperature. Remove the cinnamon sticks and mix in all remaining liquid ingredients. Chill overnight in the refrigerator. When ready, present the sangria in a clear self-serve container and put in rinsed rose petals, apple chunks, and cherries. Decorate the table with remaining rose petals and roses and glasses of ice with an apple chunk, cherry, and rose petal on top.

Hawaiian Luau Jungle Juice

Serves 40

2 bottles (750-milliliter) dark rum

2 bottles (750-milliliter) light rum

1 gallon orange juice

1 gallon pineapple juice

1 gallon sweet-and-sour mix

1 bottle grenadine

5-gallon Igloo water cooler

1 bag ice

1 black Magic Marker

Brown mailing paper to fit cooler

1 jar maraschino cherries

Pineapple slices, for garnish

1 box paper parasols

Pour the dark rum, light rum, orange and pineapple juice, sweet-and-sour mix, and grenadine in the cooler, then add a bag of ice and stir. Use the marker to make tiki totem pole designs on the brown paper, and wrap it around the cooler. Cut a hole in the paper for the spigot. Set the cherries, pineapple slices, and parasols out around this self-serve tropical oasis.

Housewarming Sangria

Serves 12

2 tablespoons sugar

2 ounces blackberry brandy

1 cup orange juice

1 cup pineapple juice

½ cup cherry juice

3 bottles chilled Lambrusco red wine

3 cups maraschino cherries

12 thinly sliced orange wheels

12 thinly sliced lemon wheels

12 thinly sliced lime wheels

Combine all ingredients except for the wine and fruits and refrigerate. When ready to serve, pour the chilled wine and chilled mixture together and garnish with the fruit. Prep glasses of ice with fruit as well.

Pineapple Upside-Down Birthday Cake

Serves 1

2 ounces vanilla vodka

1 ounce Irish cream

2 ounces pineapple juice

¼ ounce grenadine

1 cherry

1 canned pineapple ring

1 squirt whipped cream

1 birthday candle

Shake the first three ingredients with ice and strain into a martini glass. Pour in the grenadine (it will sink to the bottom), then drop in the cherry. Float the pineapple ring on top. Squirt whipped cream in the hole of the pineapple ring (this will hold the candle in place). Stick the candle in the whipped cream and light.

Pink Pajama Party Shots

Serves 10

1 bottle chilled Tequila Rose

Chocolate shot glasses

Pour chilled Tequila Rose cream liqueur into the chocolate shot glasses and serve on a tray. You can buy chocolate shot glasses on the Internet or make your own. You can find a recipe for them in Chapter 11.

Scorpion Bowl

Serves 5

2 ounces gin

2 ounces grenadine

2 ounces dark rum

6 ounces orange juice

2 ounces 151 rum

6 ounces pineapple juice

2 ounces light rum

Seasonal fruit of choice and paper parasols, for garnish

Pour all the liquid ingredients into a pitcher and stir. Pour into glasses of ice. Garnish with fruit and parasols.

Spa Party Martini

Serves 1

1 ounce organic Rain vodka

½ ounce organic honey liqueur

½ ounce organic ginger liqueur

1 ounce organic fresh lemon juice

½ ounce organic honey

1 organic cucumber slice

Shake all liquid ingredients with ice and strain into a martini glass. Slip an organic cucumber slice in the glass.

Wedding Cake Martini

Serves 1

1 ounce vanilla vodka

½ ounce amaretto

½ ounce white chocolate liqueur

1 ounce cream

Shake all ingredients with ice and strain into a martini glass.

Wedding Reception Bubbles

Serves 1

½ ounce strawberry vodka

1 ounce strawberry liqueur

Dry champagne to fill

1 strawberry

Pour the strawberry vodka and the strawberry liqueur into a champagne flute and fill with champagne. Garnish the rim with a strawberry.

Holiday and Seasonal Drinks

Humans will find just about any reason, season, or holiday to celebrate. If you plan to throw a big shindig, save money by purchasing liquors and mixers in bulk. However, you'll need to invest in smaller containers to transfer the bulk amount and make serving easier. Using clean gallon jugs helps solve this problem, and when the punch bowl runs out, all you have to do is grab another gallon from the fridge and refill.

January–April

These recipes cover seasons and holidays found in January, February, March, and April.

Chinese New Year Champagne

Serves 1

½ ounce lychee liqueur

½ ounce tangerine juice

Champagne to fill

Pour the lychee liqueur and tangerine juice into a champagne flute, then add the champagne.

Green Beer (St. Patrick's Day)

Serves 1

1 pint pilsner (yellow beer)

1 drop green food coloring

Pour up a pint of beer, then add 1 drop green food coloring.

Kama Sutra (Valentine's Day)

Serves 1

1/2 ounce Passoã passion fruit liqueur

1/2 ounce Alizé Red Passion

1/2 ounce DeKuyper Cheri-Beri Pucker

Ginger ale to fill

Maraschino cherries, for garnish

Pour the first three ingredients into a tall glass, then add ice. Fill to the top with ginger ale and garnish with maraschino cherries.

Calculating Amounts

Guests at a party will drink about 2 or 3 drinks each. One bottle of wine will yield 4 6-ounce glasses of wine, and a (750-milliliter) bottle of liquor will give you around 25 ounces of alcohol. You will also need about 1/2 pound of ice per person.

Kiss from a Rose (Valentine's Day)

Serves 1

1 ounce rosé wine

1 ounce Tequila Rose

2 ounces cream

Shake all ingredients with ice and strain into a martini glass.

Nutty Irishmantini (St. Patrick's Day)

Serves 1

1 ounce Irish cream

1 ounce Frangelico

1/2 ounce Irish whiskey

1 ounce cream

Shake all ingredients with ice and strain into a martini glass.

Ragin' Cajun Mardi Gras Punch

Serves 20

2 (40-ounce) bottles chilled purple grape juice

2 (48-ounce) cans chilled pineapple juice

1 bunch green seedless grapes

1 needle and fishing line

1 bottle (750-milliliter) chilled citrus vodka

1 (2-liter) bottle chilled ginger ale

Make an ice ring: fill half a ring mold with grape juice, freeze, fill with pineapple juice, and freeze again. String the grapes with the needle and fishing line to make beads. Pour the vodka, remaining juices, and ginger ale in a punch bowl. Place the ice ring and the string of grape beads in the bowl.

Green, Gold, and Purple

This festive punch combines the traditional Mardi Gras colors of green, representing faith; gold, symbolizing power; and purple, denoting justice. It's delicious with or without the alcohol.

Sparkling New Year Cheer

Serves 1

1 sugar cube

6 dashes Angostura bitters

Chilled champagne to fill

1 lemon twist

Dash a sugar cube with Angostura bitters and drop into the bottom of a champagne flute. Fill the flute with champagne. Twist a lemon twist to release the oils, then rub the rim of the glass with the twist and drop it into the drink.

Super Bowl Drop Kick

Serves 1

1 glass beer of your choice

1 ounce American whiskey

Fill a beer glass with a beer, then pour American whiskey into a shot glass. Here's where the drop kick comes in: Drop the shot into the beer and kick the whole thing (beer and all) down your throat in one fell swoop.

How Many People Will Be Invited to the Party?

It's very important to know the approximate number of people who will be invited, since this is the basis of the math you will do for everything related to the party. How else will you be able to calculate the amounts of food and drink, invitations, napkins, and glasses? Make a list, check it twice, and always invite the naughty and the nice for a memorable party.

White Chocolate Eastertini

Serves 1

1 ounce vanilla vodka

1 ounce white chocolate liqueur

2 ounces eggnog

1 ounce cream

Jellybeans, for garnish

Pour the liquids into a shaker tin of ice and shake, then strain into a martini glass. Hide your little Easter eggs by dropping some jellybeans in the glass to sink to the bottom.

May–August

These recipes cover seasons and holidays found in May, June, July, and August.

Blue Skyy Summer

Serves 1

1 ounce Skyy melon vodka

1 ounce blue curaçao

White (clear) cranberry juice and club soda to fill

Pour vodka and curaçao into a tall glass of ice. Fill with equal parts of white (clear) cranberry juice and club soda.

Born on the 4th of July Martini

Serves 1

1½ ounces cherry vodka or rum

3 ounces white (clear) cranberry juice

1 maraschino cherry

½ ounce blue curaçao

Pour the cherry vodka or rum and the white (clear) cranberry juice into a shaker tin of ice and shake; then strain into a martini glass. Drop the cherry in to sink to the bottom, then carefully float the blue curaçao on top by pouring it over the back of a spoon.

Canadian Crown (Canada Day)

Serves 1

2 ounces Crown Royal Canadian blended whisky

1 ounce fresh lemon juice

½ ounce simple syrup

½ ounce grenadine

1 maraschino cherry

Shake all liquid ingredients with ice and strain into a martini glass. Add the cherry.

Chatham Artillery Punch

Serves 40

1 bottle sweet red wine

½ bottle light rum

½ bottle rye whiskey

½ bottle gin

½ bottle brandy

1 cup lemon juice

4 cups strong tea

1 cup orange juice

1 cup packed brown sugar

2 bottles dry champagne

Mix together all ingredients except champagne. Cover and refrigerate for several days; then stir in the champagne just before serving. This is the historical summer punch drunk by U.S. military soldiers at regimental functions.

Champagne Fountain

You can rent a champagne fountain at a local party store and pour in anything you want as long as it doesn't have pulp or seeds. Even though the fountain will have a chiller, it's best to pour in your chosen mixture when cold.

Cinco de Mayo Martini

Serves 1

1 ounce aged tequila

1 ounce coconut-flavored tequila

½ ounce agave liqueur

2 ounces fresh lime juice

1 ounce simple syrup

Shake all ingredients with ice and strain into a martini glass.

Horse's Neck (Kentucky Derby)

Serves 1

1 lemon rind spiral (historic bar garnish)

2 ounces Kentucky whiskey

Dash Angostura bitters

Ginger ale to fill

To make the horse's neck, simply slice into the top of a whole lemon and carefully peel the entire peel off in a spiral. Lower the spiral into a highball glass, then slowly add ice so that the horse's neck is spiraled all the way up the glass. Pour in the whiskey, dash the bitters, and fill with ginger ale.

Mint Julep Punch (Kentucky Derby)

Serves 25

1 cup mint jelly

4 cups distilled water

¼ cup fresh lime juice

1 quart (can) pineapple juice

1 bottle Kentucky bourbon

1 liter lemon and lime soda

Mint sprigs, for garnish

Heat mint jelly in saucepan with 2 cups of the water until the jelly melts, then cool. Add the liquid ingredients except the soda and stir. Pour into a punch bowl over a block of ice. Add soda and mint and stir gently.

Summertime Slushy

Serves 20

1 bottle (750-milliliter) vanilla vodka (or any other flavor you want)

1 bottle (750-milliliter) coconut rum

1 gallon orange juice

1 gallon pineapple juice

2 (2-liter) bottles citrus soda (such as Fresca)

Pour the vodka, rum, orange juice, and pineapple juice in a big bowl or pot and stir. Set in the freezer for at least 24 hours or until frozen. When frozen, serve by placing 2 scoops in each tall glass and filling with the citrus soda.

September–December

These recipes cover seasons and holidays found in September, October, November, and December.

Autumn in New York

Serves 1

1 ounce applejack brandy

1/2 ounce Tuaca

Hot apple cider to fill

Whipped cream, for garnish

Pour the applejack brandy and Tuaca into a mug and fill with hot apple cider. Top with whipped cream.

Devil's Blood (Halloween)

Serves 1

3/4 glass cranberry juice

2 ounces Blavod black vodka

Pack a tall glass with ice, then pour the cranberry juice three-quarters to the top. Slowly pour the black vodka on top.

Bloody Punch Bowl Hand

Make a bloody hand to float around in a Halloween punch from cranberry juice and a latex glove. Fill the glove with the juice, tie, freeze, then rip the glove off. Some gloves have talcum powder inside—make sure you rinse it out first.

The Grinch's Sour Caramel Apple Pie

Serves 1

Raw sugar and crushed graham crackers, for rimming

1 ounce cream

1 ounce green apple vodka or rum

1 ounce sour apple schnapps

1 ounce butterscotch schnapps

Cinnamon, for sprinkling

In a saucer, mix raw sugar and graham crackers; wet the rim of a martini glass with cream and dip it into the sugared crumbs. Shake the liquid ingredients with ice and strain into a martini glass. Sprinkle with cinnamon.

Holly Berry

Serves 1

1 1/2 ounces raspberry vodka

1/2 ounce triple sec

1/4 ounce Rose's lime juice

3 ounces cranberry juice

Washed holly sprig without berries (optional)

Pour the liquid ingredients into a shaker tin of ice, shake, then strain into a martini glass. Garnish with the washed holly sprig without the berries for a festive touch. (Don't eat the berries—they are toxic. Use a plastic replica if you wish.)

Pumpkin Pie

Serves 1

Raw sugar and nutmeg, for rimming

1 ounce cream

2 ounces vanilla vodka

1 ounce pumpkin schnapps

In a saucer, mix a little raw sugar (the brown kind) and nutmeg; then wet the rim of a martini glass with cream and dip the glass into the sugar and spice. Shake the rest of the ingredients, including the cream, with ice and strain into a martini glass.

Thanksgiving Turkey Cosmo

Serves 1

1½ ounces Wild Turkey bourbon

½ ounce triple sec

¼ ounce lime juice

2 ounces cranberry juice

Shake all ingredients with ice and strain into a martini glass.

Ice Punch Bowl

To make a bowl out of ice you need a very large plastic bowl, a medium-sized plastic bowl, a reach-in freezer, some weights (such as canned food, exercise weights, bags of frozen veggies), and water. Place the large bowl in the bottom of the freezer and fill halfway with water, then place the medium-size bowl in the water and the weights in the medium bowl. Let it freeze for at least 2 days. Take it out when you need it and let it thaw naturally until the bowls pop off. (Running water on it weakens it.) Set the ice bowl on top of a platter that has a couple of folded towels under linen to absorb the melting ice. It really doesn't melt as fast as you'd think. Decorate all around the bowl.

Wassail
(historic holiday punch)

Serves 12

1 cup filtered water
¼ teaspoon nutmeg
¼ teaspoon cardamom
¼ teaspoon powdered ginger
2 cloves
2 cinnamon sticks
2 bottles medium dry sherry
1 cup raw sugar
3 organic egg yolks
6 organic egg whites
½ cup brandy
4 baked apples, sliced

Put the water and spices in a saucepan and simmer for 10 minutes. Add the sherry and sugar; heat, but do not boil. Remove from heat. Lightly beat egg yolks and whites separately (they should just be frothy). Pour a cup of the spiced sherry mix into a punch bowl and stir in the egg yolks, then add the brandy. Beat in the egg whites with a whisk until foamy. Float apples.

You Don't Know Jack-O-Lantern Punch

Serves 15

1 whole pumpkin
1 round glass bowl (such as a goldfish bowl) to fit inside the hollowed pumpkin
½ bottle (750-milliliter) chilled Jack Daniel's
¼ bottle (750-milliliter) chilled triple sec
Equal parts of chilled lemonade and Sprite to fill
Glow sticks

Hollow out a large pumpkin and carve out a face. Insert a round, clear bowl inside and place in the freezer overnight. When ready to serve, pour the Jack Daniel's, triple sec, lemonade, and Sprite into the bowl and stir. Add the glow sticks and place in a dark area for the best effect.

CHAPTER

14

starting from scratch: homemade recipes

Running a lemonade stand probably taught you the basics of making a homemade mix. All you needed was the right proportions of lemon juice, sugar, and water—and *voilà*! Making your own syrups, mixes, infusions, and liqueurs is fun and can let you create wonderful personalized gifts as well. Why not create a theme basket around your choice? This is truly a gift that can't be bought.

Homemade Supplies

You'll discover that in order to make these homemade recipes you'll need a few things you don't normally have in the drawers and cabinets in your kitchen. The recipes included in this chapter may ask for filters. Sieves, mesh, cheesecloth, paper towels, and coffee filters will all work. You will also need wide-mouthed jars with tight, secure lids (such as canning jars), bottles (plain or decorative), gallon containers, saucepans, measuring spoons and cups, plastic bags, a funnel, and corks.

Oxygen might be crucial for you to live, but it will kill your creations. It's very important that all containers have tight, secure lids. Once your creations are made, continue to keep the air out by making sure you have a tight seal on your bottle. Lots of people like to use corks. You can buy them at hobby stores and sites online. Also, make sure everything is scrubbed, sanitized, and squeaky clean before starting—especially your hands!

Homemade Syrups

When you mix a spoonful of sugar in iced tea, the sugar granules sink to the bottom of the glass. This is the reason why syrups mix better in cocktails. Fresh syrups are easy to make at home, so there is no need to buy bottles at the store that are filled with additives and preservatives. Once you learn how to make basic simple syrup from sugar, Splenda, honey, agave, or maple syrup, then you can let your imagination run wild with a variety of added flavors from fruit, vegetables, and herbs.

Basic Simple Syrups

Agave Syrup

1 cup water

1 cup agave

Bring water to a boil. Stir in the agave until dissolved, then remove from heat and allow to cool for 1 hour. Strain into a sterilized container or bottle.

Honey Syrup

1 cup water

1 cup Grade A honey

Bring water to a boil. Stir in the honey until dissolved, then remove from heat and allow to cool for 1 hour. Strain into a sterilized container or bottle.

Maple Syrup

1 cup water

1 cup Grade B maple syrup

Bring water to a boil. Stir in the maple syrup until dissolved, then remove from heat and allow to cool for 1 hour. Strain into a sterilized container or bottle.

Simple Sugar Syrup

1 cup water

1 cup sugar (raw, brown, or white)

Bring water to a boil. Stir in the sugar until dissolved, then remove from heat and allow to cool for 1 hour. Strain into a sterilized container or bottle.

Simple Syrup (sugar-free)

1 cup water

1 cup Splenda

Pour the water and Splenda into a sterilized container with a lid and shake until dissolved. Strain into a sterilized container or bottle.

The Law

In case you were wondering, you are not allowed to distill your own alcohol without a license. None of the recipes in this book teaches you to distill alcohol, and you are allowed to make as much homemade wine, liqueur, or beer as you wish. You just cannot sell it. But you can share it, so go ahead and get started!

The Simplicity of Syrup

To make flavored syrup, combine flavored water from fruit, vegetables, and herbs with the sweetener of your choice.

Flavored Syrups

Ginger Agave Syrup

1/2 cup fresh ginger, sliced
1 cup water
1 cup agave

Bring the ginger and water to a boil, then strain. Pour the water back into the pot and stir in the agave until dissolved. Remove from heat and allow to cool for 1 hour. Strain into a sterilized container or bottle.

Ginger Maple Syrup

1/2 cup fresh ginger, sliced
1 cup water
1 cup maple syrup

Bring the ginger and water to a boil, then strain. Pour the water back into the pot and stir in the maple syrup until dissolved. Remove from heat and allow to cool for 1 hour. Strain into a sterilized container or bottle.

Ginger Syrup

1/2 cup fresh ginger, sliced
1 cup water
1 cup sugar

Bring the ginger and water to a boil, then strain. Pour the water back into the pot and stir in the sugar until dissolved. Remove from heat and allow to cool for 1 hour. Strain into a sterilized container or bottle.

Ginger Syrup (sugar-free)

1/2 cup fresh ginger, sliced
1 cup water
1 cup Splenda

Bring the ginger and water to a boil, then strain. Pour the water back into the pot and stir in the Splenda until dissolved. Remove from heat and allow to cool for 1 hour. Strain into a sterilized container or bottle.

Grenadine

1 cup pomegranate juice
1 cup sugar

Bring juice to a simmer and add the sugar. Stir until dissolved, then remove from heat and allow to cool. Pour into a sterilized bottle or container.

Mint Agave Syrup

1/2 cup fresh mint leaves
1 cup water
1 cup agave

Bring the mint and water to a boil, then strain. Pour the water back into the pot and stir in the agave until dissolved. Remove from heat and allow to cool for 1 hour. Strain into a sterilized container or bottle.

Herb Syrups

Use the basics of making fresh mint syrup to substitute a fresh herb of your choice. Try basil, thyme, jasmine, lemongrass, lavender, parsley, cilantro, rosemary, sage, etc.

Mint Honey Syrup

½ cup fresh mint leaves

1 cup water

1 cup Grade A honey

Bring the mint and water to a boil, then strain. Pour the water back into the pot and stir in the honey until dissolved. Remove from heat and allow to cool for 1 hour. Strain into a sterilized container or bottle.

Mint Maple Syrup

½ cup fresh mint leaves

1 cup water

1 cup Grade B maple syrup

Bring the mint and water to a boil, then strain. Pour the water back into the pot and stir in the maple syrup until dissolved. Remove from heat and allow to cool for 1 hour. Strain into a sterilized container or bottle.

Mint Syrup

½ cup fresh mint leaves

1 cup water

1 cup sugar (raw, brown, or white)

Bring the mint and water to a boil, then strain. Pour the water back into the pot and stir in the sugar until dissolved. Remove from heat and allow to cool for 1 hour. Strain into a sterilized container or bottle.

Mint Syrup (sugar-free)

½ cup fresh mint leaves

1 cup water

1 cup Splenda

Bring the mint and water to a boil, then strain. Pour the water back into the pot and stir in the Splenda until dissolved. Remove from heat and allow to cool for 1 hour. Strain into a sterilized container or bottle.

Orgeat Syrup (simple method)

1 cup room temperature, unsweetened almond milk

½ cup sugar

6 drops almond extract

4 drops orange flower water

Pour all ingredients into a jar with a lid, then shake until sugar is dissolved. Strain into a sterilized container or bottle.

Raspberry Agave Syrup

1 pound fresh raspberries

2 cups water

1 cup agave

Bring the raspberries and water to a boil in a medium pot. Cook over medium heat for 20 minutes. Strain with a cheesecloth into another pot by squeezing out as much juice as you can, then discard the cheesecloth and raspberry pulp. Bring your strained juice to a boil, add agave, and stir until dissolved. Simmer for 5 minutes; remove from heat and allow to cool for 1 hour. Strain into a sterilized container or bottle.

Raspberry Honey Syrup

1 pound fresh raspberries

2 cups water

1 cup Grade A honey

Bring the raspberries and water to a boil in a medium pot. Cook over medium heat for 20 minutes. Strain with a cheesecloth into another pot by squeezing out as much juice as you can, then discard the cheesecloth and raspberry pulp. Bring your strained juice to a boil, add honey, and stir until dissolved. Simmer for 5 minutes; remove from heat and allow to cool for 1 hour. Strain into a sterilized container or bottle.

Fruit Syrups

Use the basics of making raspberry syrup to substitute a berry of your choice. Try blueberries, blackberries, huckleberries, or strawberries.

Raspberry Maple Syrup

1 pound fresh raspberries

2 cups water

1 cup maple syrup

Bring the raspberries and water to a boil in a medium pot. Cook over medium heat for 20 minutes. Strain with a cheesecloth into another pot by squeezing out as much juice as you can, then discard the cheesecloth and raspberry pulp. Bring your strained juice to a boil, add maple syrup, and stir until dissolved. Simmer for 5 minutes; remove from heat and allow to cool for 1 hour. Strain into a sterilized container or bottle.

Raspberry Syrup

1 pound fresh raspberries

2 cups water

1 cup sugar

Bring the raspberries and water to a boil in a medium pot. Cook over medium heat for 20 minutes. Strain with a cheesecloth into another pot by squeezing out as much juice as you can, then discard the cheesecloth and raspberry pulp. Bring your strained juice to a boil, add sugar, and stir until dissolved. Simmer for 5 minutes; remove from heat and allow to cool for 1 hour. Strain into a sterilized container or bottle.

Raspberry Syrup (sugar-free)

1 pound fresh raspberries

2 cups water

1 cup Splenda

Bring the raspberries and water to a boil in a medium pot. Cook over medium heat for 20 minutes. Strain with a cheesecloth into another pot by squeezing out as much juice as you can, then discard the cheesecloth and raspberry pulp. Bring your strained juice to a boil, add Splenda, and stir until dissolved. Simmer for 5 minutes; remove from heat and allow to cool for 1 hour. Strain into a sterilized container or bottle.

Strawberry-Mint Agave Syrup

1 pound fresh strawberries

1 cup mint leaves

3 cups water

1 cup agave

Bring the strawberries, mint, and water to a boil in a medium pot. Cook over medium heat for 20 minutes. Strain with a cheesecloth into another pot by squeezing out as much juice as you can, then discard the cheesecloth and strawberry pulp. Bring your strained juice to a boil, add agave, and stir until dissolved. Simmer for 5 minutes; remove from heat and allow to cool for 1 hour. Strain into a sterilized container or bottle.

Strawberry-Mint Honey Syrup

1 pound fresh strawberries

1 cup mint leaves

3 cups water

1 cup Grade A honey

Bring the strawberries, mint, and water to a boil in a medium pot. Cook over medium heat for 20 minutes. Strain with a cheesecloth into another pot by squeezing out as much juice as you can, then discard the cheesecloth and strawberry pulp. Bring your strained juice to a boil, add honey, and stir until dissolved. Simmer for 5 minutes; remove from heat and allow to cool for an hour. Strain into a sterilized container or bottle.

Combination Syrups
Use the basics of making strawberry-mint syrup to substitute a combination syrup of your choice. Try peach-ginger, raspberry-vanilla, strawberry-peppercorn, apple-cinnamon, etc.

Strawberry-Mint Maple Syrup

1 pound fresh strawberries

1 cup mint leaves

3 cups water

1 cup maple syrup

Bring the strawberries, mint, and water to a boil in a medium pot. Cook over medium heat for 20 minutes. Strain with a cheesecloth into another pot by squeezing out as much juice as you can, then discard the cheesecloth and strawberry pulp. Bring your strained juice to a boil, add maple syrup, and stir until dissolved. Simmer for 5 minutes; remove from heat and allow to cool for an hour. Strain into a sterilized container or bottle.

Strawberry-Mint Syrup

1 pound fresh strawberries

1 cup mint leaves

3 cups water

1 cup sugar

Bring the strawberries, mint, and water to a boil in a medium pot. Cook over medium heat for 20 minutes. Strain with a cheesecloth into another pot by squeezing out as much juice as you can, then discard the cheesecloth and strawberry pulp. Bring your strained juice to a boil, add sugar, and stir until dissolved. Simmer for 5 minutes; remove from heat and allow to cool for 1 hour. Strain into a sterilized container or bottle.

Strawberry-Mint Syrup (sugar-free)

1 pound fresh strawberries

1 cup mint leaves

3 cups water

1 cup Splenda

Bring the strawberries, mint, and water to a boil in a medium pot. Cook over medium heat for 20 minutes. Strain with a cheesecloth into another pot by squeezing out as much juice as you can, then discard the cheesecloth and strawberry pulp. Bring your strained juice to a boil, add Splenda, and stir until dissolved. Strain into a sterilized container or bottle.

Sweet Potato Syrup

1 cup sweet potato juice

1 cup sugar (raw, brown, or white)

Juice the sweet potatoes in a centrifugal juicer and allow to stand for 1 hour so the starch settles to the bottom. Fine-strain the juice three times, and then add to a medium pot and heat over medium heat. (Add a few whole cloves and a cinnamon stick if desired.) Stir in the sugar until dissolved. Remove from heat, fine-strain, and allow to cool for an hour. Strain into a sterilized container or bottle.

Tea Syrup

1 bag of tea (flavor of your choice)

1 cup water

1 cup sugar

Bring the tea bag and water to a boil in a medium pot, and then remove the tea bag. Stir in the sugar until dissolved. Remove from heat and allow to cool for an hour. Strain into a sterilized container or bottle.

Spice Syrups

Use the basics of making vanilla syrup to substitute a spice of your choice. Try anise, cinnamon sticks, fresh grated nutmeg, whole cloves, peppercorns, chilies, etc.

Vanilla Agave Syrup

3 vanilla beans, diced

1 cup water

1 cup agave

Bring the vanilla beans and water to a boil in a medium pot, then strain. Pour the water back into the pot and stir in the agave until dissolved. Remove from heat and allow to cool for an hour. Strain into a sterilized container or bottle.

Vanilla Honey Syrup

3 vanilla beans, diced

1 cup water

1 cup Grade A honey

Bring the vanilla beans and water to a boil in a medium pot, then strain. Pour the water back into the pot and stir in the honey until dissolved. Remove from heat and allow to cool for an hour. Strain into a sterilized container or bottle.

Vanilla Maple Syrup

3 vanilla beans, diced

1 cup water

1 cup Grade B maple syrup

Bring the vanilla beans and water to a boil in a medium pot, then strain. Pour the water back into the pot and stir in the maple syrup until dissolved. Remove from heat and allow to cool for an hour. Strain into a sterilized container or bottle.

Vanilla Syrup

3 vanilla beans, diced

1 cup water

1 cup sugar (raw, brown, or white)

Bring the vanilla beans and water to a boil in a medium pot, and then strain. Pour the water back into the pot and stir in the sugar until dissolved. Remove from heat and allow to cool for an hour. Strain into a sterilized container or bottle.

Vanilla Syrup (sugar-free)

3 vanilla beans, diced

1 cup water

1 cup Splenda

Bring the vanilla beans and water to a boil in a medium pot, and then strain. Pour the water back into the pot and stir in the Splenda until dissolved. Remove from heat and allow to cool for an hour. Strain into a sterilized container or bottle.

Homemade Mixes

Fresh is always best. Once you taste a fresh cocktail made with fresh mix, then you will never want to make another cocktail with artificial flavors and preservatives again. Sadly, generations born after 1960 have grown accustomed to inferior mixes that sit on store shelves. It's time to get back to freshness the way your grandmothers and great-grandmothers made everything decades ago.

Basic Bar Punch

Makes 1 gallon

3 cups fresh squeezed orange juice

1 cup homemade grenadine

3 cups sweet-and-sour mix

3 cups pineapple juice

Water to fill

Pour all ingredients except the water into a gallon container. Fill the rest of the way with water, leaving enough room at the top for agitation. Mix.

Bloody Mary Mix

Makes 1 gallon

4 ounces lemon juice

8 ounces Lea & Perrins Worcestershire sauce

8 ounces A.1. sauce

4 ounce raw horseradish (optional)

1 heaping tablespoon celery seed

1 heaping tablespoon black peppercorns

2 (46-ounce) cans whole plum tomatoes

Water as needed

Tabasco sauce (optional)

Add the lemon juice, Worcestershire sauce, A.1. sauce, and horseradish into a large container. Pour the celery seed and peppercorns in a blender and blend on high for 30 seconds, and then dump into the large container. Fill the blender halfway with the whole plum tomatoes and then add water to fill. Blend on high for 10 seconds. Fine-strain into the container. Continue this step until all the tomatoes have been blended and strained. Mix all ingredients, pour into sterilized jars or bottles, and refrigerate. You can add many types of ingredients to a basic Bloody Mary mix that you desire: beef bouillon cube, wasabi, garlic, avocado, chili powder, or bitters.

Cran-Apple Juice
Makes 1 (750-milliliter) bottle

4 cups fresh cranberries

1 cup apple juice

Water to taste

Process the cranberries in a juicer. Mix together the cranberry juice and apple juice. Add water, little by little, and taste-test along the way until it reaches the desired tart-and-sweet balance. Refrigerate.

Cranberry Juice
Makes 1 (750-milliliter) bottle

4 cups fresh cranberries

1 cup sugar

Water to taste

Process the cranberries in a juicer, and then pour into a wide-mouthed container with a lid. Add the sugar and shake until dissolved. Add water, little by little, and taste-test along the way until it reaches the desired tart-and-sweet balance. Refrigerate.

Cranberry Juice (sugar-free)
Makes 1 (750-milliliter) bottle

4 cups fresh cranberries or frozen cranberries, thawed

1 cup Splenda

Water to taste

Process the cranberries in a juicer, and then pour into a wide-mouthed container with a lid. Add the Splenda and shake until dissolved. Add water, little by little, and taste-test along the way until it reaches the desired tart-and-sweet balance. Refrigerate.

The Cranberry
Cranberries are one of the three fruits that are native to North America. The other two are Concord grapes and blueberries.

Eggnog

Makes 1 (750-milliliter) bottle

6 organic eggs

¼ cup sugar

¼ teaspoon salt

1 quart milk

1 teaspoon pure vanilla extract

¼ teaspoon fresh ground nutmeg

¼ teaspoon fresh ground cinnamon

Beat eggs, sugar, and salt in a medium saucepan. Stir in 2 cups of the milk over low heat. Cook until thick, stirring constantly. The mixture will thinly coat a wooden spoon. Remove from heat and mix in the remaining milk and the vanilla extract. Cover and chill overnight. Stir in the nutmeg and cinnamon.

Ginger Beer

Makes 4 cups

1 large piece of gingerroot, peeled

6 ounces simple syrup

4 ounces lemon juice, strained

20 ounces water

⅛ teaspoon yeast

Juice the gingerroot until you get 2 ounces, and then add to a large bowl. Add the rest of the ingredients and stir. Funnel into a sterilized jar or bottle and allow to sit in the refrigerator for 2 days.

Hot Buttered Rum Mix

Makes 25 servings

3 cups brown sugar

½ cup butter

2 tablespoons honey

1 tablespoon rum extract

1 tablespoon vanilla extract

½ teaspoon ground nutmeg

1 teaspoon ground cinnamon

½ teaspoon ground allspice

Combine all ingredients and beat with a mixer until smooth. Put in jar with a tight lid. Store in the refrigerator.

Hot Buttered Rum Ice Cube

You can fill sections of an ice cube tray halfway with the hot buttered rum mixture. Just pop a cube out when needed. To make a hot buttered rum drink, simply pour 1½ ounces of light or dark rum in a coffee mug, add one frozen cube, and fill with hot water.

Instant Cappuccino Mocha Mix

Makes 25 servings

6 tablespoons plus 2 teaspoons instant espresso coffee powder

3 heaping tablespoons unsweetened cocoa

1¼ cups powdered nondairy creamer

½ cup sugar

2 teaspoons ground cinnamon

Mix all ingredients in a bowl or plastic bag. Store tightly covered until needed. Make a cup by using 4 tablespoons in 1 cup of hot water.

Margarita Mix

Makes 6 cups

2 cups fresh lime juice

2 cups simple syrup

2 cups water

Shake all ingredients together in a large lidded container, adjusting the amount of simple syrup and water according to your personal preference; refrigerate. Some people like this mix sweeter and others like it sourer. Keep taste-testing until you find your preference. This will only last 2 days.

Margarita Mix (sugar-free)

Makes 5 cups

2 cups fresh lime juice

2 cups sugar-free simple syrup

1 cup water

Shake all ingredients together in a large lidded container, adjusting the amount of simple syrup and water according to your personal preference; refrigerate. Some people like this mix sweeter and others like it sourer. Keep taste-testing until you find your preference. This will only last 2 days.

Orange Blossom Water

2 cups rinsed orange blossoms

3 cups filtered water

1 ounce vodka

Pour water and blossoms into a medium pot and bring to a boil. Simmer with a lid for 30 minutes. Cool, then strain into a sterilized container or bottle. Add vodka for preservation.

Piña Colada Mix

Makes 10 cups

1 (46-ounce) can pineapple juice (or homemade pineapple juice)

2 (15-ounce) cans Coco Lopez coconut cream

6 drops vanilla extract

Blend the pineapple juice, coconut cream, and vanilla extract in a blender for five seconds, then refrigerate.

Pineapple Juice

Makes 10 ounces

1 ripe pineapple

2 tablespoons sugar

Dice the pineapple meat and place into a blender with the sugar. Blend for 10 seconds, and then fine-strain and refrigerate.

Rose Water

Makes 3 cups

3 cups filtered water

2 cups rinsed rose petals

1 ounce vodka

Pour water and petals into a medium pot and bring to a boil. Simmer, covered, for 30 minutes. Cool, then strain into a sterilized container or bottle. Add vodka for preservation.

Spiced Cider (simple)

Makes 1 gallon

1 gallon unfiltered apple cider

1 teaspoon allspice

1/2 teaspoon ground cinnamon

1/2 teaspoon ground cloves

1 cinnamon stick

Pour all ingredients into a medium pot and simmer for 1 hour. You can also put everything into a slow cooker and set on warm. Serve warm.

Strawberry Daiquiri Mix

Makes 5 cups

2 cups unsweetened frozen strawberries, thawed

1/2 cup fresh lime juice

1 cup simple syrup

Blend the thawed strawberries, lime juice, and simple syrup in a blender. Adjust the amount of simple syrup and strawberries according to your personal preference. Refrigerate.

Strawberry Daiquiri Mix (sugar-free)

Makes 4 cups

2 cups frozen strawberries, thawed

1/2 cup fresh lime juice

1 cup sugar-free simple syrup

Blend the thawed strawberries, lime juice, and sugar-free simple syrup in a blender. Adjust the amount of simple syrup and strawberries according to your personal preference. Refrigerate.

Sweet-and-Sour Mix (often called Sour Mix)

Makes 6 cups

2 cups fresh lemon juice
1/2 cup fresh lime juice
2 cups simple syrup
4 organic egg whites
1 cup water

Shake all ingredients together in a large lidded container, adjusting the amount of simple syrup according to your personal preference, then refrigerate (it will keep for less than a day). Some people like this mix sweeter and others sourer. Keep taste-testing until you find your preference.

Sweet-and-Sour Mix (sugar-free)

Makes 5 cups

2 cups fresh lemon juice
1/2 cup fresh lime juice
2 cups sugar-free simple syrup
4 organic egg whites
1 cup water

Shake all ingredients together in a large lidded container, adjusting the amount of simple syrup according to your personal preference, then refrigerate. Some people like this mix sweeter and others sourer. Keep taste-testing until you find your preference.

Homemade Infusions

Commercial infusions and flavored spirits can often have a sweet chemical taste and smell. Making your own infusions is easy, because alcohol does a great job of extracting flavors from fruit, vegetables, spices, herbs, and fats. Give it a try!

Basic Infusion Recipe

Washed fruit, vegetable, spice, or herb of your choice
Vodka, gin, rum, tequila, brandy, or whiskey

Place your chosen fruit, vegetable, spice, or herb in a sterilized container. Add the alcohol and close the lid tightly. Remove from direct sunlight and let sit from 1 day to 2 weeks. Shake once a day. Strain and bottle when finished.

Start with Small Batches

There's no need to use full bottles of alcohol for infusing. Simply invest in some small canning jars or recycle mayonnaise and other jars. Make small batches with a cup or half bottle of spirit before investing in a large batch.

Infusing Times

Fruits, vegetables, spices, and herbs each have different infusing times because each has a different density and intensity of flavor. Some take a day and others take weeks. Here is a good time guideline to follow:

1–3 days: Whole herbs, cracked spices, split vanilla beans, chopped hot peppers, dried fruit, and cracked coffee beans.

3–6 days: Whole berries, sliced stone fruits, sliced melons, sliced sweet peppers, and citrus zest/peels.

5–7 days: Chopped apples, chopped pears, sliced cucumbers, chopped mango, and chopped vegetables.

7–14 days: Skinned and sliced pineapple, peeled and diced ginger, and whole peppers.

Certain flavors infuse better with particular spirits, the same way certain food flavors mix together well. Here are some guidelines for matching your infusions with spirits.

Vodka: Since vodka is basically a neutral grain spirit, it infuses well with any fruit, vegetable, spice, or herb of your choice.

Gin: cucumber, apple, pear, citrus, lavender, fennel, basil, tea, berries, rosemary, lemongrass, rhubarb, and star anise.

Light Rum: Light rum adapts to infusions much like vodka, so many flavors can be infused with light rum. Try pineapple, mango, papaya, lychee, dried coconut, and dates.

Dark Rum: vanilla bean, cinnamon sticks, citrus, prunes, coffee beans, and chili peppers.

Tequila: ginger, pineapple, citrus, hot peppers, mango, pomegranate seeds, berries, dried coconut, watermelon, and mint.

Whiskey: apples, cherries, figs, walnuts, cinnamon sticks, peaches, plums, mint, vanilla bean, orange zest, and ginger.

Fat-Washing Infusions

Fat-washing infusions uses fatty foods such as bacon grease, butter, and even nut butters. The process is much like other infusions with an added step of freezing your infusion until the fat rises to the top for removal.

Basic Fat-Washing Infusion Recipe

Fatty food of your choice

Vodka, gin, rum, tequila, brandy, or whiskey

Place your chosen fat in a sterilized container. Add the alcohol and close the lid tightly. Remove from direct sunlight and let sit for 1 to 2 days. Shake once a day. Place in the freezer until the fat rises to the top. Remove the solid fat and then strain through a fine strainer or cheesecloth to filter out any remnants. Bottle when finished.

> **Bacon-Infused Bourbon**
> The first known fat-washed cocktail was a bacon-infused Old-Fashioned created by Don Lee at New York's speakeasy bar, PDT (Please Don't Tell).

Fats for Infusing

Basic fats for infusing include bacon grease, unsalted butter, peanut butter, cashew butter, almond butter, macadamia butter, pistachio butter, walnut butter, coconut oil, sesame oil, truffle oil, avocado, and plantains.

Creative fats that craft bars have experimented with are jalapeño poppers, grilled cheese sandwiches, sausages, burgers, duck fat, pizza, potato chips, PB&J sandwiches, and lasagna. Here are some flavor guidelines for matching your fat-washed infusions with spirits.

- **Vodka:** Any fat of your choice.
- **Gin:** Sesame seed oil.
- **Light Rum:** Coconut oil, nut butters, unsalted butter, and plantains.
- **Dark Rum:** Same as light rum.
- **Tequila:** Plantains, coconut oil, truffle oil, and avocado.
- **Whiskey:** Meat grease, nut butters, and plantains.

Homemade Bitters

Bitters has been used for medicinal purposes for centuries, such as to aid digestive health. Historical cocktail books show that bitters also served as an essential ingredient in cocktails. A couple of dashes in a cocktail adds a bright burst of complex flavor. Bitters is made with barks, roots, herbs, seeds, fruits, spices, and vegetables, and then preserved with high-proof alcohol.

Basic Bitters

Makes 16 ounces

1 cup dried bitter orange peel
Pinch cardamom
Pinch caraway or anise
Pinch coriander seeds
2 cups grain alcohol

Combine all the ingredients into a sterilized jar with a lid and allow to sit in a cool, dark place for 20 days, agitating it every day. Strain through a coffee filter into another jar, and then transfer to dropper bottles or bitters bottles.

Creative Bitters

Get creative making your own bitters! You can use coriander, anise, allspice, thistle seed, wormwood, various barks and leaves and blossoms, cardamom, celery seed, and any fruit or vegetable desired. The combinations are unlimited.

Bourbon Bitters

Makes 16 ounces

¼ cup roasted pecans

¼ cup roasted walnuts

1 cinnamon stick

2 whole cloves

1 vanilla bean, split

1 tablespoon cinchona bark

1 tablespoon wild cherry bark

1 tablespoon gentian root

2 cups high-proof bourbon

2 tablespoons maple syrup

Combine all the ingredients, except maple syrup, into a sterilized jar with a lid and allow to sit in a cool, dark place for 20 days, agitating it every day. Strain through a coffee filter into another jar. Add the maple syrup, stir, and then transfer to dropper bottles or bitters bottles.

Cocoa Bitters

Makes 16 ounces

½ cup cracked cocoa nibs

¼ cup orange peels

1 tablespoon wild cherry bark

½ cinnamon stick

2 cups high-proof rum

Combine all the ingredients into a sterilized jar with a lid and allow to sit in a cool, dark place for 20 days, agitating it every day. Strain through a coffee filter into another jar, and then transfer to dropper bottles or bitters bottles.

Coffee Bitters

Makes 16 ounces

½ cup cracked coffee beans

¼ cup orange peels

¼ cup cracked cacao nibs

½ cinnamon stick

2 cups grain alcohol

Combine all the ingredients into a sterilized jar with a lid and allow to sit in a cool, dark place for 20 days, agitating it every day. Strain through a coffee filter into another jar, and then transfer to dropper bottles or bitters bottles.

Green Apple Bitters

Makes 16 ounces

2 green apples, chopped

Pinch cinchona bark

1 clove

Pinch cassia chips

Zest of 1 lemon

2 tablespoons simple syrup

2 cups grain alcohol

Combine all the ingredients except the simple syrup into a sterilized jar with a lid and allow to sit in a cool, dark place for 20 days, agitating it every day. Strain through a coffee filter into another jar. Add the simple syrup, stir, and then transfer to dropper bottles or bitters bottles.

Lavender Bitters

Makes 16 ounces

1 cup dried lavender

½ cup orange peels

1 vanilla pod, split

2 cups grain alcohol

Combine all the ingredients into a sterilized jar with a lid and allow to sit in a cool, dark place for 20 days, agitating it every day. Strain through a coffee filter into another jar, and then transfer to dropper bottles or bitters bottles.

Orange Bitters

Makes 16 ounces

1 cup orange peels

1 teaspoon fennel seed

2 cardamom pods

Pinch coriander seeds

10 drops gentian extract

2 cups grain alcohol

Combine all the ingredients into a sterilized jar with a lid and allow to sit in a cool, dark place for 20 days, agitating it every day. Strain through a coffee filter into another jar, and then transfer to dropper bottles or bitters bottles.

Pear Bitters

Makes 16 ounces

2 pears, chopped

Pinch cinchona bark

1 clove

1 vanilla bean, split

Zest from 1 lemon

1 peppercorn

2 cups grain alcohol

2 tablespoons simple syrup

Combine all the ingredients except simple syrup into a sterilized jar with a lid and allow to sit in a cool, dark place for 20 days, agitating it every day. Strain through a coffee filter into another jar. Add the simple syrup, stir, and then transfer to dropper bottles or bitters bottles.

Homemade Barrel-Aged Spirits and Cocktails

In the 1600s, barrels were used to store wine because it caused less breakage than storing it in clay or glass containers. It also made transportation of the wine easier. In the 1700s, the insides of barrels were torched to create a layer of charcoal, and were then used to age whiskey. In 2010, the first people to entertain the idea of aging cocktails in charred white oak barrels were Tony Conigliaro and Jeffrey Morgenthaler, mixologists from London and Portland, Oregon, respectively. Today, it's common for craft cocktail bars to have barrel-aged cocktails listed on their menus.

You can barrel-age your own spirits and cocktails by buying a barrel and experimenting in the comfort of your own home. Barrel aging adds a deeper and softer flavor to spirits and cocktails. Depending on the size of your barrel, the average aging time is six weeks, but you need to taste-test throughout the aging period to determine when you should empty the barrel into a sterilized bottle. The goal is to avoid a woody cocktail taste.

The preparation steps before using your barrel are easy: Rinse out the barrel with water and let it soak in water (wood swells). Fill the barrel with water to check for any leaks and then pour out the water. Allow the barrel to dry. You are now ready to funnel in your chosen cocktail or spirit.

The following recipes are for filling a 1-liter barrel. You'll need to adjust and do the math to fill larger barrels.

Barrel-Aged B and B

16 ounces brandy

16 ounces Bénédictine

Funnel the ingredients into the barrel for aging. Roll the barrel once a day. Bottle contents before your ingredients begin to taste woody.

Barrel-Aged Bijou

11 ounces gin

11 ounces green Chartreuse

11 ounces sweet vermouth

11 dash orange bitters

Funnel the ingredients into the barrel for aging. Roll the barrel once a day. Bottle contents before your ingredients begin to taste woody.

Barrel-Aged Black Russian

21 ounces vodka

11 ounces coffee liqueur

Funnel the ingredients into the barrel for aging. Roll the barrel once a day. Bottle contents before your ingredients begin to taste woody.

Barrel-Aged Chrysanthemum

20 ounces dry vermouth

10 ounces Bénédictine

2 ounces absinthe

Funnel the ingredients into the barrel for aging. Roll the barrel once a day. Bottle contents before your ingredients begin to taste woody.

Tip

When barrel-aging a cocktail, only use alcohol-based ingredients in the barrel. Mixers such as lemon, lime, grapefruit, or orange juice, etc. should not be used because they will spoil.

Barrel-Aged El Presidente

20 ounces rum

5 ounces orange curaçao

5 ounces dry vermouth

1 ounce grenadine

Funnel the ingredients into the barrel for aging. Roll the barrel once a day. Bottle contents before your ingredients begin to taste woody.

Barrel-Aged Godfather

16 ounces amaretto

16 ounces Scotch

Funnel the ingredients into the barrel for aging. Roll the barrel once a day. Bottle contents before your ingredients begin to taste woody.

Barrel-Aged Godmother

16 ounces amaretto

16 ounces vodka

Funnel the ingredients into the barrel for aging. Roll the barrel once a day. Bottle contents before your ingredients begin to taste woody.

Barrel-Aged Spirits and Alcohol

Previously used barrels have been used to age alcohol for many years. Some tequilas are aged in used Jack Daniel's barrels, some Scotches are aged in used sherry barrels, and some beers are aged in used wine barrels. While aging, some of the taste of what was aged before seeps into the new batch. So after aging your cocktail, why not try aging your own spirit to gain similar results.

Barrel-Aged Last Word

11 ounces gin
11 ounces Luxardo maraschino liqueur
11 ounces green Chartreuse

Funnel the ingredients into the barrel for aging. Roll the barrel once a day. Bottle contents before your ingredients begin to taste woody. When making your cocktail, you will use 3 ounces of the Barrel-Aged Last Word and 1 ounce fresh squeezed lime juice. Shake and strain into a chilled cocktail glass.

Barrel-Aged Manhattan

21 ounces rye whiskey
11 ounces sweet vermouth
10 dashes Angostura or Abbott's bitters

Funnel the ingredients into the barrel for aging. Roll the barrel once a day. Bottle contents before your ingredients begin to taste woody.

Barrel-Aged Martini

21 ounces gin
11 ounces dry vermouth

Funnel the ingredients into the barrel for aging. Roll the barrel once a day. Bottle contents before your ingredients begin to taste woody.

Barrel Resources

You can purchase 1- to 5-liter barrels at *http://redheadoak barrels.com* for $60 to $100. Red Head will even engrave the front of the barrel for you, so it makes a great gift! Their website gives you detailed instructions on barrel aging. They are also very helpful about answering questions via phone or e-mail.

Barrel-Aged Negroni

11 ounces gin

11 ounces Campari

11 ounces sweet vermouth

Funnel the ingredients into the barrel for aging. Roll the barrel once a day. Bottle contents before your ingredients begin to taste woody.

The Most Popular Cocktail to Barrel-Age

The Negroni wins for the most experimentation in barrel-aging. Many styles of gin from sweet to dry can be used, a lighter version of Campari called Aperol can be used, and there are many choices of vermouth.

Barrel-Aged Rob Roy

21 ounces Scotch

11 ounces sweet vermouth

10 dashes Angostura bitters

Funnel the ingredients into the barrel for aging. Roll the barrel once a day. Bottle contents before your ingredients begin to taste woody.

Barrel-Aged Rusty Nail

21 ounces Scotch

11 ounces Drambuie

Funnel the ingredients into the barrel for aging. Roll the barrel once a day. Bottle contents before your ingredients begin to taste woody.

Barrel-Aged Stinger

21 ounces cognac

11 ounces white crème de menthe

Funnel the ingredients into the barrel for aging. Roll the barrel once a day. Bottle contents before your ingredients begin to taste woody.

Barrel-Aged Vesper

20 ounces gin

8 ounces vodka

4 ounces Cocchi Americano

Funnel the ingredients into the barrel for aging. Roll the barrel once a day. Bottle contents before your ingredients begin to taste woody.

Homemade Liqueurs

There is something extra special about a delicious homemade gift. If you are giving your friends and loved ones some of your homemade liqueurs as gifts, try to make them extra special by hunting for special bottles at local thrift stores, antique stores, or the Internet; attaching a cocktail recipe to the bottle; or making a basket filled with needed glassware.

Amaretto

Makes 1 (750-milliliter) bottle

2 cups sugar

1 cup brown sugar

2 cups water

3 cups vodka

¼ cup almond extract

4 teaspoons vanilla extract

Heat sugars and water until boiling and sugars are dissolved. Remove from heat and allow to cool. Add vodka, almond extract, and vanilla extract. Pour into a bottle and seal.

Flexible Ice Pack

To make a flexible ice pack, add 1 cup vodka and 1 cup water in a freezer bag, then get as much of the air out as possible before sealing. Put bag into the freezer. The next time you need a slushy ice pack to soothe your face or any other body part, it'll be ready for you.

Coffee Liqueur

Makes 1 (750-milliliter) bottle

4 cups sugar

1 cup brown sugar

5 cups water

1 cup instant coffee granules

5 tablespoons vanilla extract

½ (750-millileter) bottle premium vodka

Heat the sugars and the water until mixture boils. Stir until all sugar is dissolved. Remove from heat. Let cool to room temperature. Mix the sugar water, instant coffee, vanilla extract, and vodka together. Bottle the mixture and let it sit undisturbed in a cool, dark place for at least 1 month.

Faux Absinthe
Makes 1 (750-milliliter) bottle
2 teaspoons dried wormwood
1 fifth premium vodka
4 crushed cardamom pods
2 teaspoons chopped angelica root
2 teaspoons crushed anise seed
1/2 teaspoon crushed fennel seed
1/2 teaspoon ground coriander
1 teaspoon marjoram
1 sugar cube per serving

Place wormwood in vodka for 2 days. Filter and add remaining spices and herbs. Let sit for 1 week. Filter and bottle. When serving, drop a sugar cube in the bottom of a cordial glass. The drink will taste faintly like licorice, which comes from the anise.

Faux Aquavit
Makes 1 (750-milliliter) bottle
1 fifth potato vodka
2 teaspoons caraway seeds
2 teaspoons dill seeds
2 star anise
2 teaspoons cumin seeds
1 teaspoon fennel seeds
1 teaspoon coriander seeds
1 whole clove
1 cinnamon stick

Pour the vodka into a jar and add the rest of the ingredients. Seal tightly and shake. Store in a cool, dark place for 2 to 3 weeks, shaking every 3 or 4 days. Strain and bottle. Place in the freezer.

Faux Drambuie
Makes 1 (750-milliliter) bottle
2/3 (750-milliliter) bottle premium blended Scotch whisky
1 teaspoon fresh chopped rosemary
1 cup honey

Pour the Scotch into a wide-mouth jar. Add the rosemary. Cover and let stand for 24 hours, then strain into another jar. Add honey and shake the mixture. Let age in a dark place for 2 to 3 weeks. Strain through a coffee filter and pour into a clean bottle.

Faux Galliano
Makes 1 (750-milliliter) bottle
3 cups filtered water
2 cups sugar
1 cup white Karo corn syrup
1 fifth 100 proof premium vodka
6 drops anise extract
3 drops banana extract
1 split vanilla pod
2 or 3 drops yellow food coloring

Boil water and sugar for 5 minutes to make a simple syrup. Remove from heat and let cool. Add Karo syrup, vodka, anise extract, and banana extract. Stir thoroughly, then pour into a wide-mouthed container and drop in the split vanilla pod. Let sit for 24 hours in a dark place. Strain into a sterilized fifth bottle and add food coloring.

Faux Pimm's No. 1

Makes 1 (750-milliliter) bottle

14 ounces premium gin

1 ounce Cointreau

7 ounces sweet vermouth

3 ounces sweet sherry or ruby port

1 clean 750-milliliter bottle

Pour all ingredients into a fifth bottle (750-milliliter). Cap or cork. Turn over once or twice and it's ready to serve.

Faux Tia Maria

Makes 1 (750-milliliter) bottle

4 cups sugar

1 cup brown sugar

5 cups water

1 cup instant coffee granules

5 tablespoons vanilla extract

½ bottle (750-milliliter) premium rum

Heat the sugars and the water in a medium pot until mixture boils. Stir until all sugar is dissolved. Remove from heat and let cool to room temperature. Mix the sugar water, instant coffee, vanilla extract, and rum together. Bottle the mixture and let it sit undisturbed in a cool, dark place for at least 1 month.

Irish Cream

Makes 1 (750-milliliter) bottle

¾ cup Irish whiskey

1 (14-ounce) can Eagle Brand sweetened condensed milk

1 cup whipping cream

4 eggs

2 tablespoons chocolate-flavored syrup

2 teaspoons instant coffee granules

1 teaspoon vanilla extract

Blend all ingredients until smooth. Store in a tightly covered container in the refrigerator. It can be served within 24 hours and will last for 1 month. Always stir before serving.

Limoncello

Makes 1 (750-milliliter) bottle

Zest from 7 organic lemons

1 (750-milliliter) bottle vodka

1 cup simple syrup

Wash the lemons well. Pour half of the vodka in a gallon glass jar and add zest. Cover and let sit at room temperature for 20 days. Add the simple syrup and remaining vodka and let sit for another 20 days. Strain and bottle, then place in the freezer.

Mead
Makes 4 (750-milliliter) bottles

1 gallon water
2½ pounds honey
Juice from 1 lemon
½ tablespoon nutmeg
1 package ale or champagne yeast

Boil the water and honey. Add the lemon juice and nutmeg. Skim the foam that rises to the surface. Remove from heat and cool to room temperature. Add the yeast. Cover and let sit at room temperature for 15–17 days—any longer and the yeast will make the mixture explosive. Bottle in glass containers with tight lids or corks and age for 2 weeks. Refrigerate.

Orangecello
Makes 1 (750-milliliter) bottle

Zest from 7 organic navel oranges (thick skinned)
1 (750-milliliter) bottle vodka
1 cup simple syrup

Wash the oranges well. Pour half of the vodka in a gallon glass jar and add the zest. Cover and let sit at room temperature for 20 days. Add the simple syrup and remaining vodka and let sit for another 20 days. Strain and bottle, then place in the freezer.

Peppermint Schnapps
Makes 1 (750-milliliter) bottle

⅔ cup granulated sugar
4 cups corn syrup
4 cups vodka
1½ tablespoons peppermint extract

Combine sugar and corn syrup in a saucepan over medium heat until sugar dissolves. Remove from heat. Allow mixture to cool. Add the vodka and peppermint extract. Pour in a bottle and seal. To make cinnamon, root beer, or any other flavored schnapps, simply use that flavored extract.

Raspberry Liqueur
Makes 2½ cups

1 pint fresh raspberries
2½ cups vodka
1 vanilla bean
¼ teaspoon whole allspice
½ cup simple syrup

Wash berries and lightly crush to release flavor. Place berries in a large-mouthed bottle and add vodka, vanilla bean, and allspice. Stir and store in a bottle in a cool, dark place for 3 weeks. Strain mixture through a cheesecloth and squeeze as much juice as possible from the pulp. Pour back in bottle and add simple syrup to taste. Age another 3 to 5 weeks.

Homemade Ice

Ice plays an important role when it comes to cocktails. Career bartenders take ice very seriously and consider it sacred. The most important role ice plays in a cocktail is its dilution rate. Melted ice adds water into a cocktail whether it is stirred, shaken, built, blended, or swizzled. The amount of water added to a cocktail changes the taste, so the proper dilution rate is crucial. Large solid cubes of ice will keep a cocktail cold, but also dilutes less water into a drink. Smaller ice dilutes more water into the cocktail.

Today, serious craft cocktail bars incorporate "ice programs" that offer a myriad of ice options such as blocks of ice cut into large cubes and other shapes, ice spheres (balls), rods, crushed ice, and shaved ice. Ice machine companies have also met the demand by producing machines that make square-inch cubed ice, crushed ice, and pebble ice.

Ice History

In the early 1800s, ice was harvested from lakes and ponds, and by the early 1900s, almost every bar, household, and grocer had large blocks of ice delivered regularly by an iceman. The ice blocks were stored in an icebox (the first refrigerator). Bartenders in particular would hand-pick or hand-saw blocks of ice into large pieces, shards, or shaved ice depending on the cocktail they were making.

Purchasing an industrial-sized ice machine or cutting up a block of ice with a chainsaw in your home is not cost-effective or wise. However, you can have fun with ice on a smaller scale by purchasing molds or specialty ice trays, or by recycling paper containers from your refrigerator.

Ice Essentials

The following are tips and techniques for making ice.

Purify Water: Ice starts with water, so always start with the purest water available. You can use a home water filter, boil water, or purchase filtered water.

Clear Ice: You can make clear ice at home by boiling water. Simply bring a pot of water to boil and then allow to cool. Bring to a boil a second time and allow to cool again. Then bring the water to a boil a third time; after it is cooled, it is ready to be used.

Square Cubed Ice Trays: The best trays for making cocktail ice are the square cubed silicon trays. The 1" cubed trays work well for most cocktails, and the large 2" silicone trays work wonderfully when using a single spirit like Scotch on the rocks—but in this case, it would be Scotch on the rock.

Ice Spheres/Balls: You can purchase an expensive ice ball maker for around $700, but it also requires 5" blocks of ice. It's more economical to purchase ice ball molds. There are many types available.

Novelty Ice Trays: Novelty shaped ice trays are available in a myriad of shapes and are not normally used in bars. But you can have fun with them in your home bar. Refrain from purchasing the small trays because they lose their shape in the drink almost instantly. Look for larger novelty ice trays to make more of an impact.

Block of Ice: Let's say that you decide to make an old-fashioned historic punch and the recipe calls for a block of ice to float in the punch bowl. No problem! Simply save a half-gallon milk or juice carton, cut off the top, clean it, fill it with water, and then freeze it. When ready, tear off the paper and you have an ice block for your punch.

Ice Blocks Around Bottles of Booze: A fun idea for a party is to freeze an ice block around a bottle of booze. Use a half-gallon milk or juice carton, cut off the top, clean it, and set your chosen bottle in it. Then fill it with water (you can also add any sliced fruits, herbs, flower petals, etc. in the water for decoration if desired). Place it in the freezer for at least 24 hours. When ready, tear off the paper and you have an ice block around your spirit bottle. Your guests will be impressed. Suggested boozes to use are limoncello, schnapps, or any favorite vodka, gin, rum, tequila, or whiskey.

Cubed Ice Fun
Have fun with ice cubes by making flavored cubes or freezing items in the cube. Flavored cubes can be made with orange, cranberry, pineapple, or other fruit juices; coffee; cucumber water; chai tea mix; or anything you desire. You can also freeze berries, pieces of fruit, herbs, flowers, vegetables, dice, candy, etc. inside ice cubes.

Crushed Ice: Crushed ice machines can be purchased for home use for under $100. The best ones to buy use regular ice cubes from your freezer. These machines will produce a snow-cone type of ice. You can also use a linen napkin and a mallet (or meat cleaver) to crush ice. Simply put ice in the napkin, fold, and start pounding with a mallet. Or you could purchase a canvas bag (often called a Lewis bag). You can also sew one together yourself. Simply put ice into the canvas bag and pound with a mallet.

Pebbled Ice: Pebbled ice is also called nugget ice. It's a chewable ice. Scotsman makes the best nugget ice machines. Most are for industrial use, but they do sell a residential ice machine you can add to your kitchen for about $4,000. If that doesn't fit into your budget, then simply drive into your local Sonic Drive-In and purchase a 10-pound bag of nugget ice for $1.

CHAPTER
15

mocktails

Mocktails are exactly what they sound like—mock cocktails. They are also called nonalcoholic drinks, alcohol-free drinks, or virgin drinks. In their most basic form, simply omitting the alcohol from a cocktail will create a mocktail. However, you want to be a little more creative than just leaving the vodka out of a Screwdriver.

Reasons for Mocktails

There are countless reasons to select a mocktail, including pregnancy, being the designated driver, taking certain medications, dislike of alcohol, being under drinking age, personal choice, or allergies. Mocktails can be frozen, juicy, creamy, sour, sweet, hot, fizzy, spicy, or any other category, just like regular cocktails.

The most famous mocktail is called a Shirley Temple (today, people also call it a Kiddie Cocktail or a Cherry Sprite). It was named after the famous child actress from the 1930s and believed to be created by a Hollywood bartender from Chasen's restaurant. The Shirley Temple consisted of ginger ale and grenadine garnished with a maraschino cherry.

Syrups
Torani and Monin syrups are the most popular beverage syrups on the market. They are prevalent in coffee shops. There are about sixty flavors, ranging from Blood Orange to Mojito Mint, including sugar-free alternatives. You'll find that they add a ton of flavor without any alcohol.

The Roy Rogers is probably the second most popular mocktail. It came out in the 1950s and consists of cola and grenadine (Cherry Coke) garnished with a maraschino cherry. Its namesake was a clean-cut, strait-laced singing cowboy with his own TV show in the 1950s.

Today, mocktails can be made with veggies (such as cucumbers), herbs, nonalcoholic wine, rum extracts, flavored syrups, and just about anything else you can imagine.

Anna Banana

1 banana, sliced
5 ounces pineapple juice
½ ounce coconut cream

Combine ingredients in a blender with ice. Blend thoroughly, then pour into a tall glass.

Apple Lemonade

1 scoop lemon sorbet
2 ounces apple juice
2 ounces lemonade

Place the scoop of sorbet into a cocktail glass. Shake the juice and lemonade in a shaker tin of ice, then strain into the cocktail glass.

Apricot Bubbles

1 ounce apricot nectar
5 ounces sparkling cider

Pour ingredients into a champagne glass.

Apricot Dream

3 ounces apricot nectar
3 ounces cream

Shake both ingredients in a shaker tin of ice, then strain into a chilled cocktail glass.

Apricot Spice

2 ounces white grape juice
3 ounces apricot nectar
1 ounce ginger-infused simple syrup
Sprinkle of ground clove

Shake all the ingredients in a shaker tin of ice, then strain into a chilled cocktail glass.

Arnold Palmer

Equal parts of lemonade and unsweetened tea to fill
1 lemon wedge

Fill a tall glass with ice, then fill with equal parts of lemonade and unsweetened tea. Garnish with lemon wedge.

Baby Bellini

2 ounces peach nectar
Chilled sparkling cider to fill

Pour peach nectar into a champagne flute. Fill with sparkling cider.

Banana Baybreeze

Equal parts of cranberry and pineapple juice to fill
1 capful banana extract

Fill a tall glass with ice and fill with equal parts of cranberry and pineapple juice. Stir in banana extract.

Big as the MoonPie

4 vanilla wafers

2 scoops banana ice cream

Cream for consistency

Whipped cream, for garnish

Crush 3 of the vanilla wafers and put into a tall glass. Put the banana ice cream in a blender and add cream little by little to reach a smooth consistency. Pour into a glass and garnish with whipped cream and the fourth vanilla wafer.

MoonPie

The Chattanooga Bakery in Tennessee conceived the MoonPie—a graham cracker and marshmallow confection dipped in chocolate—in the early 1900s. It was developed for the local miners who wanted a snack that fit in their lunch pails. They wanted something that was solid and filling.

Blue Hawaiian Shake

1/2 cup blueberries, fresh or frozen

2 ounces coconut cream

4 ounces milk

Combine ingredients in a blender with ice. Blend thoroughly, then pour into a tall glass.

Blushin' Berry Mary

1/2 cup fresh raspberries

1/2 cup strawberry milk

1 cup lemon yogurt

1/2 cup milk

Whipped cream, strawberries, blueberries, and raspberries, for garnish

Add the 1/2 cup fresh raspberries, strawberry milk, lemon yogurt, and milk in a blender. Blend until mixture reaches a smooth consistency. Pour into a tall glass. Garnish with whipped cream, strawberries, blueberries, and raspberries.

Caped Cod

Equal parts of cranberry juice and limeade to fill

Fill a tall glass with ice, then fill with equal parts of cranberry juice and limeade.

Cherry Bubbles

1/2 ounce grenadine

5 ounces sparkling cider

1 cherry

Pour liquid ingredients into a champagne glass. Garnish with cherry.

Cherry Coconut Dream

1 ounce cherry juice

1 ounce pineapple juice

1 ounce Coco Lopez

1 ounce cream

Shake all the ingredients in a shaker tin of ice, then strain into a chilled cocktail glass.

Cherry Coke

2 ounces grenadine

Cola to fill

1 maraschino cherry

Pour liquid ingredients over ice in a highball glass. Garnish with cherry.

Chocolate-Dipped Strawberry

1 tablespoon chocolate or white chocolate syrup

1 ounce light cream

Strawberry soda to fill

Pour chocolate and cream into a tall glass. Stir. Fill the glass with ice and soda.

White Chocolate

White chocolate doesn't actually contain chocolate. It contains cocoa butter, milk solids, sugar, lecithin, and vanilla flavorings. Cocoa butter is the fat from cocoa beans.

Coconut Catholic School Girl

1 tablespoon honey, for rimming

Shredded coconut, for rimming

3 ounces Coco Lopez

Juice from 1 lime

Dip the rim of a martini glass into the honey and the shredded coconut. Chill the glass in the freezer to add a nice touch. Pour the Coco Lopez and lime juice into a shaker tin of ice. Shake, then strain into the martini glass.

Coffee Almond Float

¼ cup coffee

1 teaspoon brown sugar

1 teaspoon almond syrup

1 ounce milk

1 scoop coffee or chocolate ice cream

Pour all the ingredients except for the scoop of ice cream into a shaker of ice. Shake and strain into a martini glass and top with a scoop of ice cream. Can be served with a spoon.

Cool as a Cucumber

1/2 peeled cucumber
Juice from 1/2 lime
2 mint leaves
1/2 peeled ripe kiwi
1 tablespoon sugar or Splenda
1 ounce water
1 sprig of mint

Put all ingredients except mint in a blender. Add ice until you reach a frozen yet pourable consistency. Pour into a martini glass and garnish with mint.

Cranberry and Cream

3 ounces cranberry juice
2 ounces apple juice
1 ounce fresh lime juice
1 ounce cream
Dash grenadine

Combine ingredients in a blender with ice. Blend thoroughly. Pour into a tall glass.

Cranberry Fresca

Equal parts of cranberry juice and Fresca to fill

Fill a tall glass with ice, then fill with equal parts of cranberry juice and Fresca.

Creamy Cherry

4 ounces cherry soda
2 scoops vanilla ice cream
1 tablespoon honey
1 ounce cream
Dash grenadine

Combine ingredients in a blender. Blend thoroughly. Pour into a tall glass.

Down the Rabbit Hole

3 ounces carrot juice
3 ounces pineapple juice
Sparkling cider to fill

Fill a tall glass with ice, then add the juices. Fill with sparkling cider.

Earth Angel Sangria

3/4 glass grape juice or nonalcoholic red wine
Soda water to fill
Orange wheel, lime wheel, pineapple slice, and cherry, for garnish

Fill a tall glass three-quarters full with grape juice or nonalcoholic red wine. Fill with soda water. Garnish with orange wheel, lime wheel, pineapple slice, and cherry.

Nonalcoholic Wine

Ariel is a pioneer in producing award-winning nonalcoholic wines. It is the only nonalcoholic wine that won a gold medal against eight alcoholic wines at the Los Angeles County Fair's blind wine tastings.

Easy Alexander

1 teaspoon instant coffee granules
1 teaspoon brown sugar
1 ounce boiling water
1 ounce cream
Sprinkle of nutmeg

Dissolve coffee and sugar in boiling water. Let cool. Combine with cream in a shaker half filled with ice. Shake well and strain into a cocktail glass. Serve with a sprinkle of nutmeg.

Eye of the Hurricane

1 ounce rum extract
2 ounces passion fruit juice
1 ounce fresh lime juice

Combine everything in a shaker tin of ice. Strain over a tall glass of ice.

Faux Kir Royale

1 ounce raspberry syrup
Chilled sparkling white grape juice to fill
1 lemon twist

Pour raspberry syrup into a champagne flute. Fill with sparkling white grape juice. Garnish with lemon twist.

Frozen Mocha Russian

2 ounces cold black coffee
2 scoops chocolate ice cream
1 ounce cream
Sprinkle of chocolate shavings

Combine the first three ingredients in a blender without ice. Blend thoroughly and pour into a tall glass. Top with chocolate shavings.

Good Ship Lollipop

1 large scoop orange sherbet
Cold Nehi peach soda to fill
3 small cantaloupe balls
3 small watermelon balls

Drop a scoop of orange sherbet into the bottom of a tall glass. Fill with cold soda. Drop in the fruit balls. You can replace the orange sherbet with pineapple or lime.

Ancient Sherbet

The Chinese taught Arab traders how to combine syrups and snow to make sherbet. Arab traders showed the Venetians, and the Venetians showed the Romans.

Hairless Reggae

½ banana, sliced

1 ounce fresh orange juice

1 ounce fresh lime juice

½ ounce grenadine

Seasonal fruit, chopped, for garnish

Combine first four ingredients in a blender with a cup of ice. Blend. Pour into a tall glass and garnish with chopped fruit.

Hot Clamato

6 ounces Clamato juice

1 ounce fresh lime juice

¼ teaspoon horseradish

Dash Tabasco sauce

Dash Worcestershire sauce

1 lemon wedge

Pour liquid ingredients into a glass over ice; stir. Garnish with lemon.

Tabasco

Tabasco, the popular hot sauce, comes from Avery Island, 140 miles west of New Orleans. It has been produced since 1868. A 2-ounce bottle contains at least 720 drops.

Hot Not Toddy

1 tablespoon honey

Dash cinnamon

Dash ground cloves

Dash nutmeg

6 ounces hot tea

Splash lemon juice

In a coffee mug, dissolve the honey and spices in 1 ounce of tea. Stir. Add the lemon juice and the rest of the tea. Stir well.

Italian Cream Soda

1 ounce hazelnut syrup

Club soda to fill

Whipped cream, for garnish

Pour hazelnut syrup into a tall glass of ice. Fill with club soda. Top with whipped cream and a straw.

Root Beer Float

It may seem odd to put whipped cream on top of a drink with ice, but it's quite all right. You can use anise extract, cola, and cream over ice, then put whipped cream on top—it will taste like a Root Beer Float.

Juicy Julep

1 ounce fresh lime juice
1 ounce pineapple juice
½ ounce raspberry syrup
2 sprigs of mint (1 for garnish)
Club soda to fill

Combine the first three ingredients and 1 mint sprig in a shaker half filled with ice. Shake well. Strain into a Collins glass of ice. Add club soda and stir gently. Garnish with the remaining sprig of mint.

Just Say No Cocoa

1 packet cocoa mix
¾ cup hot water
Eggnog to fill
Whipped cream

Pour a packet of hot cocoa mix in a cup. Fill three-quarters of the way with very hot water and stir well. Fill the rest of the way with eggnog. Top with whipped cream.

Kiss on the Cheek

2 ounces apricot nectar
1 ounce fresh lemon juice
Club soda to fill

Pour apricot nectar and lemon juice into a mixing glass nearly filled with ice. Stir well. Strain into a highball glass over ice. Fill with club soda.

Liberated Cuba Libre

Equal parts of cola and limeade to fill
1 lime wedge

Fill a tall glass with ice, then fill with equal parts of cola and limeade. Garnish with lime wedge.

Like a Blessed Blackberry Virgin

Handful of blackberries
1 teaspoon sugar or Splenda
Lemonade to fill
Lemon slice and blackberries, for garnish

Blend the blackberries and sugar or Splenda in a blender until mixed well. Pour into a tall glass. Fill the glass with lemonade and ice. Garnish with lemon slice and some blackberries.

Knott's Berry Farm
In the 1920s, Rudolph Boysen crossed blackberries and raspberries, and the result was the boysenberry. After he abandoned his farm, a fruit seller named Walter Knott rescued some of the canes. Today his farm is called Knott's Berry Farm.

Lime Cola 🍸

1 ounce lime juice or juice from ½ lime
Cola to fill
1 lime wedge

Pour lime juice over ice in a highball glass; fill with cola. Garnish with lime wedge.

Lime in the Coconut

1½ ounces Coco Lopez coconut cream
Coconut flakes, for rimming
3 ounces limeade
3 drops vanilla extract

Pour ½ ounce of the coconut cream on a saucer and the coconut flakes on another saucer. Dip the rim of the cocktail glass in the cream then in the coconut flakes. Shake the liquid ingredients in a shaker tin of ice, then strain into the glass.

Mango Virgo

3 ounces mango nectar
Juice from ½ lime
2 ounces cream
1 slice star fruit

Pour the mango nectar, lime juice, and cream into a shaker tin of ice. Shake and strain into a chilled martini glass and garnish with 1 slice star fruit on the rim.

Mimi's Mimosa

2 ounces fresh orange juice
Chilled sparkling white grape juice to fill

Pour orange juice into a champagne flute. Fill with sparkling white grape juice.

Morally Pure Mudslide

1 scoop chocolate ice cream
1 scoop vanilla ice cream
1 ounce cold black coffee
2 tablespoons Café Vienna
1 ounce chocolate syrup
Milk or cream to blend

Put the chocolate ice cream, vanilla ice cream, coffee, Café Vienna, and chocolate syrup into a blender and blend. Add milk or cream little by little until the mixture reaches a smooth consistency. Pour into a tall glass.

Mulled Cranberry Juice

6 ounces cranberry juice
Splash fresh lemon juice
1 teaspoon honey or more to taste
2 whole cloves
Dash nutmeg

Combine ingredients in a saucepan and heat to simmer. Do not boil. Stir well. Pour into a coffee mug.

Nada Colada

¼ ounce rum extract
¼ ounce vanilla extract
3 ounces pineapple juice
3 ounces Coco Lopez
Milk or cream to blend
1 pineapple slice and 1 maraschino
cherry

Pour the rum extract, vanilla
extract, pineapple juice, and
Coco Lopez into a blender with a
cup of ice. Add milk or cream
and blend until the mixture
reaches a smooth consistency.
Pour into a tall glass and garnish
with pineapple slice and maraschino cherry.

Orange Julius

6 ounces frozen orange juice
½ cup cream
1 teaspoon vanilla extract

Put everything in a blender with
1 cup of ice and blend. Pour into
a tall glass.

Peach Dream

3 ounces peach nectar
3 ounces cream

Shake the ingredients in a shaker
tin of ice, then strain into a
chilled cocktail glass.

Peaches and Cream

1 peach, chopped
1 teaspoon sugar
2 ounces light cream
1 peach slice

Combine first three ingredients
in a blender with 1 cup of ice
and blend. Pour into a tall glass
and garnish with slice of peach.

Georgia Peach

Georgia is known for many
things, but the most beloved
is the Georgia peach. Peaches originated in Asia. Per-
sians brought the peach to
Persia and then introduced
them to Italy. The Italians
introduced them to Spain,
and then Spanish explorers
brought them to Georgia.
The Georgia peach industry
began during Reconstruc-
tion after the American Civil
War. Today, more than forty
varieties of peaches are
grown in Georgia.

Pineapple Twist

4 ounces pineapple juice

1 ounce lemon juice or juice from
1/2 lemon

2 ounces orange juice or juice from
1/2 orange

1 maraschino cherry

Combine juices in a blender with ice. Blend thoroughly. Pour into a cocktail glass and serve with a cherry.

Pink Pineapple

4 ounces pineapple juice

3 ounces cherry soda

1 tablespoon honey

1 ounce cream

Dash grenadine

Pour ingredients into a tall glass of ice. Stir.

Planter's Punch (nonalcoholic)

2 ounces pineapple juice

3 ounces fresh orange juice

1 ounce fresh lemon juice

1/2 ounce grenadine

Fruit, for garnish

Combine all liquid ingredients in a shaker half filled with ice. Shake well. Strain into a tall glass of ice. Garnish with fruit. This is the nonalcoholic version of the rum-flavored punch of the same name.

Pom Mimosa

1 ounce pomegranate juice

5 ounces sparkling cider

Pour ingredients into a champagne glass.

Pomegranate Lemonade

1 ounce pomegranate syrup

Lemonade to fill

Pour the pomegranate syrup in a tall glass of ice and fill with lemonade.

Pure Polynesian Pepper Pot

4 ounces pineapple juice

1/2 ounce almond syrup

1 ounce fresh lemon juice

4 dashes Tabasco

Dash curry powder

Combine the first four ingredients in a shaker half filled with ice. Shake well. Strain into a tall glass of ice. Sprinkle curry on top.

Quiet Passion

3 ounces white grape juice

3 ounces grapefruit juice

1 ounce passion fruit juice

Combine ingredients in a shaker half filled with ice. Shake well. Strain into a tall glass of ice.

Raspberry Cloud

¼ cup raspberries, fresh or frozen
1 ounce milk
1 tablespoon honey

Put berries in a blender and blend well. Add milk, honey, and 2 ice cubes. Pour into a tall glass.

Reno Cocktail

2 ounces grapefruit juice
1 ounce lime juice or juice from ½ lime
½ ounce grenadine
1 teaspoon fine sugar

Combine ingredients in a shaker nearly filled with ice. Strain into a cocktail glass.

Safe Sex on the Beach

1 ounce Torani or Monin peach syrup
Equal parts of orange juice and cranberry juice to fill
1 orange slice and 1 cherry

Pour the peach syrup into a tall glass of ice. Fill with equal parts of orange juice and cranberry juice. Garnish with orange slice and cherry.

Salty Puppy

1 lime wedge
Coarse salt, for rimming
4–5 ounces grapefruit juice

Rub the rim of a tall glass with the lime wedge. Pour the salt into a dish and dip the rim of the glass into the mixture. Add ice and pour in grapefruit juice.

Slumbering Bull

5 ounces V8 juice
2 ounces beef bouillon
Dash Tabasco
Dash Worcestershire sauce
Dash celery salt
1 lime wedge

Pour all liquid ingredients and celery salt into a highball glass over ice and stir well. Garnish with lime wedge.

Sunshine State

4 ounces cherry soda
½ cup orange sherbet
1 ounce fresh lemon juice

Combine ingredients in a blender with ice. Blend well. Pour into a tall glass.

Sweet Spice

1 ounce fresh lemon juice
3 ounces fresh orange juice
½ ounce grenadine
Ginger ale to fill
Cherries, for garnish

Fill a tall glass with ice and add the juices and grenadine. Fill with ginger ale. Garnish with cherries.

Sweet Sunrise

Orange juice to fill
1/2 ounce grenadine
1 orange slice

Fill a tall glass with ice, then fill with orange juice. Slowly pour the grenadine into the drink. It will sink to the bottom of the glass, making it look like a sunrise. Garnish with orange slice.

Touched by a Fuzzy Angel

1 ounce peach syrup
Orange juice to fill
1 orange or peach slice

Pour the peach syrup into a tall glass of ice. Fill with orange juice, and garnish with fruit. It's a Virgin Fuzzy Navel.

Tropical Cream

2 ounces pineapple juice
1 ounce grapefruit juice
1 ounce coconut milk
1 ounce cream

Shake all the ingredients in a shaker tin of ice, then strain into a chilled cocktail glass.

Vice Presidente

2 ounces pineapple juice
1 ounce lime juice or juice from 1/2 lime
1/2 ounce grenadine
1 teaspoon fine sugar

Combine ingredients in a shaker nearly filled with ice. Strain into a cocktail glass. This is a virgin version of the rum-flavored El Presidente.

Virgin Island Seabreeze

1 part pink grapefruit juice
1 part cranberry juice
1 lime slice

Fill a tall glass with ice. Pour in equal amounts of the pink grapefruit juice and cranberry juice. Garnish with slice of lime.

Wild Blueberry Beginner

5 mint leaves
Handful of blueberries
1 tablespoon sugar or Splenda
1 ounce water
7UP to fill
Sprig of mint and blueberries, for garnish

Put the first four ingredients into a tall glass and mash with a muddler or wooden spoon to release the oils in the mint. Fill the glass with ice and 7UP and garnish with mint and blueberries.

CHAPTER 16

american cocktail culture information

In 1862, the first known cocktail book, *How To Mix Drinks: Or, The Bon-Vivant's Companion*, by Jerry Thomas, sparked the first golden era of the cocktail. For almost sixty years, the craft of making cocktails and the professionalism of bartenders were taken quite seriously. That is, until the American Prohibition happened from 1920–1933. After Prohibition, the American cocktail culture slowly made a comeback, but was soon squelched again because of inferior products being produced by large corporations.

Cocktail mixers and ingredients filled with additives and preservatives prevailed. Fortunately, by the late 1980s a few cocktail enthusiasts began to resurrect classic cocktails and cocktails made with fresh ingredients. Thanks to these cocktail pioneers' efforts, there is now a second golden era of the cocktail.

Top Cocktail Celebrities to Follow

Today there are many cocktail celebrities doing many wonderful things. They hold positions such as consultants, bartenders, bar owners, bloggers, authors, and more. These top cocktail movers and shakers will point you in the right direction and then lead you to even more influential cocktail people to follow. Make sure you friend them on Facebook to keep up with all the latest news.

Dale "King Cocktail" DeGroff

Dale DeGroff is called King Cocktail for a reason. He is at the top of the cocktail culture pyramid. In 1988, he pioneered a gourmet approach to recreating the great classic cocktails with fresh ingredients.

www.kingcocktail.com

Gary "Gaz" Regan

You can stay on the leading edge of the cocktail culture by subscribing to Gary Regan's free newsletter. Gary has written several books, but his most famous is *The Joy of Mixology*. He is heavily steeped in the cocktail culture.

www.gazregan.com

Tobin Ellis

Tobin Ellis is the first award-winning flair bartender to cross over into the mixology world to become an award-winning mixologist. Tobin has a long list of accomplishments gained from traveling the world consulting, designing, judging, writing, and organizing all things cocktail. The famous chef Bobby Flay, from the TV show *Throwdown with Bobby Flay*, chose Tobin as America's best bartender. Tobin continues to break new ground with his creativity, tenacity, and passion for the cocktail culture.

www.barmagic.com

www.socialmixologyvegas.com

Ted Haigh

Ted Haigh's day job is designing movie posters for Hollywood. His hobby is collecting rare and unique barware, cocktail books, and spirits. Ted, aka Dr. Cocktail, is a cocktail archaeologist. Much of his collection is showcased at the Museum of the American Cocktail in New Orleans. His cocktail database should be bookmarked on your favorite browser as a reference for any historic and classic cocktail you may be looking for.

www.cocktaildb.com

Jeff "Beachbum" Berry

Beachbum Berry first became fascinated with tiki cocktail culture at eight years old. Today, he is the foremost tiki historian and author in the world. He is often credited with reviving the tiki culture. In 2014, the Bum opened his first fresh tiki bar in New Orleans.

www.beachbumberry.com

Tony "The Modern Mixologist" Abou-Ganim

In 1995, Tony opened one of the first fresh craft bars in San Francisco. In 1998, he was hired by the Petrossian Bar in the Bellagio Las Vegas. Today, he often works alongside famous chef Mario Batali, and he travels the world teaching, writing books, designing bar tools, and headlining at cocktail festivals.

www.themodernmixologist.com

Robert "Drinkboy" Hess

Robert's day job is working for Microsoft and his hobby is cocktails. He has played an instrumental role in the revival of the cocktail since the late 1990s. Among other accomplishments, Robert also cofounded the Museum of the American Cocktail.

www.drinkboy.com

David Wondrich

David is an English professor turned cocktail historian. In 1999, *Esquire* magazine asked him to update the online version of Esquire's 1949 *Handbook for Hosts*, and today he is one of the top drink historians of our time.

www.esquire.com/drinks

Cocktail Festivals and Events

Cocktail festivals are fun. They are filled with seminars, brand parties, cocktail enthusiasts and professionals, tasting rooms, and more. You will meet like-minded people and cocktail celebrities from all over the world.

January

San Antonio Cocktail Conference
www.sanantoniococktail conference.com
Four-day charity cocktail event that was founded in 2010. Ticket prices range between $30 and $150, and there are approximately 1,000 attendees.

February

Arizona Cocktail Week
www.arizonacocktailweek.com
Seven-day event for cocktail veterans and aspiring home mixologists that was founded in 2012. The event is statewide with a focus on Phoenix, Scottsdale, and Tucson. Ticket prices range between $30 and $100, and there are approximately 2,000 attendees.

March

Après-Ski Cocktail Classic
www.apresskicocktailclassic.com
Four-day event in Aspen/Snowmass, CO, that attracts rookies and industry pros. Ticket prices range between $31 and $365, and there are approximately 4,000 attendees.

Nightclub & Bar Convention and Trade Show
www.ncbshow.com
Two-day convention in Las Vegas showcasing new products. Ticket prices range between $100 and $500, and there are approximately 50,000 attendees.

April

Miami Rum Renaissance Festival
www.rumrenaissance.com
Three-day event in Miami, FL, exhibiting the best rum brands. It was founded in 2008. Ticket prices range between $20 and $125, and there are approximately 2,000 attendees.

May

Manhattan Cocktail Classic
www.manhattancocktailclassic.com
Five-day event in New York
City for spirit professionals and
enthusiasts. It can be expensive
because events are grand and
spread out all over NYC. It was
founded in 2010; ticket prices
range between $25 and $350,
and there are approximately
5,000 attendees.

June

San Francisco Cocktail Week
www.sfcocktailweek.com
Seven-day event that was
founded in 2007. Ticket prices
range between $50 and $150, and
there are approximately 7,000
attendees.

Food and Wine Classic in Aspen
www.foodandwine.com/classic
This is a three-day event in Aspen,
CO.

July

Tales of the Cocktail
www.talesofthecocktail.com
Five-day event in New Orleans,
LA. Founded in 2002, it is the #1
cocktail event in the world. Ticket
prices range between $50 and
$100, and there are approximately
30,000 attendees.

Festival Tips
A cocktail festival is like
the Walt Disney World for
grownups. The best tips to
navigate your way through
several days of fun is to
pace yourself, drink plenty
of water, stock your favorite
hangover remedies, and
bring a lot of business cards.
To get the most out of your
experience, it's best to arrive
a couple of days before and
stay a couple of days after so
you can enjoy the city sights.

August

San Diego Spirits Festival
www.sandiegospiritsfestival.com
Two-day weekend festival in San
Diego, founded in 2009. Ticket
prices range between $30 and
$150, and there are approximately
1,000 attendees.

Hawai'i Food & Wine Festival
*www.hawaiifoodandwinefestival
.com*
Seven-day festival that features
over 80 internationally renowned
master chefs, culinary personali-
ties, and wine and spirit personali-
ties. Ticket prices range between
$200 and $500, and there are
approximately 5,000 attendees.

September

Milwaukee Cocktail Week
www.milwaukeecocktailweek.com
Seven-day event founded in 2013.
Ticket prices range between $30
and $90, and there are approximately 1,000 attendees.

Pittsburgh Cocktail Week
www.pghcocktailweek.com
Seven-day event founded in 2014.
Ticket prices range between $50
and $100 and there are approximately 1,000 attendees.

October

Portland Cocktail Week
www.portlandcocktailweek.com
Seven-day event founded in 2010.
Ticket prices range between $30
and $90, and there are approximately 2,000 attendees.

Speakeasy Cocktail Festival
www.speakeasycocktailfestival.com
One-day event founded in 2012 in
Atlanta, GA.

The Best Cocktail Blogs

These cocktail blogs will help you learn the ins and outs of bartending. Make sure to check out their blogrolls for even more blogs you may enjoy.

A Dash of Bitters
Run by spirits, cocktail, barware,
and bars writer Michael Dietsch.
www.adashofbitters.com

Alcademics
Run by award-winning cocktail
and spirits writer Camper English.
www.alcademics.com

Art of Drink
Run by chemist turned bartender
turned award-winning author
Darcy O'Neil.
www.artofdrink.com

Booze Nerds
This blog takes a witty and nerdy
approach to cocktails.
www.boozenerds.com

Death to Sour Mix
Blog from a Boston bartender
filled with beautiful cocktail
photography.
www.deathtosourmix.com

Imbibe Unfiltered

A blog from the #1 drink magazine in America. It will keep you up on all the latest cocktail happenings.
www.imbibemagazine.blogspot.com

Jeffrey Morgenthaler

In the cocktail world, Jeffrey's nickname is Jeffrey Morgenblogger. He first published this blog in 2004 and it has opened up opportunities for him to travel the world to speak on cocktail subjects. He is currently the head bartender at Clyde Common in Portland, OR.
www.jeffreymorgenthaler.com

Liquor

Liquor will keep you abreast of all the latest cocktail news, spirits, and events. It's filled with the most current drink trends and videos.
www.liquor.com

Professor Cocktail

Run by cocktail and spirits columnist David J. Montgomery.
www.professorcocktail.com

Spirits and Cocktails

Godfather molecular mixologist and bar owner Jamie Boudreau may not post much because he's busy running his bar Canon in Seattle, but his site has informative, well-photographed archives to click through.
http://spiritsandcocktails.word press.com

The Cocktail Chronicles

An ongoing exploration of fine spirits, creative cocktails, and classic mixology, this site is run by Paul Clarke, who has written hundreds of magazine articles on cocktails and spirits.
www.cocktailchronicles.com

The Liquid Muse

Run by author, bartender, and consultant Natalie Bovis. Natalie makes mixology approachable for cocktail enthusiasts of all types.
www.theliquidmuse.com

The Straight Up

Brought to you by Nick Caruana, a self-taught cocktail enthusiast with a passion for classic cocktails.
www.drinkstraightup.com

The Best Drink Apps

There are thousands of cocktail apps to download these days, so it can be hard to know which ones are the most helpful. These drink apps will get your fingers started off in the right direction:

BarNotes
A social craft cocktail app that allows you to upload a cocktail recipe, connect with friends, make comments, and more.
Cost: Free

Bartender's Choice
Put together by bartender Sam Ross who worked at the legendary Milk & Honey.
Cost: $2.99.

Beachbum Berry's Total Tiki
Put together by tiki guru, Beachbum Berry.
Cost: $9.99

Latitude 29
The next time you visit New Orleans, you have the opportunity to meet Beachbum Berry in person! He opened his first tiki bar, called Latitude 29, in 2014. It's in the Bienville House Hotel at 320 Decatur Street in the French Quarter.

Cocktail Flow
Features a virtual liquor cabinet.
Cost: $2.99

Delectable Wine
An app to snap a photo of the wine label to get information.
Cost: Free

Mixology
Put together by tiki guru, Beachbum Berry.
Cost: $9.99

Pintley
A beer database connected with a social network.
Cost: Free

Speakeasy Cocktails: Learn from the Master Mixologists
Put together by Jim Meehan, mastermind of the legendary PDT bar in New York City and James Beard winner.
Cost: $9.99

Untappd
A social beer app that allows you to take a photo of the beer you're drinking, share reviews and ratings with friends, and find nearby craft beer bars.
Cost: Free

Wine Simplified
This app offers an educational experience with videos, pronunciations, and how to decode labels.
Cost: $9.99

APPENDIX A

the wrath of grapes—
all about hangovers

The buzz from drinking alcohol can be compared to the high an addictive shopper feels from a day of credit-card shopping. The hangover happens the next day when you realize you have to pay.

The Top Five Hangover Preventions

After drinking, the most common prevention is to take aspirin and drink a big glass of water before going to sleep. What you want to take is ibuprofen and water. Tylenol (acetaminophen) causes extreme liver damage when combined with alcohol.

- Drink water while drinking alcohol.
- Snack while drinking.
- Drink high-quality alcohol.
- Take vitamin B-complex and vitamin C.
- Take ibuprofen.

The Top Five Hangover Cures

There has never been one cure-all for a hangover the day after. As you can imagine, there are thousands of common folk hangover cures that have been passed down from generation to generation. There are also modern-day powders and potions that claim to be cure-alls. You'll just have to determine what is best for you.

The Hair of the Dog. This refers to drinking a bit more alcohol to cure you. Supposedly the term has been around since the 1500s and refers to placing a few dog hairs over a dog's bite wound to cure the wound. Somehow it evolved into a drinking metaphor.

Drinking a Bloody Mary is considered a classic hangover cure, especially when you add hot sauce, an egg, lemon juice, and other ingredients to the mix.

Drinking Powerade or Gatorade will supposedly rehydrate the body with essential nutrients.

Eating raw egg yolks is supposed to help because they are high in cysteine (SIS-tuh-een). There is also an over-the-counter supplement called N-aceltycysteine (NAC).

A hot bath or shower is supposed to help you sweat out the toxins from the alcohol.

Global Hangover Cures

As you can imagine, there are as many hangover cures around the world as there are ways to get rid of the hiccups.

- **America circa 1800:** Soak feet in mustard and eat eggs Benedict.
- **Ancient Egypt:** Eat boiled cabbage.
- **Ancient Romans:** Eat fried canary.
- **England:** Have clam chowder.
- **France:** Eat or drink hot onion soup.
- **Germany:** Have pickled herring with a beer.
- **Haiti:** Stick thirteen black-headed pins in the cork of the bottle you drank from.
- **Ireland:** Have an Ulster Fry (potato bread, fried egg, bacon, sausage, tomato, mushrooms, and soda bread).
- **Japan:** Wear a sake-soaked surgical mask.
- **Puerto Rico:** Rub a lemon under your drinking arm.
- **Russia:** Have salted cucumber juice or black bread soaked in water.

APPENDIX

B

drinking words through time

These won't help you win a trivia contest, but they will make you chuckle.

1300s: Drunk as a whistle, drunk as all get-out, taverned, cupshotten, down among the dead men, drunk as an ape, dizzy, feebleminded, mad, double-tongued, drunk as a mouse, drunk as a Pope.

1400s: Drowned the shamrock, dronke, drunk as a swine, overseen, pissed as a skunk, served up, off me pickle, aroused.

1500s: Aled up, befuddled, drinking deep, malt above the meal, swallowed a tavern token, shattered, shaved, swilled up, whittled, rowdy, has more than one can hold, has on a barley cap.

1600s: Admiral of the narrow seas, beastly drunk, cap-sick, bubbled, caught a fox, D and D (drunk and disorderly), boozed, dull in the eye, elevated, giggled up, got bread and cheese in one's head, muddled up, drinking merry-go-round, on the rampage, seeing double.

1700s: Addled, rotten drunk, cherry-merry, clips the King's English, cracked, cranked, dizzy as a coot, fuddled up, full as a goat, got a snootful, groggy, happy-juiced, in the altitudes, jacked up, juiced to the gills, lapping it up, cockadoodled, drinking like a fish, and stewed, screwed, and tattooed.

1800s: A bit on, a couple of chapters into the novel, a cup too much, a date with John Barleycorn, a drop too much, a little in the suds, peg too low, piece of bread and cheese in the attic, a public mess, on a bender, above par, altogether drunk, apple palsy, at peace with the floor, lifting the little finger, been looking through a glass, banged up on sauce, bemused, blue around the gills, breath strong enough to carry coal with, can't see a hole in a ladder, caught the flavor, corked, dead to the world, doped up, woozy, drunk as Bacchus, drunk as forty billygoats, electrified, feeling glorious, fired up, fogged in, full to the brim, ginned, groggified, half gone, haywire, inked, lushed, moonshined, off the deep end, on the rocks, pie-eye, polished, sloppy drunk, sloshed, stinking, soaked, swazzled, tanked, whacked out of one's skull.

1900s: Lit, high, party animal, three sheets to the wind, tipsy, slave to drink, aboard, blown away, done, gone, liquored up, bashed, buzzed, acting like a fool, baked, blasted, bombed, blitzed, bonkers, canned, creamed, crocked, fried, hammered, stoned, toasted, double vision, wasted.

2000s: Boneless, get the fade on, tight, torqued, bulletproof, shined, Picassoed, locked out of your mind, jagged up, in the paint, pixilated, punch drunk, drunk as hell.

Index